EDITOR
MAX FRASER

MANAGING EDITOR
IDA VIZNEROVA

DESIGN
RICHARD ARDAGH
ELEPHANTSGRAVEYARD.CO.UK

COVER DESIGN
ALISTAIR HALL
DAVID PEARSON
& PAUL FINN

PUBLISHING DIRECTOR
MAX FRASER

CONTRIBUTORS
MICHELLE ALGER
ANNA BATES
ANNABEL FRASER
TIM GREENHALGH
NINA HERTIG
ELLEN HIMELFARB
JULIEN LOMBRAIL
KIERAN LONG
JOHN MILLER
ANGEL MONZON
TRACEY NEULS
TIM PARSONS
KATI PRICE
LYNDA RELPH-KNIGHT
DUNCAN RICHES
GILLIAN RUSSELL
CHRYSTINA SCHMIDT
MICHAEL SODEAU
THORSTEN VAN ELTEN

Welcome to *London Design Guide*, the first publication to comprehensively report on the best places in London for great design. After months of research, countless conversations, endless reviewing and numerous trips around the capital, I am delighted to introduce you to the results, whether you're a design expert, enthusiast or novice.

London is a vast, cosmopolitan city, offering a myriad of cultural influences and never-ending variety. As a born-and-bred Londoner, I still find the magnitude of offerings overwhelming and the task of locating them daunting. This guide is a focused compendium, easily digestible in our information-rich lives. It concentrates on a niche – that of contemporary and vintage design – highlighting and reviewing the design shops and galleries where you can buy; the institutions and museums were you can learn; and the bookshops where you can read about it.

Within each chapter, the city is subdivided according to areas of concentrated design activity, with every place we reviewed marked onto maps, helping you navigate around the maze of streets. In unfamiliar neighbourhoods, you can follow a walking tour tailor-made by an informed local. Furthermore, there are suggestions for restaurants, bars, cafés, specialty shops and hotels – all selected with the design-savvy visitor in mind. Ultimately, the guide celebrates life in London, where design plays a vital role.

Each year, the guide will provide a platform for commentary on various design-related subjects, including manufacturing, history, new movements, collectible furnishings and the visceral experience of living with them. In this edition, the critical analyses are accompanied by a section on design 'tribes', which aims to define the city's most prominent designers by the approaches and philosophies they share.

London Design Guide is not an aspirational 'lifestyle guide' – it is a practical resource to be used from cover to cover. Above all, you should consider it a foundation on which you can build your own interpretation of the vibrant capital. Don't just drain the city of what it has to offer but interact with it as well. And in the process, slow down, absorb and enjoy the finer details.

Max Fraser

We welcome feedback and recommendations for the next edition. Contact us by email: info@londondesignguide.com

GUIDELINES AND CRITERIA

The definition of 'design' in this guide refers to three-dimensional objects in the broadest sense, and furniture, lighting, ceramics, glass, textiles and tableware more specifically. The focus is on contemporary design, but we've also included vintage originals. The guide reviews businesses open to the public, so it doesn't include references to studios, or interior and architecture practices.

We have chosen to exclude the following: shops devoted to 'permanents', such as bathroom and kitchen appliances, tiles, flooring, light fixtures, etc; office-furniture showrooms; shops with stock comprising more than 50 per cent clothing; businesses with an 'appointment only' opening policy; businesses that are utterly unbearable to deal with (you know who you are). In very few cases, there are exceptions to this criteria.

London's boundary is defined by the M25 orbital motorway. No neighbourhood was predetermined – all were defined after we had researched, visited and approved every place. We defined each area by the high concentration of design activity within it, afterwards adding recommendations for the *Eat & Drink*, *Indulge* and *Sleep* sections concluding each chapter. The maps that open each chapter are illustrative and include streets that are relevant to the entries in the guide. We recommend carrying a comprehensive street map for a greater overview.

Most importantly, no person or business has paid to be included in the editorial portions of this guide, nor can any exert pressure on us to tailor the reviews. Research visits were anonymous and unannounced to ensure a genuine customer experience. Clothes worn were casual with no outward display of wealth.

Now that's clear, please enjoy!

Contents

LONDON

Notting Hill
& Holland Park

Marylebone

Mayfair

Soho

Chelsea,
Knightsbridge
& Brompton

DISCOVER KING'S ROAD

Chelsea. A name synonymous with glamour, style and fashion. And nowhere more so than the legendary King's Road. With its eclectic mix of cutting-edge boutiques, contemporary bars and independent restaurants, this iconic, vibrant and ever-evolving corner of London has long been a must-see destination for anyone serious about fashion, entertainment or dining.

Isn't it time you discovered the King's Road for yourself?

www.discoverkingsroad.com

Chelsea, Knightsbridge & Brompton

ST LUKE'S CHURCH, SYDNEY STREET

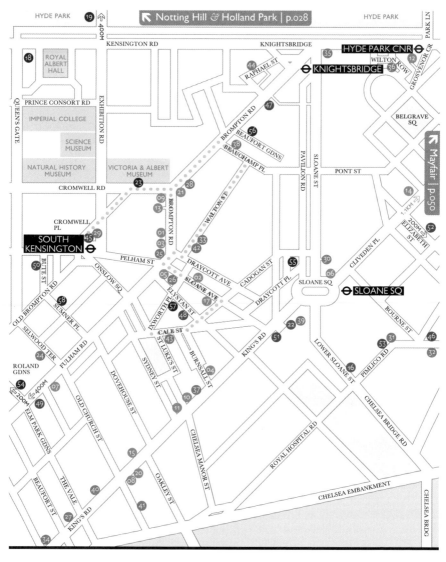

● Design galleries & institutions
● Design shops & C20th vintage
● Design bookshops

● Eat & Drink
● Indulge
● Sleep
  (pp.022-023)

••• Take a walk route

01	B&B ITALIA	13	MINT
02	BISAZZA	14	PHILLIPS DE PURY & COMPANY
03	BOFFI	15	POLIFORM
04	CHRISTOPHER FARR	16	POTTERTON BOOKS
05	THE CONRAN SHOP	17	RABIH HAGE
06	DAVID MELLOR	18	RCA
07	DE PARMA	19	SERPENTINE GALLERY
08	DESIGNERS GUILD	20	SIGMAR
09	FEW AND FAR	21	SKANDIUM
10	HABITAT (p.067)	22	TASCHEN
11	HEAL'S (p.090)	23	VICTORIA AND ALBERT MUSEUM
12	JACQUELINE RABUN		

Chelsea, Knightsbridge & Brompton

TAKE A WALK
Chrystina Schmidt *

From South Kensington station, head along Thurloe Place and snake through the residential backstreets to the exquisite Few and Far boutique by Priscilla Carluccio, and the fabulous mint design gallery by Lina Kanafani – both neighbours to my Scandinavian design store Skandium. Walking up Brompton Road, pick up fresh bread from the Quarter Grocer on Egerton Terrace, before turning right into Beauchamp Place. On your left, Penhaligon's perfumers have a cosy traditional shop and, across the road, 36 Opticians is an absolute must for aficionados of glassware. At No.38, Maroush never lets you down, serving simple but delicious Lebanese food. Further up the road there is The Beauchamp, always charming, with good food, and a great stop for a drink.

Reaching the end of the street, turn right into Walton Street. Here you find some true Chelsea gems. To unwind, pop into The Enterprise pub and restaurant or get a few delights from La Picena, one of the few original Italian Deli shops that, luckily, still grace our city. The Orientalist specialises in rare and unusual antique tribal Caucasian and Anatolian rugs, carpets, kilims, tapestries and artefacts, while The Walton Street Stationery Company offers bespoke stationery for all occasions. Further down Walton Street, pop into Coskun art gallery. If it is not a Damien Hirst exposé you find, then it will surely be another 'hot grafter' of the moment. The wonderful perfumery Santa Maria Novella sells handmade toiletry products from the famous Florentine pharmacy started by Dominican monks back in 1221.

Keep walking until you reach Sloane Avenue, home of The Conran Shop and other upmarket interior shops such as Rabih Hage, with the most eclectic and highly collectible interiors in town. Turn right into Whiteheads Grove until you access Cale Street and discover The Little Pie Man, which must be the smallest shop in London, offering excellent pies and other necessities to local foodies. Or pop in to Tom's Kitchen for a (well-deserved) relaxing lunch. Afterwards, peek into St Luke's Church and admire the fabulous East window, or find a free bench in the tranquil garden and enjoy the birdsong.

Co-founder of Skandium (p.020 & 042) skandium.com

01 B&B ITALIA
250 BROMPTON ROAD SW3 2AS
020 7591 8111
LONDON.BEBITALIA.COM
MON-SAT 10-6, SUN 12-5
SOUTH KENSINGTON

02 BISAZZA
60 SLOANE AVENUE SW3 3DD
020 7584 8837
BISAZZA.COM
MON-SAT 10-6
SOUTH KENSINGTON

Since it opened its doors in 2001, the B&B Italia flagship showroom at Brompton Cross has been a destination for connoisseurs of sophisticated Italian furniture and design devotees in general. Originally a car showroom, the site was converted in a collaboration between two contemporary-design pioneers: architects John Pawson and Antonio Citterio. Their shared principles of superior quality and refined detail have resulted in a fresh, light, contemporary space – the ideal environment in which to exhibit the B&B look. Furthermore, B&B recently expanded its shop frontage, making this showroom the biggest of its kind in London.

Indeed from the street it appears monumental. With its minimal aesthetic and dazzling materials – sheet glass, natural stone and bronze – it certainly stands out from the grandiose houses of the neighbourhood. Inside, a ramp carries the visitor from the entrance area into the main space, a cavernous 120-metre-long cathedral-like gallery divided into different room sets and furniture displays. Huge windows mark the endpoint of the showroom, where there is even room for a display of outdoor furniture.

The showroom team regularly updates the displays of B&B Italia's collections – accompanied as they are by the more conservative ranges from sister company Maxalto, as well as a smattering of quirkier designs from part-owned Dutch brand moooi. B&B Italia, however, carries the most regard and can boast a leading international reputation for high-end, comfortable 'lifestyle' living, which this immense showroom strives to convey. And it succeeds.

Bisazza's London ambassador showcases some of the finest interior decoration possibilities that mosaic tiles can offer. The two-storey flagship, presented as an ornate private living space, is an environment where clients, architects and designers can truly experience Bisazza's directional style.

A floral mosaic sweeps across the walls of the expansive ground floor in a pixellated pattern reminiscent of a William Morris fabric. The palette is a mixture of shimmering browns from the *Le Gemme* collection and white-gold *Oro*, a composition of hand-applied 24-carat gold leaf between two layers of glass. An iridescent gloss mosaic obscures the staircase leading to the subterranean level, an extensive display area for Bisazza's ranges, accompanied by a library of mosaic options and an area where clients can work with the professional team to create bespoke schemes.

This is not your average retail space but a tranquil environment where the company can allow its product to show its full potential and awaken the customer's imagination. Over the years, Bisazza has commissioned leading designers – including Patricia Urquiola, Fabio Novembre, Marcel Wanders, Studio Job, Jaime Hayón, and Tord Boontje – to push the envelope of mosaic design. The results may be over-the-top, but – above all – it is encouraging to see this age-old decorative technique reinvigorated by this visionary Italian brand.

 BOFFI

254 BROMPTON ROAD SW3 2AS

020 7590 8910

BOFFI-CHELSEA.COM

MON–SAT 10–6

SOUTH KENSINGTON

Boffi is a relatively new addition to the Brompton Cross design district. Kitchens are not included within the editorial remit of this guide, but this flagship is more of a temple to exquisite high-end detailing and craftsmanship than a boring, old kitchen shop. This is a destination in which to experience the Italian brand's signature designs in all their glory against a rather raw, industrial, yet gallery-like backdrop.

Designed by Boffi's creative director Piero Lissoni, the 600-square-metre showroom houses a sizable portion of Boffi's catalogue. Immaculate and gleaming under the spotlights, against a dark graphite backdrop, you will find some of the company's instant classics – my favourite being the textured *Duemilaotto* kitchen designed by Piero Lissoni, and Naoto Fukasawa's truly sensuous *Sabbia* and *Terra* bathtubs. Whatever the design, tactility is core to the experience.

The overall aesthetic is Minimalist. Boffi's handling of materials is modern and confident yet timeless in its appeal. The precision detailing is evident at first glance but becomes even more apparent in all the hidden, functional design interventions. Anyone with reservations as to what extent a kitchen, bathroom or partition wall can leave you wanting more obviously hasn't yet handled a Boffi bathroom tap. Get a grip, I hear you say. And you'd be right. But at this end of the market you expect perfection. And in an era of cost-cutting and mediocrity, it is refreshing to see that true quality can still prevail.

04 CHRISTOPHER FARR
🏠 6 BURNSALL STREET SW3 3ST
☎ 020 7349 0888
🔗 CHRISTOPHERFARR.COM
🕐 MON-FRI 10-6
⊖ SLOANE SQUARE

05 THE CONRAN SHOP
🏠 MICHELIN HOUSE, 81 FULHAM ROAD SW3 6RD
☎ 020 7589 7401
🔗 CONRANSHOP.CO.UK
🕐 MON-FRI 10-6, WED-THU 10-7, SA 10-6.30, SU 12-6
⊖ SOUTH KENSINGTON

In 1988 Christopher Farr began his business designing and producing high-quality contemporary rugs and has built up an envious reputation in this area since then. Trained as a painter, Farr chose to swap oil on canvas for wool and dye, and his modern creations soon attracted attention as a welcome antidote to the ornate antique-rug market. Farr, together with business partner Matthew Bourne, has released a considerable number of designs commissioned from a diversity of talents, including artists, fashion designers, furniture designers and architects. It hardly seems respectful to walk on rugs by the likes of Romeo Gigli, Allegra Hicks, Andreé Putman, Timorous Beasties, Sarah Morris and Ilse Crawford – which is why many customers choose to hang them instead.

The business is currently located in this Chelsea space, tucked away off the King's Road. The quiet office showroom attracts interior designers and architects, many of whom are regularly drawn back here by the unique qualities a Christopher Farr rug lends to their projects. For others, this is a tranquil environment in which to admire the collection and get a lesson from the team about Farr's production processes. Each rug uses the highest quality wool, which is hand-dyed and hand-spun by skilled weavers in Turkey. In my opinion, the designs are enhanced by the variation in tones, pattern and textures that come about from this skilled hands-on approach. I highly recommend experiencing these nuances for yourself.

Since launching in 1973 The Conran Shop has been synonymous with great design and quality, a consistent leader in the contemporary-homewares market. As its name suggests, it is the brainchild of Terence Conran – founder of Habitat and one of the UK's best-known food and design entrepreneurs. Possessing a keen eye for old spaces with character, Conran was moved to restore the iconic Michelin Building (the 1911 headquarters of the eponymous tyre company) and move The Conran Shop there in 1987.

Conran has always been a strong advocate of good design and he has made it his mission to increase the public's awareness of it by reimagining subjects to be more accessible and appealing. In many respects his stores are a physical manifestation of his design mores, boasting a well-edited combination of modern classics and cutting-edge releases sourced from around the world.

The product selection is focused on the home and caters to varying budgets. The ground floor boasts eye-catching window displays as well as styled room settings, while the lower level comprises more categoric displays of lighting, tableware, kitchenware and accessories. While Conran offers centrepiece sofas, voluptuous vases and lively lighting, it also provides smarter alternatives to everyday products that don't cost a fortune, and manages to steer many practical items away from the mundane.

The mini-emporium at Brompton Cross is a landmark in this neighbourhood and continues to attract a loyal following, whether seeking a gift or a complete domestic overhaul.

06 DAVID MELLOR
4 SLOANE SQUARE SW1W 8EE
020 7730 4259
DAVIDMELLORDESIGN.COM
MON-SAT 9.30-6, SUN 11-5
SLOANE SQUARE

07 DE PARMA
247 FULHAM ROAD SW3 6HY
020 7352 2414
DEPARMA.COM
MON-SAT 10-6
SOUTH KENSINGTON

The David Mellor shop is an established glass-fronted fixture in upmarket Sloane Square, where it has been trading kitchenware since 1969. The man behind it, David Mellor CBE, sadly passed away in 2009, leaving a legacy of work spanning his illustrious career. A Royal Designer for Industry, Mellor became a key figure in British design and manufacturing best known for his classic cutlery, all of which is produced at his factory near Sheffield and sold in this store. What few people realise is that Mellor was responsible for designing – among other civil interventions – the British traffic lights that we drive past daily.

The shop, spread over two floors, houses the entire collection of David Mellor's stainless-steel and silver cutlery, and the friendly staff will happily advise on the differences, aesthetic and otherwise. An impressive selection of tableware and kitchenware complements Mellor's own-brand offerings and makes this store a destination for anyone in the market for products of this genre. Mellor was a believer that well-designed equipment can improve your life, and this criteria has been carried through his stock.

The shop is a sophisticated environment for affluent Chelsea shoppers, although I wouldn't say it has high prices to match. My main frustration here is that it somehow fails to exhibit the full design achievements of this brand and its founder, so the story somehow passes the newcomer by.

At time of going to press, De Parma was just moving into its new Fulham Road premises from its Notting Hill gallery, where it operated under the Domus Gallery trading name. De Parma belongs to collector and dealer Gary De Sparham, who first dealt in traditional antiques before switching to what has become his ultimate passion: 20th-century design.

A regular participant in antiques and decorative-arts fairs, the gallery has become a respected and sought-after forum for quality mid-20th-century pieces, ranging from affordable furnishings to museum-calibre masterpieces. The key designers and producers represented hail largely from Italy and include Gio Ponti, Franco Albini, Ico Parisi, Stilnovo, Fornasetti and Fortana Arte. Standouts dotted among the Italian classics are a pair of *Steltman* chairs by Gerrit Rietveld, a Fritz Hansen reclining chair and Harry Bertoia's monoprints. Everything is in good condition, with the gallery's workshop sympathetically refurbishing where necessary.

Stepping further into the furniture market, De Sparham maintains retail/workshop premises in Chelsea's Gas Works (CORE 1, THE GAS WORKS, 2 MICHAEL ROAD SW6 2AN), an immense space that allows him to display larger pieces – dining tables, sofas, cabinets – and where he designs and produces bespoke furniture, an ever-growing sidestep from selling originals.

08 DESIGNERS GUILD
- 267 & 277 KING'S ROAD SW3 5EN
- 020 7351 5775
- DESIGNERSGUILD.COM
- MON-SAT 10-6, SUN 12-5
- SLOANE SQUARE/SOUTH KENSINGTON

09 FEW AND FAR
- 242 BROMPTON ROAD SW3 2BB
- 020 7225 7070
- FEWANDFAR.NET
- MON-SAT 10-6, SUN 12-5
- SOUTH KENSINGTON

Distinctly colourful and decorative, and at times overwhelmingly so, Designers Guild will wow anyone looking to add vibrancy to their home furnishings. The business was founded in 1970 by Tricia Guild, who has worked tirelessly to develop her brand into an award-winning contemporary-textiles outfit with global distribution. Today, it specialises in the design, manufacture and sale of furnishing fabrics, wall coverings, bed and bath collections and some furniture and home accessories.

This King's Road store is the dedicated London outlet for the brand and the perfect location for attracting affluent Londoners. The showroom is split into two entities, with the more prominent corner showroom, at No.277, housing an extensive range of wallpaper designs and more than 2,000 interior fabrics, all coordinated according to colour and pattern.

The larger neighbouring store is more lifestyle-driven and deals with a broader array of home products, including furniture, linens and bath and home accessories. The space is spread across several levels with items arranged in abundantly styled room sets that ooze confidence. In reality, I'm not sure many people would go the whole hog in their own homes, but there is something to be said for inspiring new ideas and possibilities. Quite frankly, any business encouraging punters away from identikit beige interior blandness should be thanked and supported.

When, in 2008, Priscilla Carluccio opened her own store in Brompton, there was little doubt it would be a culmination of her redoubtable professional life. Her energy and ambition have steered her through a number of instrumental creative positions at The Conran Shop (p.012 & 041), Habitat (p.067) and Heal's (p.090), through to the formation of the highly successful Carluccio's restaurant and food retailing brand with her husband Antonio.

One gets the impression that Priscilla has always been hungry for new challenges, but she remains humble in her self-titled role as a 'shop-keeper'. She is very clear about what she wants of Few and Far: a shop with a point of view, where product quality and impeccable service replace the faceless monotony of much retailing today. This shop tells the story of its keeper, as everything has been chosen with the criteria that Priscilla would have it in her own home.

The result is a boutique filled with a varied range of quirky items and one-off pieces from around the world, ranging from contemporary and antique furniture, to clothes from Morocco, India and Italy, to lighting by Ingo Maurer, to kitchenware and hand-crafted children's toys. Theatrical window displays are styled according to the theme of that season – an opportunity to regularly transform the space along with the merchandise.

There are elements of this store that don't factor on my radar, such as the clothing, but for a fresh and individual perspective and previously unseen products, Few and Far hits the mark.

12 JACQUELINE RABUN

➤ 32 GROSVENOR CRESCENT MEWS SW1X 7EX

☎ 020 7245 0524

↖ JACQUELINERABUN.COM

🕐 MON-FRI 10-6, SAT 10-1

🚇 HYDE PARK CORNER

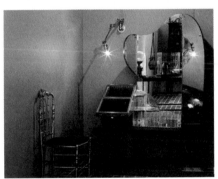

Concealed within an elegant, peaceful, gated mews, Jacqueline Rabun's store-cum-gallery could not provide a more welcome contrast to the hustle and bustle of Hyde Park Corner just minutes away.

A calm descends as you pass through the heavy glass door, and one can't escape that thrilling feeling of having discovered a wonderful secret. This converted stable oozes stylish tranquillity and is the ideal environment in which to explore Rabun's graceful and sensual jewellery.

The well-executed design for this stable conversion was undertaken as a collaboration between the jeweller and Lyndsay Milne. The original features of the space, including the neatly tiled floor and stall partitions, have been lovingly restored with a clean, modern aesthetic (the beams and walls are boxed and painted a uniform lichen grey), which successfully creates a number of intriguing, private environments – like the intimate consultation room, should you be after a bespoke piece of Rabun's magic.

In each stall is a new treasure to discover – with the jewels themselves displayed on playfully customised furnishings. You may find yourself gazing down into a glass-topped billiard table at a sparkling diamond in a golden cage (part of the *Grace* collection), or puzzling over a 1950s Danish Surrealist dresser in whose drawers lie bulbous silver forms to adorn the finger and wrist. A covetable gold necklace diverts your attention from the silver-plated school desk within which it is concealed.

A sweeping staircase leads up to the spacious design studio, encouraging an easy relationship between designer and client – not to mention the most civilised working environment for Rabun and her team. Along with her own collection on display here, a selection of pieces from her ongoing work with Georg Jensen is also present as an extra temptation.

Rabun's work and her presentation of it are a million miles from the industry's mainstream players. Her immaculate pieces, as well as the space in which they're presented, should be inspiration to those in the market for jewellery and those who appreciate truly individual, refined and sophisticated retailing.

13 MINT
📍 2 NORTH TERRACE SW3 2BA
☎ 020 7225 2228
🖅 MINTSHOP.CO.UK
🕐 MON-SAT 10.30-6.30, THU 10.30-7.30, SUN 12-5
⊖ SOUTH KENSINGTON

14 PHILLIPS DE PURY & COMPANY
📍 HOWICK PLACE SW1P 1BB
☎ 020 7318 4010
🖅 PHILLIPSDEPURY.COM
🕐 MON-FRI 10-6
⊖ VICTORIA

By no exaggeration, Mint is the most unique, dynamic and visionary design store in London. A veteran of Wigmore Street, it recently relocated to the Brompton Design District after the original location fell into developers' hands. No matter: this new space, a former kitchen showroom converted by Paul McAneary Architects, is the perfect blank canvas on which owner Lina Kanafani can layer the treasures from her next retail adventure.

Kanafani has always listened to her heart when selecting Mint's distinctive pieces, which range from quirky tabletop accessories to extraordinary lighting and larger furnishings. Her reputation for spotting emerging design talent has earned her a loyal following of customers eager to track down unconventional items that add narrative to the home.

At the time of going to press Mint had only just opened, but had done so with aplomb and a canny mix of mass-production pieces and handcrafted ceramics, glass and textiles. Items by design greats including Matali Crasset, Maarten Baas, Patricia Urquiola, Tord Boontje, Jaime Hayón, Studio Job and Doshi Levien are juxtaposed with conceptual pieces that even the design-savvy won't have seen before. This is the magic of this ever-evolving space: it is playful, escapist, impassioned. And it never stands still. A visit here is made all the more inviting by the presence of Kanafani and her friendly, knowledgeable team.

Twice a year all eyes are on the Phillips de Pury 'design' auctions of modern and contemporary furniture, lighting and *objets*. They have become a barometer for the country's appetite for collectible design and, in certain circles, are considered the hub of the 'design art' market. Recently Phillips de Pury added to its established programme of auctions, private sales and exhibitions with a new series of themed auctions, which also includes design lots.

The company lives in a converted Victorian post-sorting station in Howick Place; the volume and scale lends itself perfectly to showcasing the spectacular contemporary art, photography, jewellery and design. Contemporary, cutting-edge talents like Mario Testino, Guy Bourdin, Zaha Hadid, Rolf Sachs and Ross Lovegrove have all shown their work.

Where rival houses project a more traditional and elitist image, Phillips de Pury seems to favour the more youthful, edgy, controversial collections. Younger collectors have the opportunity to acquire high-quality works at relatively reasonable prices in the quarterly sale, *Saturday@Phillips*, which features works with no reserve – meaning no minimum sale price has been stipulated by the seller. In general, you'd best check the website for exhibition/auction schedules prior to your visit.

15 POLIFORM

278 KING'S ROAD SW3 5AW

020 7368 7600

POLIFORMUK.COM

MON–SAT 10–6

SLOANE SQUARE/SOUTH KENSINGTON

16 POTTERTON BOOKS

93 LOWER SLOANE STREET SW1W 8DA

020 7730 4235

POTTERTONBOOKSLONDON.CO.UK

MON–FRI 10–6, SAT–SUN 11–5

SLOANE SQUARE/SOUTH KENSINGTON

This immense award-winning showroom from furniture brand Poliform sits confidently in its Cubist fixture on the King's Road – a London presence one might expect from such a high-end Italian brand. The vast floor-to-ceiling windows treat passers-by to a treat of slick sofas, beds, wardrobes, storage systems and kitchens dominating this 750-square-metre space. This Minimalist box was originally designed by architect Paolo Piva (with a redesign in 2006) and forms an unobtrusive backdrop for the company's contemporary look, which the company describes as 'comfortable Minimalism'. Precision kitchen designs from subsidiary company Varenna also share the space.

The showroom is uncompromisingly modern, aesthetically polished and luxurious in its command of space. The high ceilings and strict architectural lines set the scene for the chic simplicity and functionality of a working kitchen by Paolo Piva, a bold Cubist sofa by Paola Navone, a sleek sideboard by Carlo Colombo and a dream bed by Marcel Wanders.

There is no doubt that designs from Poliform and Varenna can boast top-quality materials and manufacture, which goes some way to justifying the high price tags. As is my issue with the presentation of so many Italian brands, these two tend to forget about adding some personality, warmth and human touch to soften the rather hard-edged surfaces and finishes. If you struggle to picture these pieces in your own home, the on-site bespoke design team and helpful showroom staff may hopefully bring that vision into focus.

You can tell this is not just any bookshop as soon as you walk through the doors. Potterton Books is simply inspirational – as are its glossy tomes that are simply published works of art. The company has been in business for more than a quarter of a century; its head office is in Sessay, North Yorkshire, and there are branches in New York and Los Angeles. But it's the London shop that is the most comprehensive and, consequently, the most difficult to leave. Based around the corner from Chelsea's antiques district, Potterton stocks a thorough selection of titles on interior design, fine and decorative art, architecture, fashion, lifestyle and culture. And if it doesn't have exactly what you're looking for, someone will source it for you. There's also a wide range of rare, vintage and out-of-print books – such as David Hicks's *Living with Taste* or *Vogue's Book of Houses, Gardens, People* from 1968.

The shop has a relaxed atmosphere and just enough elbow room for lingering. Themed displays make shopping easier and staff are always on hand to offer friendly advice on suitable titles. It is a draw for smart local professionals – in fact anyone seeking a conversation-piece for the coffee table or to give as a gift. It is also worth keeping an eye out for the regular signings and book events – a cut above the rest.

17 RABIH HAGE
- 69-71 SLOANE AVENUE SW3 3DH
- (020 7823 8288
- RABIH-HAGE.COM
- MON-SAT 10-6
- SOUTH KENSINGTON

18 ROYAL COLLEGE OF ART
- KENSINGTON GORE SW7 2EU
- (020 7590 4444
- RCA.AC.UK
- DAILY 10-6 (DURING EXHIBITIONS)
- SOUTH KENSINGTON

Paris-trained architect Rabih Hage opened this gallery in 2002, introducing his collection of artwork and design he curates personally from talents he meets and nurtures around the world. Hage has always been successful at combining the functional with the non-functional – an approach more prevalent in Parisian galleries. And he inadvertently preempted the 'design art' movement that has exploded in recent years, whereby certain design and designers have gained the 'collectible' status enjoyed by the art world. In tandem with his ground-floor gallery, he runs a successful interior-design business from his lower-ground office.

The relatively small Sloane Avenue gallery hosts several exhibitions a year. Past shows include commissioned works by established names like Matali Crasset and Aki Kuroda and more recent talents Paul Cocksedge, Assa Ashuach, Karen Ryan and Moritz Waldemeyer. Rabih Hage is also the UK dealer for Dutch designer and manufacturer Piet Hein Eek, whose strikingly diverse furniture, lighting and accessories are normally a feature in the space – most notably his signature *Scrapwood* range.

Most certainly you'll sense a lack of pretension here – which, frankly, comes as a welcome relief from the snobbery we often associate with the art and antiques scene. You will always be warmly welcomed at Rabih Hage, and if the personable owner himself is in the building, you will more than likely find yourself engrossed in conversation.

The Royal College of Art (RCA) is the world's only university of art and design devoted solely to postgraduate degrees in fine art, applied art, design, communications and the humanities. It was founded in 1837 as the Government School of Design, and its staff, students and alumni comprise an internationally renowned community of artists, designers and academics who play a significant role in the shaping of modern culture. The RCA has produced past masters like Christopher Dresser, David Mellor and Alan Fletcher and today's leading talents: Tracey Emin, James Dyson, Thomas Heatherwick, Jasper Morrison and Konstantin Grcic, to name a few.

The college's galleries and lecture theatres are regularly home to a lively programme of exhibitions, events, academic symposiums and talks by leading art and design figures. The annual *Secret* postcard exhibition invites artists, celebrities and students to transform blank postcards into works of art. Throughout the academic year, the RCA proudly presents the work of its current students, the grand finale traditionally being the graduate Summer Show – always a big hit and a great opportunity for the public to buy work from emerging contemporary artists before they are snapped up by galleries and collectors. Further to the RCA's in-house events, external exhibitions from selected partners occur at varying intervals in the year. It is not advised to just turn up, so be sure to check the RCA website before making the journey.

19 SERPENTINE GALLERY

- KENSINGTON GARDENS W2 3XA
- 020 7402 6075
- SERPENTINEGALLERY.ORG
- DAILY 10-6
- KNIGHTSBRIDGE/SOUTH KENSINGTON/LANCASTER GT.

20 SIGMAR

- 263 KING'S ROAD SW3 5EL
- 020 7751 5801
- SIGMARLONDON.COM
- MON-SAT 10-6, SUN 12-5
- SLOANE SQUARE/SOUTH KENSINGTON

For 40 years the Serpentine Gallery has staged pioneering exhibitions of modern and contemporary art and consequently secured itself a fine international reputation. The always changing programme of exhibitions features seminal artists such as Ellsworth Kelly, Gerhard Richter, Dan Flavin, Bridget Riley, Damien Hirst and Cindy Sherman, all showing works across a range of media.

Housed in a classical 1934 tea pavilion, the gallery is, to me, an ideal size for exhibitions – not too big, not too small. Wandering through the building, you glimpse occasional views out to Hyde Park and the adjacent Serpentine Lake, after which the gallery was named.

Each summer the grounds come alive with a temporary pavilion designed by an internationally acclaimed architect who has never before completed a building on English soil. Recent honorees have included giants like Rem Koolhaas, Oscar Niemeyer, Toyo Ito, Daniel Libeskind and Frank Gehry, who have contributed to the programme with some memorable structures; the 2009 pavilion was built by Japanese architecture practice SANAA. It is well worth checking out the busy calendar of events, talks, film screenings, concerts and parties that take place at the pavilion during the summer months.

A trip here is always worth combining with a walk around the tranquil park. The gallery closes for periods between exhibitions, but its popular bookshop, operated by Koenig Books (p.077) remains open regardless.

To find a refined dealer of 20th-century European decorative art and design is a welcome treat on the busy King's Road. If you aren't paying attention, you could easily pass right by this small outlet, its frontage purposefully devoid of the usual retail fanfare. If you do miss Sigmar, be sure to backtrack as it is certainly worth enjoying the well-edited interior products that share a focus on fine craftsmanship and longevity, be they vintage or new.

Sigmar was founded by Ebba Thott and Nina Hertig on their mutual passion for Modernism and quality. The owners merge of two complementary mindsets: those of a designer and a decorative-arts dealer. Together the partners offer a strong background in 19th- and 20th-century modern and use Sigmar to underline some of the principal values of that period. Across two small floors they have displayed many otherwise hard-to-find items such as Carl Aubock's *Tea Trolley* and brass hooks; an early Arne Jacobsen brass floor light; recent Michael Anastassiades bronze *Ball Lights*; or skeletal *LinE* shelving by Yedidia Blonders.

Sigmar aims to unite function, beauty and craft in an optimal way – and Thott and Hertig apply this philosophy to their interior design service too. This business has got a clear point of view, which is steered by the vision of its passionate owners. Take a moment to chat to them in the shop and you'll soon find their integrity and enthusiasm is contagious.

21 SKANDIUM

- 247 BROMPTON ROAD SW3 2EP
- 020 7584 2066
- SKANDIUM.COM
- MON–SAT 10–6.30, THU 10–7, SUN 11–5
- SOUTH KENSINGTON

Spurred on by the success of their shop on Marylebone High Street (p.042) and concession in Selfridges (p.042), the owners of Skandium brought their brand of Modernism to the Brompton Quarter in 2005. Located on a prominent corner, the sizable two-floor retail unit is very much in the spirit of the original but is more spacious. The refreshingly bright space is home to a broader product range – not just Scandinavian Modernist housewares and furniture but other complementary pieces that command similar aesthetic formalism from companies like Knoll, Vitra, Cassina, Ercol and Isokon Plus.

Merchandise is displayed with pride of place here, with no signs of clutter, and so Skandium positions itself somewhere between a furniture shop and a design museum. Beautiful objects such as Aalto's 1930s *Paimio Chair*, Jacobsen's *AJ Royal Lamp* and Wegner's *Three Legged Shell Chair* are confidently showcased and given appropriate space to shine. Smaller accessories or gift items attract passers-by drawn to the colourful glassware of iittala or the vibrant Marimekko fabrics that help to energise the space.

Every last detail of this successful business – from the range of products sourced to the highly professional staff, sleek interior, confident branding and tidy displays – is the result of hard work from its dedicated trio of owners. Above all, Skandium has helped to open our eyes to the confident simplicity, considered functionality and material honesty of quality Nordic design.

22 TASCHEN

- 12 DUKE OF YORK SQUARE SW3 4LY
- 020 7881 0795
- TASCHEN.COM
- MON-FRI 10-6, WED, SAT 10-7, SUN 12-6
- SLOANE SQUARE

23 VICTORIA AND ALBERT MUSEUM

- CROMWELL ROAD SW7 2RL
- 020 7942 2000
- VAM.AC.UK
- DAILY 10-5.45, FRI 10-10
- SOUTH KENSINGTON

Located beside the new Saatchi Gallery on the recently developed Duke of York Square, the London outpost for the German publisher Taschen is a courageous, contemporary addition to the otherwise swanky Chelsea neighbourhood. Designed, like all the Taschen stores worldwide, by design maverick Philippe Starck, the space houses a bookstore and gallery, and stocks the entire range of Taschen tomes covering art, photography, architecture, fashion, film, design, travel, pop culture and sex.

With theatricality, wit and signature flair à la Starck, the fresh interior defies the fustiness and claustrophobia of many bookshops. The display stands are made of cast bronze formed in an abstract tree-trunk-like design surrounded with billowing white drapes – a fitting backdrop for Taschen's glossy titles. Added to that is an ever-changing display of prints and photographs in the basement gallery, complemented by some of Taschen's limited-edition books. Whether you're just passing by or happen to be looking for a biography of a porn star, a book on Rothko or a recent design compendium, this will certainly make for a good port of call.

The Victoria and Albert Museum is the world's largest museum of decorative arts and design, housing a collection of more than 4.5 million objects. Named after Queen Victoria and Prince Albert, the reigning monarchs when the museum was founded in 1852, it has since grown to cover some 145 galleries filled with 5,000 years' worth of artefacts in virtually every medium, from the cultures of Europe, North America, Asia and North Africa. Somewhat frustratingly, a vast number of items are in storage and never see the light of day.

In 2001 the museum embarked on an ambitious redevelopment programme that has seen a major overhaul of the departments, including the refurbishment of certain galleries – examples of which are the new Contemporary Glass and Ceramic galleries. Other new spaces include the Sackler Centre for arts education, the gift shop and the John Madejski Garden. To complement the permanent collections the V&A stages temporary exhibitions covering a broad range of subjects, from design to fashion and photography to architecture. *Cold War Modern: Design 1945-70; Vivienne Westwood: A Retrospective; Modernism: Designing a New World;* and *Telling Tales* are some of the memorable shows from recent years.

A whole diary of events take place here throughout the year. Noteworthy is the after-hours event *Friday Late*, held on the last Friday of every month. The evenings are centred around a theme or exhibition and feature live performances, guest DJs, a late bar and other fun and games.

● *Eat & Drink*

24 THE ANGLESEA ARMS 15 SELWOOD TERRACE
SW7 3QG | 020 7373 7960 | ANGLESEAARMS.COM
Traditional historic pub in what was once a
neighbourhood of Charles Dickens. Reputation
for good food and drink.

25 AUBAINE 260-262 BROMPTON ROAD SW3 2AS
020 7052 0100 | AUBAINE.CO.UK
Sophisticated but relaxed re-invention of a
classic Parisian café and boulangerie. Also
a bakery. Leisurely but glammed-up lunch.
Great for people-watching.

26 BIBENDUM RESTAURANT MICHELIN HOUSE,
81 FULHAM ROAD SW3 6RD | 020 7581 5817
BIBENDUM.CO.UK
Fresh seafood cuisine. Original setting in the
iconic Michelin House. Beautiful Art Deco
architecture. Tiles and pictures depicting great
races of the past. Great for a quick glass of wine
and a nibble or early dinner.

27 BLUEBIRD CAFÉ AND RESTAURANT
350 KING'S ROAD SW3 5UU | 020 7559 1000
BLUEBIRD-RESTAURANT.COM
Modern European food. Sophisticated design.
Rich colours, subtle lighting. Relaxed mood.
Great for elegant dinner. Quiet entrance area
ideal for a business meeting.

28 BROMPTON QUARTER CAFÉ 223-225 BROMPTON
ROAD SW3 2EJ | 020 7225 2107
BROMPTONQUARTERCAFE.COM
Part deli, part bakery, part restaurant with a
passion for fine, tasty food. Trendy, upscale yet
easy-going. Very busy on the weekends. For fresh
food and delicacies try Quarter Grocer around
the corner.

29 CASA BRINDISA 7-9 EXHIBITION ROAD SW7 2HQ
020 7590 0008 | CASABRINDISA.COM
Traditional Spanish tapas menu. Tapas bar, ham-
carving counter, cheese room and delicatessen
in the basement. Tasty, affordable lunch.

30 LE CERCLE 1 WILBRAHAM PLACE SW1X 9AE
020 7901 9999 | LECERCLE.CO.UK
Impressive Gallic dishes with a twist.
Underground space. Ask for the discreet booths.
Exposed wine cellar. Smart crowd.

31 DAYLESFORD ORGANIC 44B PIMLICO RD SW1W 8LP
020 7881 8060 | DAYLESFORDORGANIC.COM
Organic food, organic farming. Deli, butcher and
bakery. Canteen-like environment. Elegant white-
marble decor and beautiful customers. A stylish
breakfast or lunch. Gets very busy for brunch,
especially on sunny weekends.

32 THE EBURY 11 PIMLICO ROAD SW1W 8NA
020 7730 6784 | THEEBURY.CO.UK
Restaurant with a brasserie-style menu.

Large 60s-era arched windows. Wooden bar,
comfortable leather seating. Sophisticated, cool
crowd. Ideal for a cosy dinner. Great wine list.

33 ECLIPSE 111-113 WALTON STREET SW3 2HP
020 7581 0123 | ECLIPSE-VENTURES.COM
A taste of Mediterranean in the city. Opulent
leather booths. Small and cosy. Irresistible
watermelon martini.

34 EIGHT OVER EIGHT 392 KING'S ROAD SW3 5UZ
020 7349 9934 | RICKERRESTAURANTS.COM
Modern Japanese dim sum. Eastern-
influenced decor. Dark wood floors, light walls,
oriental lampshades. Smart location for a
memorable meal.

35 FIFTH FLOOR LONDON HARVEY NICHOLS,
109-125 KNIGHTSBRIDGE SW1X 7RJ
020 7235 5250 | HARVEYNICHOLS.COM
Fine modern European dining in one of
London's most fashionable stores. Fresh
ingredients from the adjoining Harvey Nichols
Foodmarket. Celebrity hotspot. For a quick lunch
or a break from your retail therapy try the airy,
open-concept Fifth Floor Café and Bar.

36 GRENADIER 18 WILTON ROW SW1X 7NR
020 7235 3074
Long enjoyed a reputation as one of the most
haunted pubs – but not the easiest to find. Always
packed with locals. Good variety of hand-
pumped ales. Great for lazy Sunday lunch.

37 THE GROCER ON KINGS 184A KING'S ROAD
SW3 5XP | 020 7351 5544 | THEGROCERON.COM
Intelligent, seasonal, fresh and ready-made food.
Small seating area at the back. There is another
one in Notting Hill (p.034).

38 KUMO 11 BEAUCHAMP PLACE SW3 1NQ
020 7225 0944 | KUMOKNIGHTSBRIDGE.COM
Japanese cocktail bar and restaurant. Well-chosen
selection of traditional Japanese food perfect
for sharing. Minimalist in style with impressive
oriental details. Glamorous crowd.

39 MANICOMIO 85 DUKE OF YORK SQUARE SW3 4LY
020 7730 3366 | MANICOMIO.CO.UK
Freshly prepared, quality Italian food. Simple,
understated decor, relaxed atmosphere. Large,
open terrace. Get freshly baked bread and other
Italian delicacies from a small shop at the front.

40 NAPKET 342 KING'S ROAD SW3 5UR
020 7352 9832 | NAPKET.COM
Uber-chic café-deli. A large 'create your own'
salad bar. Gourmet selection of freshly prepared
sandwiches, soups and desserts. Slick interior
design. Dark and glossy decor. Even the toilet
paper is black.

41 THE PIG'S EAR 35 OLD CHURCH ST SW3 5BS
020 7352 2908 | TURNINGEARTH.CO.UK/THEPIGSEAR
Well-established gastropub with a dining room

a stone's throw from King's Road. Classic British brasserie menu. A fine array of beers and wines.

42   TINI 87-89 WALTON STREET SW3 2HP
     020 7589 8558 | TINIBAR.COM

Italian aperitivo bar. Chic after-work spot. The glamour of 1950s Italy. Black-leather banquettes, copper-top tables, framed Pirelli calendars. Truly *la dolce vita*.

43   TOMS KITCHEN 27 CALE STREET SW3 3QP
     020 7349 0202 | TOMSKITCHEN.CO.UK

Casual, all-day brasserie-style venue. British and traditional French cuisine. Whitewashed brick walls, scrubbed-wood tables. Bar on the first floor. Very relaxed, unpretentious.

44   ZUMA 5 RAPHAEL STREET SW7 1DL
     020 7584 1010 | ZUMARESTAURANT.COM

Glamorous Japanese fusion food. Swanky wood, granite and stone interior. Open robata grill. Expensive, but if you can afford it, your meal will be a truly special event.

● *Indulge*

45   LA CAVE FROMAGE 24-25 CROMWELL PL SW7 2LD
     0845 108 8222 | LA-CAVE.CO.UK

The best French and British cheeses from local farmers and dairies. More than 200 cheeses available.

46   THE GARDEN 30 PIMLICO ROAD SW1W 8LJ
     020 7730 2943 | DAYLESFORDORGANIC.COM

An offshoot of Daylesford Organic. Gardening products, garden furniture and plants as well as desirable antiques like vases, buckets and baskets. Environmentally conscious.

47   HARRODS FOOD HALL 87-135 BROMPTON ROAD
     SW1X 7XL | 020 7730 1234 | HARRODS.COM

The *pièce de résistance* of the famous department store. The finest foods and luxury groceries. Lavish decor. Mouth-watering experience. Enjoy an afternoon break at the picturesque Ladurée tea room.

48   HAYNES HANSON & CLARK 7 ELYSTAN ST SW3 3NT
     020 7584 7927 | HHANDC.CO.UK

Independent wine merchant. London's top Burgundy specialist. Attractive little shop with helpful staff.

49   LUIGI'S DELICATESSEN 349 FULHAM RD SW10 9TW
     020 7352 7739 | LUIGISDELICATESSEN.COM

Family-owned deli. Very popular local one-stop shop for all kinds of Italian delicacies, from pasta to cheese and wine. In business 30 years.

50   MOXONS 17 BUTE STREET SW7 3EY
     020 7591 0050 | MOXONSFRESHFISH.COM

Traditionally styled fishmongers. Great varied selection of fresh fish. Helpful and friendly staff

will happily give you advice on the best way to cook the fish you are buying.

51   PARTRIDGES 2-5 DUKE OF YORK SQUARE SW3 4LY
     020 7730 0651 | PARTRIDGES.CO.UK

A fine all-round grocer with emphasis on British deli food and cheese. Hosts an open-air Saturday food market. Small café at the back. Expensive but top-quality foods.

52   POILANE 46 ELIZABETH STREET SW1W 9PA
     020 7808 4910 | POILANE.FR

Renowned French bakery in the heart of London. Traditional methods of baking. Not the cheapest fare in town, but the freshness and aroma live up to the expectation.

53   WILD AT HEART 54 PIMLICO ROAD SW1W 8LP
     020 7229 1174 | WILDATHEART.COM

Fresh flowers with a signature style. One of the most recognised floral designers in the city. This is its flagship.

● *Sleep*

54   BLAKES 33 ROLAND GARDENS SW7 3PF
     020 7370 6701 | BLAKESHOTELS.COM

Created by internationally renowned designer and hotelier Anoushka Hempel. Pure modern decadence. Each room has its own style, inspired by Russia, Greece and India. Ideal for those who appreciate privacy and immaculate service. But it all comes at a price.

55   ELEVEN CADOGAN GARDENS 11 CADOGAN GDNS
     SW3 2RJ | 020 7730 7000 | NO11LONDON.COM

Opulent boutique hotel overlooking the beautifully secluded Cadogan Gardens. Sumptuous theatrical interior. Ideal for the modern discerning traveller.

56   KNIGHTSBRIDGE HOTEL 10 BEAUFORT GARDENS
     SW3 1PT | 020 7584 6300 | FIRMDALE.COM

A modern English rose set in three classic Victorian terraced houses. A medley of luxuriant colour, swishy sofas, marble fireplaces and linen drapery. A true metropolitan jewel.

57   MY HOTEL CHELSEA 35 IXWORTH PLACE SW3 3QX
     020 7225 7500 | MYHOTELS.COM

Softer, more feminine sibling of its sleekly modern Bloomsbury original. Embraces the distinctive character of the Chelsea surroundings. Softer pastel tones and floral patterns. Country farmhouse feel.

58   NUMBER SIXTEEN HOTEL 10 SUMNER PL SW7 3EG
     020 7589 5232 | NUMBERSIXTEENHOTEL.CO.UK

Well-groomed Kensington hideaway. Excellent location seconds from South Kensington station. Uniquely decorated rooms using flirty florals and savvy colour combinations. Reasonable prices.

It is both creative nerve centre and gentrified 'blandscape'. Designer TIM PARSONS on why London keeps his peers coming back

A VIEW FROM THE STUDIO

For most anybody, cities offer a myriad of currents that guide our emotions and behaviour. But for designers, this urban texture – the 'psychogeography' of the city – also serves as both inspiration and working context. London serves up an exhausting array of material, both physical and conceptual, to respond to. While this richness is one major draw for designers, there is much else that contributes to their experience of the city as a creative stimulus.

Perhaps most importantly, London is a place where designers can find respect for their ideas. Creating the truly new calls for intuitive leaps and can require suspension of disbelief on the part of the viewer. This open-mindedness towards new ideas, often lacking in the provinces, is engendered in London's citizens from many sources. The nature of living in a multicultural city means tolerating values in contrast to our own. This permeates the collective psyche and enables creative expression to flourish. A brave sartorial statement that would attract derision in style capitals like Paris and Milan is unlikely to raise an eyebrow on a London street. Fresh thinking is encouraged both within and beyond the cultural sector, fuelled by the graduates of the city's creative institutions and measured by critical interest from the media.

Adding to artists' sense of affirmation is the design literacy among London's consumers. The city has always had a public willing to invest in the handiwork of its creative trades. While some trades have declined or disappeared, the city has retained its workforce of creatives whose craft cannot, either for practical or ideological reasons, be outsourced to the Far East. From the tailors of Savile Row to the set-builders of theatreland, there are pockets of skilled designers quietly contributing to the visual quality of London life.

Even London's mayor has thrown his weight behind competitions to design a new Routemaster bus, and a carafe to encourage the consumption of tap water in restaurants. So there's a growing awareness of design's importance in the corridors of power.

'A brave sartorial statement that would attract derision in style capitals like Paris and Milan is unlikely to raise an eyebrow on a London street.'

That said, being a designer in London isn't without its challenges. The concentric rings of affluence that spread through the 'edgy', 'up and coming' neighbourhoods where many designers base themselves continually push them farther from the centre. In the 1980s, before the gentrification of Whitechapel, Shoreditch and Hoxton, it was possible to rent studio space a stone's throw from London's financial district for a relative pittance. Now designers who remain in the area pay heavily for the privilege. Of course this gentrification has its benefits. Shops, bars and restaurants need interiors, graphic identities, artwork... When correctly managed, such opportunities allow designers to play a role in fighting the 'blandscaping' of the city's streets by supermarket giants and chain stores.

Although the new business-oriented social-networking tools (Linked-In, Meetup.com, etc) make it easy to find like-minded practitioners, there is a flip side. Hanging with your tribe isn't necessarily the way to find challenging opinions of the kind likely to open up new avenues of thought. Inertia can lead to a blinkered outlook. With growing numbers of designers chasing the same opportunities, decision-makers often revert to the 'usual suspects' rather than attempting to decipher the cacophony of new voices. So often a scene that should be highly diverse occasionally exhibits an unhealthy insularity.

Despite its numerous paradoxes, London's design scene benefits from the relentless energy of its members and the diversity of their approaches. There is both establishment and avant-garde. There are respected academic institutions and a thriving corporate design infrastructure. And, for better or worse, there is the unflinching optimism of countless wannabes — like LA's budding actors waiting (on tables) for their big break. London is their playground, the annual design festival their showcase. And the fruits of their labour are for us all to feast upon.

TIM PARSONS IS A PRODUCT DESIGNER, WRITER AND LECTURER ON ALL MATTERS DESIGN
TIMPARSONS.INFO

Tom Dixon opens its first London Showroom

Wharf Building Portobello Dock
344 Ladbroke Grove
London
W10 5BU

Open 9am – 6pm weekdays only
+44 (0) 207 400 0500
www.tomdixon.net

Tom
Dixon

Notting Hill & Holland Park

TRELLICK TOWER, GOLBORNE ROAD

↘ Chelsea, Knightsbridge & Brompton | p.008

● *Design shops & C20th vintage*

● *Eat & Drink*
● *Indulge*
● *Sleep*
  (pp.034-035)

● ● ● *Take a walk route*

01 FLOW
02 PHILIP THOMAS
03 THE RUG COMPANY
04 SCP WEST
05 THEMES & VARIATIONS
06 TOM DIXON
07 VESSEL

Notting Hill
& Holland Park

TAKE A WALK
Angel Monzon *

From Notting Hill Gate, walk down Pembridge Villas to Arancina for an Italian coffee and the best mini-croissants in the area. Try their authentic Sicilian pasta and pizza – not the usual stodgy tourist stuff. Continue wandering through the tree-lined streets until you reach the chic chocolate shop Melt on Ledbury Road for fabulous handmade truffles.

Proceed onto Westbourne Grove for the area's finest collection of 20th-century design at Themes & Variations. Across the street, England & Co carries contemporary art. Have a seasonal snack at Daylesford Organic, or if you want truly imaginative food that's irresistibly presented, try Ottolenghi at the junction with Ledbury Road.

Continue on and you'll discover a treasure trove of high-end fashion, shoes, jewellery and stylish childrenswear. Head on to the secluded Colville Mews to visit the Museum of Brands, Packaging and Advertising, for anyone interested in nostalgic graphics. Then hit Portobello Road (Friday is the best day), where you can buy excellent organic meat and game from the family-owned Kingsland Edwardian Butcher.

Turn left onto Blenheim Crescent for the famous Travel Bookshop; Books for Cooks has the largest selection of hard-to-find cookbooks. Stock up on spices from the bewildering selection at The Spice Shop. For lunch, stop at E&O for fusion cooking and celebrity-spotting, or hang out at the beautifully refurbished Electric Cinema & Brasserie on Portobello Road. Continue down Blenheim to R Garcia & Sons, an outstanding Spanish deli-café.

Now it's straight ahead to London's legendary music store Honest Jon's Records and on through to Golborne Road, one of London's most eclectic thoroughfares. Rummage through the avant-garde clothing at Kokon To Zai, buy fresh fish at Golborne Fisheries or take home some moreish custard tarts from Lisboa Patisserie. Your walk ends at the iconic landmark Trellick Tower (1972), a Brutalist masterpiece by Erno Goldfinger, with the world-famous vintage shop Relik at its foot.

Co-owner of Vessel (p.033)
vesselgallery.com

01 FLOW
- 1-5 NEEDHAM ROAD W11 2RP
- 020 7243 0782
- FLOWGALLERY.CO.UK
- MON-SAT 11-6
- NOTTING HILL GATE

02 PHILIP THOMAS
- 4A LADBROKE GROVE W11 3BG
- 020 7229 4044
- PJTHOMAS.COM
- TUE-SAT 11-6
- HOLLAND PARK

Hidden on a side street off Notting Hill's fashionable Westbourne Grove, Flow was established by Yvonna Demczynska more than a decade ago to showcase the best of international and British applied arts. Today Flow represents some 100 artists, who work in ceramics, glass, paper, wood, textiles, metal and jewellery.

Having spent her childhood behind the Iron Curtain in a region boasting a rich history of quality handicrafts, Demczynska has a strong appreciation for the art of craft. At her gallery she eschews mass-produced products in favour of this impressive collection of both functional and non-functional objects – all original and unique. Her massive client list is a testament to the gallery's integrity.

This light, airy space is an oasis of calm and tranquillity, filled with a mix of tactile handmade pieces in muted, earthy tones and those awash in vibrant, eye-catching colours. You will find John Lewis's bright and fluid-shaped glass vases; Maria Jauhiainen's delicate brass tableware; Annette Bugansky's textured ceramic vessels; and Barry Griffiths's geometric wire furniture. In addition to the permanent display featured on the white walls, Flow produces up to six exhibitions a year; these often explore creative talent from abroad – like the recent *Land Marks* exhibition, featuring crafts from the Danish Island of Bornholm.

Blurring the distinction between functional design and decorative craft, Flow has built a following of niche clientele seeking more unusual and collectible additions for their homes.

Philip Thomas started out in the furniture business when he was only 18 years old, working on Portobello Road before progressing to an antiques shop in Westbourne Grove. It was there that he honed his knowledge of antiques, before eventually branching out into selling modern desks, sofas, chairs, lighting, mirrors and *objets* from his own boutique.

Thomas sources stock from France, Italy, Denmark and Germany, restoring and reupholstering if need be. Then he arranges them in his Ladbroke Grove space, decorating the black-framed window with choice pieces.

The quality here belies the small, disjointed space; some great pieces stray, refreshingly, from the usual suspects of mid-century Modernism. On my visit, designs by Belgian architect Jules Wabbes were prominently displayed, including an exquisite 1960s rosewood desk accompanied by a pair of his bronze table lamps from the following decade. A 70s sideboard in black lacquer and stainless steel, designed by the legendary Willy Rizzo, was topped with Italian glass fish sculptures from the 1940s and spotlit by a striking 1958 hanging light by Italian producer Stilnovo.

All in all, the shop feels tidy and approachable, its rough, wire-cut oak floor and pale green walls a clean backdrop for an accomplished selection of collectibles.

03 THE RUG COMPANY
- 124 HOLLAND PARK AVENUE W11 4UE
- 020 7229 5148
- THERUGCOMPANY.INFO
- MON–SAT 10–6, SUN 11–5
- HOLLAND PARK

04 SCP WEST
- 87–93 WESTBOURNE GROVE W2 4UL
- 020 7229 3612
- SCP.CO.UK
- MON–SAT 10–6, SUN 11–5
- BAYSWATER/QUEENSWAY

Collecting rugs was a hobby and passion for husband and wife duo Christopher and Suzanne Sharp. Their love of floor coverings led them to form the Rug Company in 1997. Today, more than 200 designs can be sourced at showrooms in London, New York, Los Angeles, Miami and Dubai.

The company originally marketed vintage Armenian, Berber, Persian and Turkish carpets in addition to its own designs. Then, working with popular stylemakers from the UK and abroad, the Sharps launched the *Designer Collection*. Since then, they have collaborated with such luminaries of fashion design as Paul Smith, Vivienne Westwood, Matthew Williamson and Diane von Furstenberg, and commissioned product designers including Tom Dixon, Ron Arad, Barber Osgerby and Committee.

Each rug is hand-knotted in Nepal and takes about four months to manufacture; considering the amount of skill and labour involved, the average price of £2,000 seems reasonable enough. Recently the Rug Company unveiled a range of soft furnishings, such as cushion covers and wallhangings.

The London store, spread across two floors, manages to communicate most of the company's sizable output – visitors can view the company's entire catalogue if a sample doesn't happen to be in store. That is, if the salespeople acknowledge your presence. In typical British fashion, I was ignored on my visit. But don't let that deter you if you're in the market for a knockout contemporary rug.

Sheridan Coakley was running this cutting-edge design and retail outfit more than 20 years ago, at a time when there were very few producers of modern furniture in Britain. He is now acknowledged to be one of the country's most respected manufacturers and suppliers of contemporary design, working with and championing a stellar lineup of British talent.

This 200-square-metre outpost on Westbourne Grove is the West London sibling of the original SCP store in East London (p.136). Designed by architects Munckenbeck & Marshall, the glass-fronted corner space is a veritable stage for a cast of tantalising furniture, lighting, and accessories bursting with character.

Before SCP opened here in 2007, this affluent area of West London was remarkably low on offerings when it came to modern furniture and lighting. Now locals have every opportunity to tap into the British and European contemporary aesthetic. Furniture-wise, the emphasis is on SCP's own range of sofas, chairs, tables and storage in its signature functionalist aesthetic – made even more appealing with colourful upholsteries, accent lighting and quirky accessories.

With such a strong range, SCP continues to attract shoppers with varying budgets – from those seeking a stylish gift to others kitting out an entire house. It has most certainly proved to be a welcome addition to this part of town.

⑤ THEMES & VARIATIONS

- 📍 231 WESTBOURNE GROVE W11 2SE
- ☎ 020 7727 5531
- ↖ THEMESANDVARIATIONS.COM
- ⏱ MON-FRI 10-1, 2-6, SAT 10-6
- ⊖ NOTTING HILL GATE

⑥ TOM DIXON

- 📍 PORTOBELLO DOCK, 344 LADBROKE GROVE W10 5BU
- ☎ 020 7400 0500
- ↖ TOMDIXON.NET
- ⏱ MON-FRI 9-6
- ⊖ LADBROKE GROVE/KENSAL GREEN

What makes the uber-chic Themes & Variations so successful? The vision of its owner, the elegant Liliane Fawcett, who set up this dealer in 20th-century furniture decades ago with a vision and determination to select objects with a point of view. Uninterested in the design hype of the past decade, which is so often accompanied by a monotonous assembly line of brands and designers, Fawcett simply buys pieces that she likes and that illustrate distinctive characteristics.

On my visit I encountered a 70s smoked-glass and chrome coffee table by Romeo Rega; the 1956 floor-to-ceiling *Infinito* bookcase by Franco Albini; and some vibrant mid-century Murano-glass designs. Living in harmony with these older classics was the playful *Margueritz* coffee table by Hubert De Gall and several signature pieces by the Fornasetti studio. The gallery occasionally offers works by design pioneers Tom Dixon, André Dubreuil, Mark Brazier-Jones and other jewels of French, Italian and Scandinavian origin.

This gallery was once a garage; Fawcett converted it for this purpose into an open, bright white space. There is an elegantly curved wall breaking the right angles of the room; it cleverly incorporates shelving for smaller collectibles. Buzz for entry and you step into a calming environment dedicated to the sorts of pieces you aspire to own.

The Tom Dixon furniture and lighting range recently got its own showroom, the first for the accomplished collection since it launched in 2002. In case it wasn't obvious, Tom Dixon is also the man behind the brand – a maverick talent firmly rooted in the British design establishment.

Dixon started his career in the music business but shifted his emphasis when he began attracting interest in his welded-metal furniture-sculptures in the 80s. Since then, the self-invented designer has worked with leading manufacturers (and completed a successful stint as creative director of Habitat) and finally become a producer himself.

His furniture business has enjoyed steady growth, perhaps helped along by certain triumphs, such as the popular *Mirror Ball* (a globe-shaped plastic polycarbonate light, metalised with chrome metal for a mirror-like finish) and the upholstered furniture collection that he designed in partnership with George Smith (the shapely *Wingback* chair is a highlight).

Fans of Dixon's work can now view his oeuvre in one single place: this industrial Victorian building on the edge of the Grand Union Canal. The fit-out of the showroom was not complete at the time of going to press, but early indications suggested that the 175-square-metre space would be a welcome experience for both the trade and fans of the man.

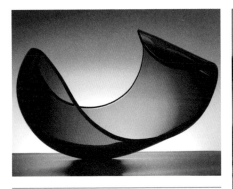

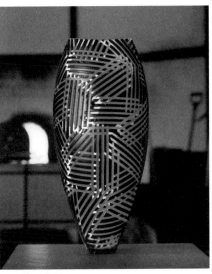

 07 VESSEL

📍 114 KENSINGTON PARK ROAD W11 2PW

📞 020 7727 8001

↖ VESSELGALLERY.COM

🕐 MON-SAT 10-6

⊖ NOTTING HILL GATE

Vessel has received critical and industry recognition on both local and international levels and gained a reputation as an authority in the contemporary European glass and ceramics market. Under the watchful eye of owners Nadia Demetriou Ladas and Angel Monzon, Vessel blurs the line between shop and gallery to allow all visitors access to excellent design without the sterility and snobbery that can accompany traditional galleries. After more than 10 years in business, Vessel still maintains its strong presence in Notting Hill.

Incorporating the building's ground and lower-ground floors, the shop provides a clean, understated backdrop against which the glass and ceramic pieces on show can really shine. Colourful Murano glass vases are deftly complemented by Nymphenburg porcelain and surrealist Fornasetti vases for Bitossi. The clean, minimal contours of the Rosenthal Studio Line pose elegantly alongside Georg Jensen's fluid stainless-steel vases and timeless classics from Scandinavian producers such as iittala, Stelton and Orrefors.

The more accessible designs are displayed on the ground floor, but Vessel has also carved out a niche in the contemporary glass-art market. Considerable statement pieces can be found in the basement, where the shop hosts well-curated exhibitions year-round. Past shows have included spectacular collectible works by the likes of Lena Bergstrom, Jaime Hayón, Timo Sarpaneva, Olgoj Chorchoj, Karim Rashid and John Pawson.

The personable owners have a skilled eye for beauty, quality and innovation in their chosen field. Their approach is to confidently mix and match their offerings, then leave the pieces alone to speak for themselves without confusing the displays with any other clutter or messages. The result is that you experience every piece on an equal playing field, free from any price, logo or designer hierarchy. Even to the trained eye, the result is refreshing. And to the uninitiated: trust your instincts or else ask one of the helpful and informative staff for some guidance.

● *Eat & Drink*

08 202 CAFÉ 202-204 WESTBOURNE GROVE W11 2RH
020 7792 6888 | NICOLEFARHI.COM
Half Nicole Farhi shop, half stylish café. Rustic
feel. Laidback but always busy. Best for brunch.

09 BEACH BLANKET BABYLON 45 LEDBURY ROAD
W11 2AA | 020 7229 2907 | BEACHBLANKET.CO.UK
Stylish bar and dining room. Distinctive
Baroque/Rococco/French chateau-style decor.
Columns, marble busts, opulent furniture.

10 BLOODY FRENCH 149 WESTBOURNE GROVE W11 2RS
020 7727 7770
Gallic bistro. Small but tasty traditional French
menu. Bare brickwork and sophisticated dark-
wood interior. Communal tables.

11 BUMPKIN 209 WESTBOURNE PARK ROAD W11 1EA
020 7243 9818 | BUMPKINUK.COM
Organic food with a homely touch. Simple,
wholesome food. Country-chic surroundings.

12 LE CAFÉ ANGLAIS 8 PORCHESTER GARDENS W2 4DB
020 7221 1415 | LECAFEANGLAIS.CO.UK
Classic Anglo-French menu. Elegant, Roaring
Twenties style. Grand room divided into two
by the sweeping-arc silhouette of a beige
leather banquette. High ceilings with imposing
rectangular Art Deco lights. An enticing dining
experience over all.

13 COCKNEY'S 314 PORTOBELLO ROAD W10 5RU
020 8960 9409
Proper cockney fare. Good old pie and mash.
Tiled interior, wooden benches, steel counters.
Fuss-free local grub.

14 THE COW 89 WESTBOURNE PARK ROAD W2 5QH
020 7221 0021 | THECOWLONDON.CO.UK
Homely and characterful Irish boozer complete
with a cosy upstairs dining room. Red Formica
tables. A good place for oysters and a Guinness.
Always busy downstairs.

15 CRAZY HOMIES 125 WESTBOURNE PARK RD W2 5QL
020 7727 6771 | CRAZYHOMIESLONDON.CO.UK
Mexican-style restaurant and bar. Traditional
Mexican dishes. Bright, kitsch decor. Bohemian,
easygoing and fun. Great value for money.

16 DAYLESFORD ORGANIC 208-212 WESTBOURNE
GROVE W11 2RH | 020 7313 8050
DAYLESFORDORGANIC.COM
Café with a traditional British menu and a
raw-food bar offering virtuous organic dishes.
Minimalist interior. Full of yummy mummies,
posh hipsters.

17 E&O 14 BLENHEIM CRESCENT W11 1NN
020 7229 5454 | RICKERRESTAURANTS.COM
Chic 'Eastern and Oriental' restaurant. Creative
interpretations of Chinese, Japanese and Thai
classics. Sleek, black and white dining room.

18 ELECTRIC BRASSERIE 191 PORTOBELLO RD W11 2ED
020 7908 9696 | ELECTRICBRASSERIE.COM
A classic brasserie and bar next to the
Electric Cinema. Cosmopolitan menu and
atmosphere. A decor of brown-leather
banquettes and chrome tables. Popular with
Notting Hill residents.

19 THE GROCER ON ELGIN 6 ELGIN CRESCENT
W11 2HX | 020 7221 3844 | THEGROCERON.COM
Posh, pre-prepared meals. A mix of café in the
basement and deli at ground level. Food with
French and Italian inspiration. Fresh, seasonal
ingredients from small artisan producers and
quality suppliers.

20 HEREFORD ROAD 3 HEREFORD ROAD W2 4AB
020 7727 1144 | HEREFORDROAD.ORG
Once a Victorian butcher's shop. Now a popular
neighbourhood restaurant. Classy, American-
style leather booths, British menu. Ideal for a
romantic dinner.

21 THE LEDBURY 127 LEDBURY ROAD W11 2AQ
020 7792 9090 | THELEDBURY.COM
Elegant gastronomic gem. Quality French
cuisine. Strong wine list. Modern-chic interior.
Outdoor patio area great in summer. Pricey.

22 LISBOA PATISSERIE 57 GOLBORNE ROAD W10 5NR
020 8968 5242
Traditional Portuguese caff/patisserie. You must
try Pastel de Nata, the famous Portuguese custard
tarts. Very popular local institution in the shadow
of the iconic Trellick Tower.

23 LUCKY 7 127 WESTBOURNE PARK ROAD W2 5QL
020 7727 6771 | LUCKY7LONDON.CO.UK
London's take on a traditional American diner.
Breakfast and burgers. Casual retro style. Booth
seating. Vintage rock posters.

24 OTTOLENGHI 63 LEDBURY ROAD W11 2AD
020 7727 1121 | OTTOLENGHI.CO.UK
Chic daytime café with innovative take-away
menu. Mediterranean cuisine with the spice of
North Africa. The best raw ingredients. Chic
all-white decor. Heaven for all customers,
including vegetarians.

25 THE PRINCE BONAPARTE 80 CHEPSTOW RD W2 5BE
020 7313 9491 | THEPRINCEBONAPARTEW2.CO.UK
Reinvigorated local gastropub. Traditional British
food with a Modern European influence. Antique
interior. Dark ceilings, fireplaces, gilt trimmings.
Pub with a soul.

26 RAOUL'S CAFÉ 105-107 TALBOT ROAD W11 2AT
020 7229 2400 | RAOULSGOURMET.COM
Popular bistro-esque restaurant-café. All-day
brunch menu. Stylish lighting, huge mirrors,
chic leather banquettes. Pop in for a full English
breakfast. It goes down a storm with brunchers
on weekends.

27 ROSA'S DINING ROOM 69 WESTBOURNE PARK RD
W2 5QH | 020 7221 5329

More an eccentric aunt's kitchen than a full-on restaurant. British home-spun cooking. Dark panelled walls, plastic tablecloths. Charming and full of character. Good prices.

28 S&M CAFÉ 268 PORTOBELLO ROAD W10 5TY
020 8968 8898 | SANDMCAFE.CO.UK

Good, old traditional sausage and mash. Reliable and unpretentious. Lively location, great atmosphere. Retro Formica interior.

● *Indulge*

29 & CLARKE'S 122-124 KENSINGTON CHURCH STREET
W8 4BH | 020 7229 2190 | SALLYCLARKE.COM

Bakery, food shop and restaurant under one roof. Fresh-baked bread every morning. Anything from fresh fruit and veg, jams and jellies to quality cheeses.

30 C LIDGATE 110 HOLLAND PARK AVENUE W11 4UA
020 7727 8243 | LIDGATES.COM

A fourth-generation family butcher. Quality meat, free-range poultry and excellent homemade pies and sausages.

31 GOLBORNE FISHERIES 77 GOLBORNE RD W10 5NP
020 8960 3100

Famed local fishmongers. Fresh fish at very reasonable prices.

32 HUNTSWORTH WINE 108 KENSINGTON CHURCH ST
W8 4BH | 020 7229 1602
HUNTSWORTHWINE.CO.UK

A wide selection of wines from across the globe. Careful: you may spend hours browsing.

33 KINGSLAND THE EDWARDIAN BUTCHER
140 PORTOBELLO ROAD W11 2DZ | 020 7727 6067

Superb traditional butchers. Typically jam-packed on Saturday with visitors to the Portobello market.

34 LE MAROC 94 GOLBORNE ROAD W10 5PS
020 8968 9783

Authentic Moroccan deli and halal butchers.

35 NEGOZIO CLASSICA 283 WESTBOURNE GROVE
W11 2QA | 020 7034 0005
NEGOZIOCLASSICA.CO.UK

Italian wine shop, bar and quality store. Great corner location on Portobello Road.

36 MELT CHOCOLATES 59 LEDBURY ROAD W11 2AA
020 7727 5030 | MELTCHOCOLATES.COM

Elegant lab-like bonbonnerie. Bespoke chocolates made daily. Open kitchen.

37 MR CHRISTIAN'S 11 ELGIN CRESCENT W11 2JA
020 7229 0501 | MRCHRISTIANS.CO.UK

The original Notting Hill grocer. Delicious-looking delicatessen counter and brilliant baked goods. Fresh bread every day.

38 R GARCIA & SONS 248-250 PORTOBELLO ROAD
W11 1LL | 020 7221 6119

London's largest Spanish delicatessen. Wide selection of meats, cheeses, salamis, wines, oils and even soaps and colognes.

39 THE SPICE SHOP 1 BLENHEIM CRESCENT W11 2EE
020 7221 4448 | THESPICESHOP.CO.UK

A little oasis for the home cook. Amazingly well stocked. Charming and colourful. Selling unusual cooking ingredients too.

40 TAVOLA 155 WESTBOURNE GROVE W11 2RS
020 7229 0571

Quality delicatessen with a range of Italian, Spanish and French gourmet fare.

41 TOM'S DELI 226 WESTBOURNE GROVE W11 2RH
020 7221 8818 | TOMSDELILONDON.CO.UK

A 'designer deli' owned by Tom Conran. Vintage grocery packaging. Extremely busy and exceptionally good. Up some stairs is a small diner/café.

42 WILD AT HEART TURQUOISE ISLAND,
222 WESTBOURNE GROVE W11 2RJ | 020 7727 3095
WILDATHEART.COM

Fresh modern florist. Housed in Piers Gough's green-tiled public lavatory on the Westbourne Grove traffic island.

● *Sleep*

43 GUESTHOUSE WEST 163-165 WESTBOURNE GROVE
W11 2RS | 020 7792 9800 | GUESTHOUSEWEST.COM

Upmarket reinvention of traditional British B&B. Stucco-fronted Edwardian house in the heart of Notting Hill. Walking distance to shops of Ledbury Road and Westbourne Grove. Family atmosphere. Manageable prices.

44 THE HEMPEL 31-35 CRAVEN HILL GARDENS W2 3EA
020 7298 9000 | THE-HEMPEL.CO.UK

Luxurious boutique residence. Created by British designer Anouska Hempel. Super minimalist architecture that some may find stark. Ornamental garden at the front. Acceptable prices.

45 PORTOBELLO HOTEL 22 STANLEY GDNS W11 2NG
020 7727 2777 | PORTOBELLOHOTEL.COM

In a converted neoclassical mansion. Offbeat, eccentric and sexy. Rooms designed on a theme, from Japanese Flower Garden to Victorian. Perfect for extravagant weekend.

46 MILLER'S RESIDENCE 111A WESTBOURNE GROVE
W2 4UW | 020 7243 1024 | MILLERSUK.COM

A small luxury 18th-century-style boutique hotel. Full of character and eccentric guests. Antique furnishings. Individually decorated rooms. Romantic, intimate hide away with discreet entrance.

DeTnk.

A NEW WAY
OF COLLECTING
DESIGN

'another chair' by Karen Ryan

KNOWING THE MARKET/ UNDERSTANDING DESIGN **www.detnk.com**

Marylebone

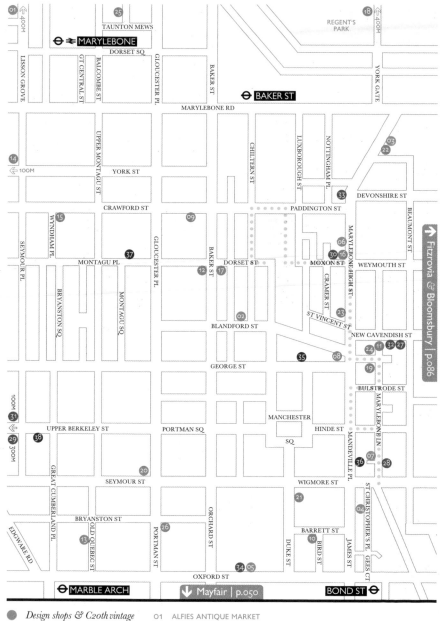

Design shops & C20th vintage

Eat & Drink

Indulge

Sleep
(pp.044-045)

••• Take a walk route

Marylebone

TAKE A WALK
Tracey Neuls *

Homogenisation of our cities is sadly becoming more and more unavoidable. Marylebone Village, on the other hand, is unmistakably British and goes even one step further – it is honestly local. The atmosphere as you walk from Oxford Street to Marylebone Lane quickly changes from department stores to shops like Biggles Gourmet Sausages, where you can buy handmade links by the dozen or in a bun to take away. Neighbours include David Penton & Son, an old world DIY shop where, more times than not, they will have what you need. And The Button Queen, which supplies buttons from the 1800s. Across the road you have Paul Rothe & Son, a family-run café where the decor has been loved yet untouched since it opened over 100 years ago.

And this is the best bit about Marylebone: popping up among the original shops are strong contenders for future classics. The side streets are always worth exploring for just that. For example, on Bulstrode Street you will find Content, which sells creams and perfumes served by the passionate owner herself, who knows her products inside and out. Remembering less is more, don't miss the Monocle magazine shop – quite possibly the smallest shop in London yet jam packed with goodies. Keep walking and you can choose between butterflies and cheese. Worth a look is Damien Hirst's boutique Other Criteria, where art multiples can be bought at a hint of the price of the original. Nearer the top of Marylebone High Street, The Fromagerie beckons. This cheese specialist and grocer supports local producers, and has a few secret tables in the back where they prepare and serve up a delicious daily menu. Pass through the tranquil innercity Paddington Street Gardens before arriving closer to the heart of residential Marylebone. A rather eccentric character called Felix sets up a rogue stall every morning selling flowers in front of Hardy's restaurant. His unique selections of cut flowers are reflective of his own individual personality. And while you are there treating your senses, have a peep across the street at St Andrews Mansion Courtyard for some rare, well-preserved London architecture.

Canadian-born shoe designer (p.043) traceyneuls.com

01 ALFIES ANTIQUE MARKET
- 📍 13-25 CHURCH STREET NW8 8DT
- ☎ 020 7723 6066
- 🔗 ALFIESANTIQUES.COM
- 🕑 TUE-SAT 10-6
- Ⓔ EDGWARE ROAD

02 CENTURY
- 📍 58 BLANDFORD STREET W1U 7JB
- ☎ 020 7487 5100
- 🔗 CENTURYD.COM
- 🕑 TUE-SAT 11-6
- Ⓔ BOND STREET/MARBLE ARCH

Opened by Bennie Gray in 1976 on the site of the Edwardian department store Jordan's, Alfies has evolved into one of the city's leading destinations for antiques and 20th-century collectible furniture, lighting, ceramics, jewellery, art and clothing. With more than 75 dealers spread across 3,500-square-metres of space over five floors, it is also one of the country's vastest indoor antiques arcades. It is largely thanks to this emporium that the rather hotch-potch Church Street is now lined with antiques dealers.

There are several major retail spaces among the bric-a-brac. Unrivaled in Italian vintage lighting and interiors is Vincenzo Cafferella Gallery, which offers an extensive collection of mainly 1950 to 1970s Italian lighting, furniture and art – including such beauties as a pair of 1960s Mazzega Murano glass chandeliers; a rare 1950s chrome floor lamp by Arredoluce; and a sculptural *L'Apoggio* chair by Claudio Salocchi. In the basement, occupying more than 500-square-metres, Decoratum has tidy room sets arranged by style or era with an emphasis on designer pieces from the 1940s through the 1970s.

Decoratum's organised displays distinguish the dealer from the rest of Alfies, where many others cram as much as possible into their tiny warrens. Swirly carpets and fluorescent lighting prevail, thankfully stripping this place of unnecessary pretension. Don't let this deceive you: dealers can be shrewd and prices inflated. With such a huge selection, the enjoyment comes from hunting down a hidden treasure.

Spread across two floors – with a hairdresser rather bizarrely sharing the ground floor – Century is on the snug side. But its size is inversely related to its impressive range of retro furnishings – including classics like Eames's *Rocking Chair*, George Nelson's *Bubble lights* and a selection of collectible textiles by Lucienne Day, Barbara Brown and Marion Mahler. The stock here is always rotating, but on my last visit there was a strong presence of vintage Ercol furniture and some 20th-century American classics, including pieces by Heywood Wakefield, Charles & Ray Eames and Warren McArthur.

As small as it is, the shop has not been stuffed to the rafters with merchandise. Instead, the careful selection of items is set out to give customers a taster of original vintage furniture, lighting and accessories. Century also incorporates a collection of new designs – including retro-inspired ceramic vases by the esteemed US potter Jonathan Adler and wall sculptures by Curtis Jere studio – which stylistically complement the vintage originals.

Owner Andrew Weaving is a published authority on Modernism. Should he be in the house on the day of your visit, test his encyclopaedic knowledge of his craft; you'll be sure to learn something new. And if you are searching for something particular, Weaving will likely be able to track it down for you.

 THE CONRAN SHOP

- 55 MARYLEBONE HIGH STREET W1U 5HS
- 020 7723 2223
- CONRANSHOP.CO.UK
- MON-WED, FRI 10-6, THU 10-7, SA 10-6.30, SU 11-5
- BAKER STREET

04 MARIMEKKO

- 16/17 ST CHRISTOPHER'S PLACE W1U 1NZ
- 020 7486 6454
- MARIMEKKO.COM
- MON-SAT 10-6.30, THU 10-7, SUN 12-5
- BOND STREET

Marylebone's Conran Shop is one of the younger in a series of major London restoration projects undertaken by the Conran Group (other listed buildings in their portfolio include Michelin House and the Bluebird Garage), which tend to act as a catalyst for the regeneration of the surrounding neighbourhood. A former stable building at the north end of Marylebone High Street, this structure was entirely rebuilt to provide accommodation for the second Conran Shop in London, as well as the elegant Orrery restaurant that adjoins.

The elegant layout of classic-modern and contemporary homewares, chosen for their 'good design' credentials, is fronted by a distinctive two-storey arched-bay elevation. Founder Terence Conran has built a lifetime reputation on his sophisticated presentation, and for his range of iconic and unusual offerings from around the world. Conran stock manages to balance quality and price in equal measures.

The Marylebone location offers yet more evidence of the strength of the Conran brand: clean, comfortable, unobtrusive, functional, timelessly modern. The company offers a consistently high benchmark, which newcomers in the trade strive to follow. Although prices can be on the high side, it is neither inaccessible nor intimidating. The three sales floors are organised in departments according to the rooms of the home, and it's just as easy to find the perfect gift here as a sweeping four-seater sofa. When you enter the Conran Shop you access a part of the design establishment.

The mid-century marvel Marimekko sparked a design revolution in Finland when it was founded by visionary textile designer Armi Ratia and her husband Viljo. Together they pioneered a new definition of fabric that altered the entire interiors industry. Today Marimekko is a publicly traded company with 1,000 retailers around the world. The original bold, colourful designs have won Marimekko international recognition, but its growing range nowadays extends to clothing, fabrics, interior design solutions, gift items, bags and other accessories.

When the Marimekko London store debuted at the top end of St Christopher's Place it sparked a regeneration of this once quiet lane. The shop presents a tightly edited cross-section of the exuberant Marimekko fashions and home furnishings portfolio, all in the brand's recognisable bold graphics and colours. Bestselling designs by the likes of Maija Isola and Vuokko Eskolin-Nurmesniemi are accompanied by more recent collaborations with younger design talents such as Maija Louekari, Sanna Annukka and Anna Danielsson.

Marimekko is a distinctive brand that has attracted a loyal customer following over the years. Its vibrant patterns add a certain irreverent cheer to any interior, be it in a simple cushion or a fabric wallhanging. I'm a big fan of most of it, although I can't help feeling that the company has applied its designs across too many products.

05 SELFRIDGES & CO
- 400 OXFORD STREET W1A 1AB
- 0800 123 400
- SELFRIDGES.CO.UK
- MON-SAT 9.30-9.30, SUN 12-6
- BOND STREET

06 SKANDIUM
- 86 MARYLEBONE HIGH STREET W1U 4QS
- 020 7935 2077
- SKANDIUM.COM
- MON-SAT 10-6.30, THU 10-7, SUN 11-5
- BOND STREET

Gordon Selfridge built his eponymous retail emporium on Oxford Street with the belief that a grand, modern store should be as important to public life as a historic landmark. One hundred years later and, like most great landmarks, there is no shortage of visitors to this central-London institution. At the time when the recession has led many retailers to recoil rather than innovate, the upmarket department store has remained valiant and ever ambitious.

This concession-based retailer is the only reason many Londoners still venture onto the clogged artery of mediocre consumerism that is Oxford Street. Once past the stately columned entrance, one encounters the scented white perfume hall, the beauty department, then designer accessories before reaching the mouthwatering displays in the food hall. Continue up the escalators, through the vertiginous atrium, and you'll cut a swathe through several floors of cutting-edge fashion before hitting the furniture and lighting concessions at the top.

Merchandise up here morphs with the trends. In the past Selfridges had its share of contemporary furniture, albeit hidden away on the fourth floor. Today most of the more interesting furniture concessions have gone, and in their place are middle-of-the-road brands like BO Concept, Natuzzi and Loft Living. This is thankfully redeemed on the lower-ground floor, where accessories from Skandium (p.020 & 042), Marimekko (p.041) and Alessi (p.052) share space with a superb bookshop that stocks a good section on visual arts, design and architecture.

Fed up with London's dearth of modern Scandinavian design in the late-90s, the entrepreneurial trio Magnus Englund, Chrystina Schmidt and Christopher Seidenfaden resolved to do something about it. The result is Skandium, a dealer in new and established Scandinavian products that has since evolved at an impressive rate. This is, frankly, unsurprising, considering the Nordic talents in store: Jacobsen, Aalto, Sarpaneva, Aarnio, Franck, Kjaerholm and Wirkkala, as well as their design heirs Lena Bergström, Harri Koskinen, Claesson Koivisto Rune, Pia Wallen and Seppo Koho.

Spread across two floors, Skandium carries expertly chosen brands including Asplund, iittala, Le Klint, Louis Poulsen, Marimekko, Muuto and Woodnotes and acts as their main UK agent. On the ground floor, the white walls and a courtyard-like glass roof provide a light, bright and fresh backdrop to the kitchenware, glass and ceramics that dominate the scene. Downstairs, a well-edited display of furniture and lighting is accessorised with vibrant Marimekko printed fabric and lacquered-wood toys from the Swedish manufacturer Brio.

Skandium is likely to bolster your opinion of Scandinavian design, which can sometime suffer from the stereotype of being rather conservative and safe. In my opinion, the designs at Skandium set a benchmark for quality and longevity – free from the fickle constraints of fashion and trends. These are items that you will enjoy and keep and likely pass down through the generations.

 TRACEY NEULS

29 MARYLEBONE LANE W1U 2NQ

020 7935 0039

TN29.COM

MON-FRI 11-6.30, SAT-SUN 12-5

BOND STREET

I first spotted Tracey Neuls's shoebox of a shop while wandering along peaceful Marylebone Lane, seemingly far from the chaos of Oxford Street. As a man, I've not had much reason to investigate women's footwear, but the captivating display at this small store had me intrigued. Shoe shops are outside of the editorial remit of the *London Design Guide* but, what the hell. There is always room for an exception.

Trained in fashion design, Canadian-born Neuls has built a reputation over the past decade for innovative, idiosyncratic cobbling. Her footwear is characterful, playful and utterly individual. As a shoe novice, I can nonetheless appreciate the attention to detail and respect for craftsmanship that is inherent in each design. On the one hand, there is clearly a confident understanding of shoemaking, which partners with Neuls's penchant for unconventional materials and production techniques. She draws on multiple influences with each range. You can't help admiring these shoes as examples of great product design – both the premium *Tracey Neuls* collection and the more accessible *TN_29* range.

The shop interior reflects Neuls's playful curiosity and her unconventional approach to visual merchandising. Shoes are displayed like installations, dangling from the ceiling on red strings. The tiny boutique is likely to change with each visit as Neuls enjoys experimental collaborations with artists like Boo Ritsen. All in all, the atmosphere is welcoming, unpretentious and rather homely. And ladies: you will even be served gourmet coffee and freshly baked bread while you try on the shoes.

● *Eat & Drink*

08   L'AUTRE PIED 5-7 BLANDFORD STREET W1U 3DB
020 7486 9696 | LAUTREPIED.CO.UK
More of a bistro, with an informal, bustling atmosphere. Unpretentious, without tablecloths or fancy silverware. Modern European. Imaginative, well-considered flavour combinations. Fairly expensive.

09   THE BEEHIVE 126 CRAWFORD STREET W1U 6BF
020 7486 8037 | THEBEEHIVE-PUB.CO.UK
One of London's oldest pubs, established in 1884. Classic-looking but with a strangely all-Italian staff. Traditional pub grub cooked to superior quality. An extensive list of beers – including the Beehive's very own honey-ed Beehive Brew bitter.

10   BUSABA EATHAI 8-13 BIRD STREET W1U 1BU
020 7518 8080 | BUSABA.COM
A canteen-style Thai fusion restaurant. Tasty fast food and simple flavours. Long communal tables. Dark wood-lined dining room. Nice buzzy atmosphere. Be prepared to queue – but not for very long.

11   CAFFÉ CALDESI 118 MARYLEBONE LANE W1U 2QF
020 7935 1144 | CALDESI.COM
Younger sibling of the La Cucina Caldesi cookery school around the corner. Celebrates diverse dishes from all regions of Italy. Authentic Italian food at its best. Wine tasting available.

12   CANTEEN 55 BAKER STREET W1U 8EW
0845 686 1122 | CANTEEN.CO.UK
Stunning canteen-style British restaurant on busy Baker Street. Superb ingredients and no-nonsense British fare. Postwar feel with relaxed, intimate atmosphere – despite the open plan.

13   CARBON OLD QUEBEC STREET W1C 1LZ
020 7479 5050 | CARBONBAR.CO.UK
Bar/nightclub hybrid. Industrial, low-key yet super-chic in the heart of Marylebone. Concrete, steel, brick and wood contrast with outsized Chesterfield sofas and bevelled mirrors. Elegantly architectural. Giant, fixed steel chains hanging from floor to ceiling.

14   DININGS 22 HARCOURT STREET W1H 4HH
020 7723 0666
One of London's best contemporary Japanese restaurants. Known for its tapas concept. The townhouse exterior contrasts with the Modernist decor. Concrete Brutalist solid-wood basement space. Good-value meals prepared by a Nobu grad. Relaxed, friendly atmosphere.

15   THE DUKE OF WELLINGTON 94A CRAWFORD ST
W1H 2HQ | 020 7723 2790 | THEDUKEW1.CO.UK
Revived pub gastro-fied with smart black façade, red ceilings, chandeliers, wood floors and gilt mirrors. Busy at ground level, more peaceful in small upstairs dining room. Great varied menu.

16   LA FROMAGERIE 2-6 MOXON STREET W1U 4EW
020 7935 0341 | LAFROMAGERIE.CO.UK
Dedicated cheese and dairy shop, deli and tasting café. Stylish, unconventional and oh so high end. Communal atmosphere. Ideal for an indulgent lunch or early-afternoon snack. Get spoilt by tantalising cheese flavours and smell of freshly baked bread.

17   GALVIN BISTROT DE LUXE 66 BAKER ST W1U 7DJ
020 7935 4007 | GALVINRESTAURANTS.COM
Parisian-style bistro. Delicious, authentic French food. Cool, restrained 1930s decor with retro touches. Cheerful, comforting buzz. Friendly and efficient staff. Not always easy to get a table.

18   THE GARDEN CAFÉ INNER CIRCLE, THE REGENT'S
PARK NW1 4NU | 020 7935 5729
THEGARDENCAFE.CO.UK
Parisian bistro style in the heart of pretty Regent's Park. Gourmet food of an extremely high standard at surprisingly reasonable prices. Light and airy space. Original 1960s decor and fittings. Friendly, efficient staff. Survey the park life as you tuck in.

19   GOLDEN HIND 73 MARYLEBONE LANE W1U 2PN
020 7486 3644
Good traditional British dishes in an old-fashioned environment. Black and white tiled floor, wooden tables, a wood coat and umbrella stand. Extremely popular. Local character and clientele. Must try the proper fish'n'chips. Take-away available.

20   LOCANDA LOCATELLI 8 SEYMOUR STREET W1H 7JZ
020 7935 9088 | LOCANDALOCATELLI.COM
High-end Italian restaurant with the famous chef at the helm. Classic Italian cooking with a few innovative twists. Decor reminiscent of the more stylish side of the New Romantic era. Tasteful drapes, elegant retro fittings. Sophisticated experience. Professional service. Still one of London's top Italian eateries.

21   THE MOOSE BAR 31 DUKE STREET W1 1LG
020 7644 1426 | VPMG.NET/MOOSE
Fun, hip cocktail bar just off Oxford Street behind Selfridges. Interior is the work of designer Shaun Clarkson. Styled like a rustic ski lodge – complete with log-cabin walls, cow-print sofas, cream timber and antler chandeliers. Ask for some of the delicious bar snacks. Relaxed, feel-good atmosphere.

22   ORRERY AND ORRERY EPICERIE 55 MARYLEBONE
HIGH STREET W1U 5RB | 020 7616 8000
DANDDLONDON.COM
French-inspired food in elegant surroundings. Terence Conran's culinary pride. Comfy and quietly confident. Extensive wine list. Pricey

but highly recommended to food-lovers. The Epicerie on the corner serves breakfast, light lunch and snacks in more informal surroundings.

23 THE PROVIDORES AND TAPA ROOM
109 MARYLEBONE HIGH STREET W1U 4RX
020 7935 6175 | THEPROVIDORES.CO.UK
A fun culinary romp. Formal dining room upstairs, casual tapas-style café downstairs. Asian-fusion cuisine with a New Zealand twist. Always packed – expect to queue for some of the best food in London.

24 LE RELAIS DE VENISE L'ENTRECÔTE
120 MARYLEBONE LANE W1U 1QG
020 7486 0878 | RELAISDEVENISE.COM
An outpost of the original, which opened in Paris more than 50 years ago. A true Parisian brasserie. Banquette seating, mirrored walls, large windows, waitresses in French maids' outfits. Buzzy, convivial atmosphere.

25 THE SWAN & EDGAR 43 LINHOPE STREET NW1 6HL
020 7724 6268 | SWANANDEDGAR.CO.UK
A real locals' pub. Charming, cosy hideaway. No larger than the average living room. Stained walls, wooden benches, tiled floors. Bar made of old paperbacks. Trad homemade pub grub. Lose yourself for hours.

26 TEXTURE RESTAURANT 34 PORTMAN ST W1H 7BY
020 7224 0028 | TEXTURE-RESTAURANT.CO.UK
Modern European cuisine combining and emphasizing different consistencies. Housed in an Adam-style room. Blends contemporary elegance with original features. A distinct gallery feel. Unusual and attractive.

Indulge

27 AROUND WINE 40 NEW CAVENDISH ST W1G 8UD
020 7935 4679 | AROUNDWINE.CO.UK
Specialists in fine wines, wine-drinking accessories and wine guides.

28 BIGGLES 66 MARYLEBONE LANE W1U 2PF
020 7224 5937 | EBIGGLES.CO.UK
The best sausages in town. A full-blown, satisfying lunch without denting the budget.

29 COCOMAYA 35 CONNAUGHT STREET W2 2AZ
020 7706 2770 | COCOMAYA.CO.UK
Fine luxury chocolates. A riot of inventiveness, wit and originality.

30 GINGER PIG 8-10 MOXON STREET W1U 4EW
020 7935 7788 | THEGINGERPIG.CO.UK
A must-go world-class butchers. Produce comes from their own farms. Very helpful and knowledgeable staff. Plus a changing daily menu of cooked meals to take home. A great local resource and well worth the visit if you're planning a special meal.

31 GREEN VALLEY 36-37 UPPER BERKELEY ST W1H 5QE
020 7402 7385
Middle Eastern grocery and delicatessen. Freshly baked flatbreads and sweets.

32 JANE PACKER 32-34 NEW CAVENDISH ST W1G 8UE
020 7935 2673 | JANE-PACKER.CO.UK
Noted British floral designer. Floristry as art. Twenty-year-old tradition in West End. Design courses available.

33 NATURAL KITCHEN 77-78 MARYLEBONE HIGH ST
W1U 5JX | 020 7486 8065
THENATURALKITCHEN.COM
Artisan, organic café and foodstore. Anything from fresh fruit to takeaway foods and wines. There's also a wine cave and an artisan tasting table. Good place for quick lunch.

34 SELFRIDGES FOOD & WINE 400 OXFORD STREET
W1A 1AB | 0800 123 400 | SELFRIDGES.COM
Extensive choice of top-quality ingredients – everything you need for a dinner party. Check out the Wonder Bar, where you can taste a wide selection of wines on their sampling machines.

Sleep

35 DURRANTS HOTEL GEORGE STREET W1H 5BJ
020 7935 8131 | DURRANTSHOTEL.CO.UK
Good, old-fashioned hotel service. A homely, traditional English atmosphere. Converted Georgian townhouse. Classic English fabrics and antiques. Wood panelling, regal colour scheme, original plasterwork and fireplaces. Discreet and friendly service. Very charming and cosy.

36 MANDEVILLE HOTEL MANDEVILLE PLACE W1U 2BE
020 7935 5599 | MANDEVILLE.CO.UK
Boutique hotel. Unmistakeably British yet modern. Luxurious fabrics and wall coverings, winged armchairs, mirrored walls, marble bathrooms. Sophisticated, stylish environment. Pop in to the deVigne bar for a cool drink.

37 MONTAGU PLACE 2 MONTAGU PLACE W1H 2ER
020 7467 2777 | MONTAGU-PLACE.CO.UK
Intimate boutique hotel in a listed Georgian townhouse. Stylish accommodation in a quiet residential street. Only 16 rooms. Original townhouse features contrast with sleek, modern decor. Cosy and welcoming, very much designed like a comfortable home.

38 THE SUMNER 54 UPPER BERKELEY STREET W1H 7QR
020 7723 2244 | THESUMNER.CO.UK
A family-owned townhouse hotel. Part of the beautifully maintained 1820s Georgian Terrace. Tradition combined with modern comfort. Intimate, elegant setting. Rooms individually decorated in modish natural tones. Moderately priced by London standards.

The fat years gave London some iconic architecture – and some eyesores. KIERAN LONG says the only way we can move forward is to stand still a while.

FROM BOOM TO BETTER

London's attitude to architecture has transformed completely in the last decade. Iconic architecture has finally arrived in the capital, and the City's skyline has changed in record time – thanks to recent prosperity and the advent of London's mayor in 2000.

For the most part, Londoners have embraced the new buildings. The 'gherkin', designed by Norman Foster, is an elongated pinecone in the financial heart of the UK, populated by elite law firms and financiers who enjoy incredible views from its plush interior. Yet even non-establishment types will admit it has added something special to the skyline, visible as it is from the north and east. It is curious how Londoners can develop affection for some of the most undemocratic symbols in the city.

Some of London's most popular and well-used buildings are substantially contemporary, or at least historic with a contemporary makeover. The Millennium Bridge (once it overcame its wobbling issues); Tate Modern; the Great Court at the British Museum; Wembley Stadium; St Pancras terminal; Canary Wharf tube station; Heathrow Terminal 5 – all major contemporary buildings that are praised by locals and visitors alike.

But perhaps the most satisfying symbols of London's contemporary development are the smaller buildings away from the media spotlight. The Museum of Childhood in Bethnal Green – recently reworked by the architect firm Caruso St John – was critically lauded but also retains the informal charm of the original. At the Young Vic Theatre, Haworth Tompkins managed to enhance the appeal of a building that had become tired and outdated, and provide London with another great public space: the first-floor balcony. Many other great contemporary buildings stand out: Robbrecht & Daem's refurbishment of the Whitechapel Gallery; David Adjaye's Bernie Grant Centre; and the Women's Library in East London by Wright & Wright.

It is easy to forget that just a decade ago London was much worse for wear. Before the first mayor, there was a lack of leadership in urban development. Today the major beneficiary of increased attention is public space: squares, gardens, parks, streets. They have transformed the way we use the city. It's easy to take for granted a stroll through

'It is easy to forget that just a decade ago London was much worse for wear'

the South Bank or Trafalgar Square, forgetting just how benighted these areas were before their renewal.

Then there is the new lease of life Greenwich peninsula got with the Dome, Deptford Creek with the Laban Dance Centre, Thames Barrier Park, Dalston's Gillett Square, Acton Town Square, Barking Town Square (which recently won the coveted European Prize for Public Space), and now Olympic Park. These are all unrecognisable from 10 years ago.

What does the future hold for London architecture? Well, the short answer is that precious little will happen while the credit crunch plays out and the property market struggles back to its feet. Some trends are clear, though. Mayor Boris Johnson has expressed a commitment to the suburbs – partly because his base is there, and partly because his predecessor Ken Livingstone neglected them. An Outer London Commission has been formed to help to build up and add character to the suburbs.

Some upsides to the credit crunch will be the cancellation of some high-density housing developments – think Stratford High Street – that were conceived in the boom and now prove unfeasible.

But despite today's sluggish development, architects continue to flock to London. The capital has eight architecture schools and is a magnet for design communities worldwide. In turn, London has become a major exporter of architecture. Ask most London-based architects what they're working on, and they're more likely to mention China, the Middle East or northern Europe than anywhere within the M25.

But life has always been like this for architects in London. The city is not quick to hand out opportunities. Even the likes of Norman Foster and Richard Rogers waited until their 60s and 70s for the opportunity to leave their mark on this great city.

KIERAN LONG IS EDITOR-IN-CHIEF OF THE ARCHITECTS' JOURNAL AND THE ARCHITECTURAL REVIEW
ARCHITECTSJOURNAL.CO.UK & ARPLUS.COM

THE MOST BEAUTIFUL CHAIR I'VE SEEN IN YEARS

Established & Sons LIMITED
2–3 Duke Street, St James's, London SW1Y 6BJ
Phone +44 (0)20 7968 2040
Email gallery@establishedandsons.com
www.establishedandsons.com

LIMITED

Mayfair

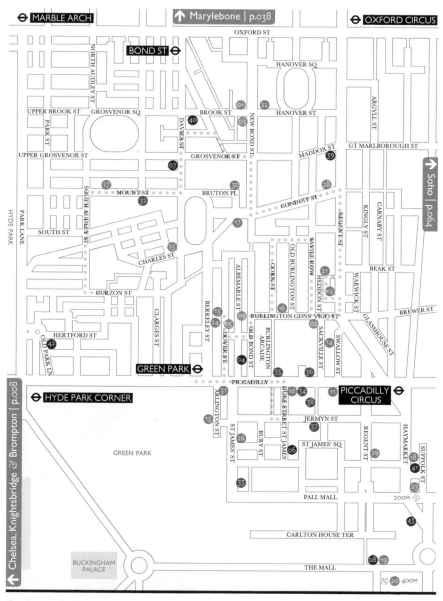

OXFORD ST

BOND ST ⊖

HANOVER SQ

ARGYLL ST

NORTH AUDLEY ST

UPPER BROOK ST
GROSVENOR SQ

BROOK ST   01

HANOVER ST

GT MARLBOROUGH ST

PARK ST

DAVIES ST

40

03

NEW BOND ST

22

CARNABY ST

KINGLY ST

UPPER GROSVENOR ST
GROSVENOR ST

MADDOX ST
39

07

REGENT ST

27
MOUNT ST

30
BRUTON PL

28

BEAK ST

SOUTH AUDLEY ST

32

CONDUIT ST

SOUTH ST

17

SAVILE ROW

OLD BURLINGTON ST

WARWICK ST

CHARLES ST

25

ALBEMARLE ST

CORK ST

21
HEDDON ST

GLASSHOUSE ST

BREWER ST

CURZON ST

CLARGES ST

BERKELEY ST

12

CURZON ST

13
24 05
09

BURLINGTON GDNS VIGO ST

16

02

SACKVILLE ST

SWALLOW ST

HERTFORD ST

42

OLD PARK LN

DOVER ST

OLD BOND ST

BURLINGTON ARCADE

14

04

GREEN PARK ⊖

35

36

PICCADILLY

31

10 34

11 PICCADILLY CIRCUS ⊖

⊖ HYDE PARK CORNER

ARLINGTON ST

DUKE ST ST JAMES'

38

15

JERMYN ST

37

Chelsea, Knightsbridge & Brompton | p.008

ST JAMES' ST

26

BURY ST

06

ST JAMES' SQ

REGENT ST

29

HAYMARKET

18

SUFFOLK ST

41

23

GREEN PARK

33

PALL MALL

200M ⇨

43

CARLTON HOUSE TER

BUCKINGHAM PALACE

08 19

THE MALL

½ 20 400M

⬤ Design galleries & institutions
⬤ Design shops & C20th vintage

⬤ Eat & Drink
⬤ Indulge
⬤ Sleep
(pp.058-059)

••• Take a walk route

01 ALESSI
02 ALMA
03 ARMANI / CASA
04 CARPENTERS WORKSHOP
05 DOVER STREET MARKET
06 ESTABLISHED & SONS LIMITED
07 GAGOSIAN GALLERY
08 INSTITUTE OF
    CONTEMPORARY ARTS

09 PAUL SMITH

Mayfair

TAKE A WALK
*Julien Lombrail**

Leaving Green Park tube, head first to the Royal Academy of Arts at Burlington House. This iconic art institution is a fine place to begin your walk through Mayfair, as it symbolises tradition and discovery in a beautiful, calm environment. From there, you can stroll to the White Cube gallery off Duke Street, the first free-standing building that has been erected in the area for decades and home to myriad British art inspirations. Christie's auction house is around the corner on King Street.

Nearby, the unconventional pleasures of Dover Street Market and its cutting-edge fashion await your perusal; stop for coffee and cake in Rose Bakery on the top floor. On Dover Street itself, you can find the Kamen YaKimov salon, in a space so striking you could mistake it for a gallery – and, indeed, it is almost a gallery for hair. You might wander past Brown's Hotel on nearby Albemarle Street (the most quintessentially British place to spend a night) en route to Cork Street, with its back-to-back art galleries. Loop round to b store, a distinctive fashion boutique dedicated to emerging talents – located on the still traditional Savile Row, home to London's establishment tailors.

Above all, Mayfair is a place for enjoyment. Just around the corner is Momo restaurant on Heddon Street, a top destination for a fun Moroccan meal. Further up the road on Conduit Street is the contemporary-ornate Sketch, a beautiful spot for fine dining in the Middle Room or cocktails in the Parlour. Continue along Conduit Street to New Bond Street, where the prestigious auction house Sotheby's resides.

From here, enjoy some shopping in the fashion stores of Bond Street or head over to La Petite Maison on Brook's Mews for an elegant rendezvous over a delicious meal. Or you may be tempted to wander over to Mount Street for some excellent fish at the iconic Scott's. Also on Mount Street you can find Allen's Butchers, which has supplied the best restaurants of Mayfair with meat for nearly 200 years. From here, you can slip over to the Curzon Cinema, take in a movie and give your legs a rest.

Co-owner of the Carpenters Workshop Gallery (p.053)
cwgdesign.com

01 ALESSI
- 22 BROOK STREET W1K 5DF
- 020 7518 9091
- ALESSI.COM
- MON-SAT 10-6.30, THU 10-7, SUN 12-6
- BOND STREET

02 ALMA
- 8 VIGO STREET W1S 3HJ
- 020 7439 0925
- ALMAHOME.CO.UK
- MON-SAT 10-6
- PICCADILLY CIRCUS

In 1921, Giovanni Alessi began producing hand-crafted nickel- and silver-plated brass tableware from a small workshop in the Italian Alps. Still a family-run business today, Alessi has transformed into a globally recognised brand responsible for some of the most iconic designs of the 20th and 21st-centuries. Its catalogue spans everything from kitchenware, clocks and watches, tableware and utensils to electrical appliances, bathroom ranges, even barbecues.

Under the creative guidance of Alberto Alessi, the company has manufactured a huge array of playful designs from talents including Achille Castiglioni, Alessandro Mendini, Jasper Morrison, Aldo Rossi, Ettore Sottsass, Philippe Starck, Marc Newson... this list only scratches the surface. Every imaginable home accessory has been tackled, from figurative bottle openers, controversial lemon squeezers and postmodern whistling kettles to monkey-faced sugar bowls and Minimalist cutlery.

There are authorised dealers dotted around town, but this three-storey flagship on Brook Street is, in every sense, the London embassy for the company's enduring brand. Even the building, with its colourful mosaic exterior and stucco facade, matches Alessi's witty and distinctive aesthetic. Personally, I'm not interested in the gimmicky plastic ranges, but I tend to appreciate the refined stainless-steel pieces that don't vie for your attention. The vast majority of designs perform their everyday function very well and, as Alberto Alessi puts it, they 'somehow make commonplace gestures more pleasing, more straightforward and more personal'.

An old-school London supplier of leather, Alma moved into interiors 15 years ago, and now produces high-quality furnishings, flooring and finishes to rival the best in the country.

Led by Saeed Khalique, Alma is known for its off-the-shelf designs, crafted in the East London workshop. But bespoke customers should head to the Mayfair showroom, a stunning 19th-century townhouse in the historic Albany development. Crossing the threshold is like stepping into a sophisticated, tailored mansion. High ceilings, creaking wooden floors, narrow corridors, original cornicing and ornate fireplaces provide an elegant backdrop to the décor, a showcase of Alma's full potential.

At the time of going to press, the Mayfair location was undergoing a major refurbishment (previous interior pictured above). A new backdrop was being put in place for a rotating display of Alma's best, ranging from contemporary to retro- and vintage-inspired pieces and dotted with 'classics with a twist'. Alma will also offer 'carry away' items and artwork by commissioned artisans. The thinking is: if Savile Row can master bespoke fashion, Alma can do it for interiors.

 ARMANI/CASA
🔖 113 NEW BOND STREET W1S 1DP
📞 020 7079 1930
🔗 ARMANICASA.COM
🕐 MON-SAT 10-6
🚇 BOND STREET

04 CARPENTERS WORKSHOP GALLERY
🔖 3 ALBEMARLE STREET W1S 4HE
📞 020 3051 5939
🔗 CWGDESIGN.COM
🕐 MON-SAT 10-6
🚇 GREEN PARK

The first of Giorgio Armani's luxury home-furnishings showrooms in the UK is a relative newcomer here on upmarket New Bond Street, but the brand is forever expanding internationally. Launched in Milan a decade ago, Armani/Casa embodies the Italian fashion designer's inimitable style – his refined sophistication, understated elegance and timeless classicism.

The interior of this London space has, like other Armani stores, a vast loft look, with black and steel floor tiles, a palette of warming earth colours, fine finishings and diffused lighting. Housed inside is a collection of his latest home products, from furniture, lighting, accessories and fabrics to kitchen and bathroom systems. Themed room sets gather around the space, each representing Armani's vision for the home environment. In the luxury market, one often expects things to be glitzy or showy, and while that does come through at times here (in the form of a lizard-skin and rosewood writing desk or a 24-carat gilded table), the overall effect is surprisingly subtle and restrained.

'My collections combine beauty with function and values elegance and sophistication over transient trends,' says Armani himself. There is a lot to be said for that as, indeed, much recent design has become so flamboyant as to have entered the realm of entertainment. Armani is holding true to the distinctive style and core values he promotes globally. That may go some way to explaining Armani/Casa's 80 stores in 45 countries worldwide.

Carpenters Workshop Gallery is the brainchild of ambitious French duo Loïc Le Gaillard and Julien Lombrail, who opened this slick gallery in the heartland of London's fine art scene, moments from the Cork Street establishment. The gallery has become a key player in the relatively new market for high-end design that converges with sculptural art, commonly referred to as 'design art'.

As collectors have grown increasingly disillusioned by the swelling of the art market, they have been turning their attentions towards design: objects created with function in mind but undertaken without constraints. Focusing on such creations, the gallery organises a diverse programme of solo and group exhibitions throughout the year. It is encouraging to watch CWG support lesser-known talent; my particular favourites include Vincent Dubourg, Sebastian Brajkovic, rAndom International, Joris Laarman, Robert Stadler and Demakersvan, who are each carving out their own niche and gaining traction with the collectors.

The gallery offers mainly limited-edition pieces that challenge the concept of functional sculpture. In doing so they inevitably lend substance to a burgeoning market that has been both hyped by the media and scrutinised by the design industry to the extent that only those with integrity stand a chance of survival. The gallery maintains its original space in a former gasworks in Fulham, where you can visit by appointment only.

 DOVER STREET MARKET
17-18 DOVER STREET W1S 4LT
020 7518 0680
DOVERSTREETMARKET.COM
MON–WED 11–6, THU–SAT 11–7
GREEN PARK

Welcome to the bizarre universe that is Dover Street Market: the fantastic vision of designer Rei Kawakubo of Japanese label Comme des Garçons. This high-fashion megastore has become somewhat of a retail phenomenon in the city and has, in the process, gained an international following.

As a rule, we don't include fashion boutiques in this guide, but we're highlighting DSM as an exception, mainly due to its interior, which has thankfully turned the age-old concept of the slick, polished flagship on its head. Transforming a six-storey office block into a jaunty retail experiment has subverted our preconceived notions of luxury. DSM has adopted a guerilla approach to its displays, whereby exquisite clothing, shoes, handbags, lingerie, jewellery and perfumes are displayed against rough-and-ready backdrops, often infiltrated with a selection of antique furniture and found objects. On every level, in stark contrast to the imaginative displays, is the buildings pre-existing suspended office ceiling, complete with harsh lighting – a nod to the store's previous tenants.

Each floor acts as a stage set for the various retail installations, some simple and pared back and others extravagant in their execution. Anything goes: old corrugated-metal and wood huts or a life-sized, velvet-draped birdcage become fitting rooms; red-painted steel structures serve as hanging racks; an upside-down building installation forms the backdrop for a new collection. On the top floor, utilitarian homewares company Labour and Wait (p.132) has a spot in the sun, as well as Rose Bakery, where you can people-watch over a reinvigorating cup of tea and a freshly baked scone.

Where Comme has been clever is to mix its own collections with those of other avant-garde talents, such as Christopher Kane, Gareth Pugh, Raf Simons, Hussein Chalayan and Sophia Kokosalaki. This approach resembles the popular concessions in department stores like Selfridges, but without the appearance of luxury-brand logos everywhere. By combining designers in this way, Dover Street encourages its customers to stop, look and touch the products, rather than 'channel-hop' between brands. After all, the fashionistas who frequent this hotspot already know what is what.

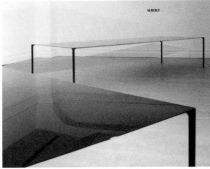

06 ESTABLISHED & SONS LIMITED

- 2-3 DUKE STREET SW1Y 6BJ
- 020 7968 2040
- ESTABLISHEDANDSONS.COM
- MON-FRI 9.30-6
- GREEN PARK

07 GAGOSIAN GALLERY

- 17-19 DAVIES STREET W1K 3DE
- 020 7493 3020
- GAGOSIAN.COM
- MON-SAT 10-6
- BOND STREET

Since British brand Established & Sons (p.115) launched in 2005, it has made a great effort to unveil high-end limited-edition designs along with its more commercial, mass-produced furniture and lighting collections. The limited editions have caused quite a stir from within the design industry and dropped Established & Sons into the middle of the fervent 'design art' debate. This rather dissatisfying term has been projected onto objects that blur the distinction between the functionalism of design and the expressive freedom of art. Offer a designer an open brief with an invitation to explore unusual materials and specialist technical skills and the results are likely to be expressive, if not excessive.

In 2007 Established & Sons opened this ethereal gallery space in Mayfair, which is devoted to a rotating programme of exhibitions featuring the company's highly collectible furnishings – visions by the country's leading designers. Barber Osgerby's colourful anodised-aluminium *Iris* tables; Amanda Levete's sinuous, solid-wood *West* bench; Terence Woodgate and John Barnard's gravity-defying carbon-fibre *Surface* table; and Zaha Hadid's already famous *Aqua* table have all made appearances in the space.

Unlike some other high-end galleries in London's more upmarket neighbourhoods, at Established & Sons you are unlikely to encounter pomposity and aloofness from unhelpful staff. This helps make your entry – by buzzer, through sliding-glass doors – a moment of anticipation, not consternation.

The Gagosian Gallery in Mayfair may well be the 'cherry on the cake' of Larry Gagosian's art empire. The space operates in tandem with the larger Britannia Street venue (p.102) and presents smaller-scale exhibitions of contemporary artists such as Richard Serra, Jeff Koons and Damien Hirst.

Virtually a storefront, the Davies Street gallery is the smallest of Gagosian's seven spaces worldwide. In just a few years it has hosted shows by some huge names, including the inaugural exhibition of eight versions of Pablo Picasso's most famous print, *La Minotauromachie*. The space, designed by Caruso St John Architects, looked rather impressive when a single sculpture was boldly displayed there in 2007: *Sacrificial Heart* by Tim Noble and Sue Webster.

Despite its art-market tendencies, the mini gallery with the mega name took a brave detour into the realm of design when, in 2008, it staged an exhibition of specially commissioned limited-edition pieces by Marc Newson. This illustrious collectible designer has put his hand to everything from bottle openers to Airbus A380 interiors, but in this instance he turned his attentions to a collection of furniture that was precision-cut from immense blocks of solid Carrara marble to extraordinary effect. It was this move that steered the gallery into my radar and into this guide, and I eagerly await further interventions of this sort in the future.

08 INSTITUTE OF CONTEMPORARY ARTS

- ☛ THE MALL SW1Y 5AH
- ☎ 020 7930 0493
- ➤ ICA.ORG.UK
- ⊙ DAILY 12-7, THU 12-9, BAR OPEN LATER
- ⊖ PICCADILLY CIRCUS/CHARING CROSS

Founded in 1947 by a collective of artists, writers and poets as a place to debate, exchange and champion contemporary culture, the ICA has evolved into one of London's leading artistic institutions. Who could have imagined that anything vaguely contemporary, controversial or cool could infringe upon the turf of London's grand establishment in the Mall? Sharing the same street as the Queen and with Whitehall and Parliament around the corner, the ICA remains safely cocooned in its regal 18th-century Nash House, free to make its own noise amid its conservative neighbours.

The ICA brings together the latest in the worlds of cinema, theatre, digital art, photography, painting, sculpture, design, music and other visual and performing arts. Management frequently dusts off old classic and cult movies to be screened in the two cinemas along with a curated programme of independent films. Two gallery spaces host a diverse range of temporary exhibitions, while the theatre and upstairs salons host debates, networking events and full-on music gigs. In the foyer, the ICA bookshop provides a good resource for books, magazines and DVDs that will appeal to the diverse audiences visiting this institution. During the day, a pitstop at the café/bar is a great way to digest the cultural exhibits or enjoy one of the regular club nights.

As it boasts such a packed programme of events, it is best to keep an eye on the website for the latest the institute has to offer.

09 PAUL SMITH 9 ALBEMARLE STREET

📌 9 ALBEMARLE STREET W1S 4BL

☎ 020 7493 4565

🖢 PAULSMITH.CO.UK

⏱ MON-SAT 10.30-6, THU 10.30-7

⊖ GREEN PARK

Many of Paul Smith's contemporaries have launched 'on brand' home collections, but true to form, this quintessentially British fashion designer has introduced something altogether more intriguing. In his Albemarle Street store, Smith has extended his lifetime passion for collecting unusual objects into an assembly of original and unique antiques, *objets d'art* and curiosities sourced from around the world. No.9 Albemarle Street is Smith's first space dedicated to such collectibles, where everything on show is available for purchase from his knowledgeable team.

The parquet-floored shop consists of two individually styled rooms – the first with soft-pink walls, and the second with distressed plaster and vintage wallpaper. Against this backdrop sits a mismatched yet simply arranged collection of furniture, lighting, art, jewellery and oddities. On my visit, highlights included a *Suvretta* bookcase by Ettore Sottsass and a 1950s revolving rosewood bookcase attributed to Gianfranco Frattini, plus smaller items such as a 1970s *Sintesi* task light by Ernesto Gismondi, a silver pot by Gio Ponti for Krupp and a collection of metal Japanese teapots. When it comes to upholstered pieces, many have been given a new lease of life with Paul Smith fabrics in his signature stripes.

The upmarket location goes hand-in-hand with upmarket prices, alas. But if you are after a collectible piece with character and individuality that can't be replicated, then a visit to this ever-evolving store comes highly recommended.

● *Eat & Drink*

10 1707 WINE BAR 181 PICCADILLY W1J 9LE
020 7734 8040 | FORTNUMANDMASON.COM
Sample any of the wines from Fortnum &
Mason's extensive selection. Designed by David
Collins. Dominant horseshoe-shaped bar.
Historical charm.

11 5TH VIEW 203-206 PICCADILLY W1J 9LE
020 7851 2433 | 5THVIEW.CO.UK
Essentially a bar attached to the Waterstone's
bookshop. Slick and airy. Some of the best
views of London rooftops. Great choice for
refreshment in the middle of town.

12 AUBAINE 4 HEDDON STREET W1B 4BS
020 7440 2510 | AUBAINE.CO.UK
Chic corner café, patisserie and restaurant
specialising in food from Southern France.
Tucked away behind busy Regent Street. Freshly
baked breads and croissants. Tables outside.
Great for people-watching.

13 AUTOMAT 33 DOVER STREET W1S 4NF
020 7499 3033 | AUTOMAT-LONDON.COM
Classic American brasserie that does a
convincing impression of a midtown Manhattan
steakhouse. Leather booths, black and white
floor tiles. Reasonably priced, reasonably trendy.
Buzzy atmosphere.

14 BENTLEY'S 11-15 SWALLOW STREET W1B 4DG
020 7734 4756 | BENTLEYS.ORG
London's reinvention of the historic fish
restaurant thanks to chef Richard Corrigan.
A history dating back to 1916. Warm, elegant
interiors. Serene, sophisticated and charming.

15 LE CAPRICE ARLINGTON HOUSE, ARLINGTON STREET
SW1A 1RJ | 020 7629 2239 | LE-CAPRICE.CO.UK
French-influenced classic-European cuisine.
Hot-ticket of the London dining scene since
1947. Charmingly dated 80s decor. Utterly
professional service.

16 CECCONI'S 5A BURLINGTON GARDENS W1S 3EP
020 7434 1500 | CECCONIS.CO.UK
A beacon of London's Italian-dining scene from
Soho House Group. Studioilse design. Black and
white-striped marble floors and bright-green
leather chairs. A classic.

17 COACH & HORSES 5 BRUTON STREET W1J 6PJ
020 7629 4123
Popular local's pub. Distinctive mock-Tudor
exterior. Wainscot panelling, wooden beams,
leaded-glass windows. A good range of draught
ales and decent selection of whiskies. A stone's
throw from the high-end boutiques of New
Bond Street.

18 ELECTRIC BIRDCAGE 11 HAYMARKET SW1Y 4BP
020 7839 2424 | ELECTRICBIRDCAGE.COM
Decadent and truly over-the-top bar. Design by
Shaun Clarkson. Carousel-like bar, fluorescent
birdcages, giant rearing horses, stucco ceiling
in fuchsia pink. Maybe too eccentric for many
people's tastes, but worth a pop-in. Good pan-
Asian food available.

19 ICA CAFÉ & BAR THE MALL, ST JAMES SW1Y 5AH
020 7930 8619 | ICACAFE.COM
A trendy drink after swilling a dose of modern
art. Minimalist interior with a pinch of bright
Modernist motifs. Turns into a late-night
DJ lounge.

20 INN THE PARK ST JAMES'S PARK SW1A 2BJ
020 7451 9999 | INNTHEPARK.COM
Tom Dixon-designed restaurant. Seasonal British
food. Spectacular seating overlooking the lake
and Duck Island of St James's Park.

21 MOMO 25 HEDDON STREET W1B 4BH
020 7434 4040 | MOMORESTO.COM
Authentic North African cuisine. Excellent
reputation. Cool Moroccan decor. Wooden
fretwork, deep-red rugs, low seating. Convivial
and infectiously upbeat party atmosphere.

22 NAPKET 6 BROOK STREET W1S 1BB
020 7495 8562 | NAPKET.COM
Essentially a sandwich and create-your-own-salad
bar. Glammed up by very slick interior design.
Coated in black gloss. Even the toilet paper
is black. Several in town.

23 THE NATIONAL DINING ROOMS THE NATIONAL
GALLERY, TRAFALGAR SQUARE WC2N 4DN
020 7747 2525 | THENATIONALDININGROOMS.CO.UK
All-things-British menu in the atmospheric
setting of the National Gallery's Sainsbury Wing.
Sleek, modern room. Floor-to-ceiling windows
with views onto Trafalgar Square. Calm and
enjoyable. Book for lunch and enjoy.

24 NOBU BERKELEY ST 15 BERKELEY STREET W1J 8DY
020 7290 9222 | NOBURESTAURANTS.COM
Acclaimed Japanese restaurant. Mix of French
chic and Japanese perfectionism. Delicate
flavours and intricate textures. Understated
decor. Try signature Nobu dish black cod in miso.
Glamorous and costly.

25 THE ONLY RUNNING FOOTMAN
5 CHARLES STREET W1J 5DE | 020 7499 2988
THEMEREDITHGROUP.CO.UK
Used to be a grotty old boozer, but has now
been stripped back and smartened up. The
ground-floor bar can be noisy; the upstairs dining
room tends to be more peaceful. Hearty food
served in both.

26 SAKE NO HANA 23 ST JAMES'S STREET SW1A 1LP
020 7925 8988 | SAKENOHANA.COM
Pure taste of traditional Japanese cooking.
Austerely elegant style. Clean, modern design by

Japanese architect Kengo Kuma. Japanese-cedar tables with foot-wells. Simple and playful.

27 SCOTT'S 20 MOUNT STREET W1K 2HE
020 7495 7309 | SCOTTS-RESTAURANT.COM

Glamorous seafood restaurant. Fresh fish prepared simply and presented beautifully. Opened as an oyster warehouse in 1851. Oak-panelled dining room and magnificent green onyx-topped bar. Real culinary treat.

28 SKETCH 9 CONDUIT STREET W1S 2XG
020 7659 4500 | SKETCH.UK.COM

Ultra-extravagant dining experience at the Lecture Room. Cosy afternoon break at the Parlour. The Gallery transforms from art gallery by day into stylish restaurant by night. Futuristic East Bar. Check out the toilets! Witty, elegant and refreshingly individual.

29 ST ALBAN 4-12 LOWER REGENT STREET SW1Y 4PE
020 7499 8558 | STALBAN.NET

Contemporary European cooking. Decadent 70s decor with modern touches. Great for people-watching.

30 UMU 14-16 BRUTON PLACE W1J 6LX
020 7499 8881 | UMURESTAURANT.COM

Located on peaceful Bruton Place. Enter via a push-button sliding door into the chic Kyoto-style restaurant. Warm, multi-textured interior that puts wood to excellent use. Expensive, but the cooking is expert.

31 THE WOLSELEY 160 PICCADILLY W1J 9EB
020 7499 6996 | THEWOLSELEY.COM

One of the most traditional restaurants in London. Inspired by Europe's grand brasseries. Originally a 1920s car showroom. Marble floors, pillars and archways. Great for breakfast or afternoon tea, but packed whatever the hour.

● Indulge

32 ALLEN'S 117 MOUNT STREET W1K 3LA
020 7499 5831 | ALLENSOFMAYFAIR.CO.UK

Mayfair's oldest butcher first opened in 1830. Suppliers to smart London eateries such as the Wolseley and Cecconi's.

33 BERRY BROS & RUDD 3 ST JAMES'S ST SW1A 1EG
0870 900 4300 | BBR.COM

Britain's longest established wine merchant dating back to 1689. Tucked into a spectacular manor house. Vaulted cellars, wood panelling.

34 FORTNUM & MASON 181 PICCADILLY W1A 1ER
020 7734 8040 | FORTNUMANDMASON.COM

One of the oldest and most famous establishments in Piccadilly. The purveyor of British tradition, food and wine. A must-see for anyone visiting the West End.

35 LADURÉE 71-72 BURLINGTON ARCADE W1J 0QX
020 7491 9155 | LADUREE.COM

Famous French patisserie dating back to 1862. Known for its delicate and colourful macaroons, available by the kilo! Beautiful presentation.

36 MINAMOTO KITCHOAN 44 PICCADILLY W1J 0DS
020 7437 3135 | KITCHOAN.COM

Traditional Japanese *Wagashi* confectioners and health-food shop.

37 PAXTON & WHITFIELD 93 JERMYN STREET SW1Y 6JE
020 7930 0259 | PAXTONANDWHITFIELD.CO.UK

Cheesemonger to Queen Victoria. Specialising in French and English artisan cheeses.

38 PRESTAT 14 PRINCES ARCADE, PICCADILLY SW1Y 6DS
020 7629 4838 | PRESTAT.CO.UK

Brightly coloured, richly scented, tiny chocolate shop. One of the world's oldest and grandest chocolate companies. The official purveyors of fine chocolates to the Queen.

● Sleep

39 NO.5 MADDOX STREET 5 MADDOX ST W1S 2QD
020 7647 0200 | NO5MADDOXST.COM

A peaceful hideaway just off Regent Street. Stylish, urban and edgy. Leather sofas, bamboo flooring, organic colour palette. Popular with the trendy and sophisticated.

40 CLARIDGES HOTEL BROOK STREET W1K 4HR
020 7629 8860 | CLARIDGES.CO.UK

The epitome of classic London style. Distinctly Art Deco interiors. Pop in for the best afternoon tea in town at the hotel's glittering Foyer or for a fine-dining experience at the Claridge's restaurant. The créme de la créme of the city's hotel scene.

41 HAYMARKET HOTEL 1 SUFFOLK PLACE SW1Y 4BP
020 7470 4000 | FIRMDALE.COM

A hip designer hotel by Tim and Kit Kemp. Bleached-oak floors, statement sculptures, wooden chandeliers. Swimming pool-cum-nightclub in the basement.

42 METROPOLITAN 19 OLD PARK LANE W1K 1LB
020 7447 1000 | METROPOLITAN.COMO.BZ

A fashionable design hotel situated on exclusive Park Lane and overlooking Hyde Park. Sleek, light, cream-toned interiors. Enjoy an eclectic Japanese cuisine in the hotel's Nobu restaurant or a cocktail in the Met Bar.

43 THE TRAFALGAR HOTEL 2 SPRING GARDENS
SW1A 2TS | 020 7870 2900 | THETRAFALGAR.COM

Super-central location. Simple Scandinavian style. Buzzing Rockwell Bar and lively lobby area. Amazing views from the hotel's roof garden onto the famous square.

Every building in every city hides a story behind its doors. ANNABEL FRASER wonders if we should strive to bring them all out in the open or leave every discovery to chance

BELOW THE RADAR

Walk down any street in London and you can be certain there is a story behind every brick in every wall and under every paving stone. The sheer number of these hidden narratives can be overwhelming. It's like the moment you realise someone's painstaking planning has overseen every stone cornice and wrought-iron rail in our urban landscape. It is practically inconceivable.

Certain stories are deemed crucial enough to recount in the public realm. The blue plaques on the façades of buildings are testament to that, as are statues and monuments that render concrete certain moments of history. But these clues are the outward manifestation of our history — tiny official fragments that only begin to skim the surface of what there is to uncover. What happens to all those tales buried beneath the layers of pavement and plaster? The ones stored in graveyards, archives and 'local history' books? As a graphic designer devoted to drawing out stories in and about the city, I experience an ongoing dilemma: should these stories be broadcast to the passer-by, or should they languish below the radar?

There does seem to be an appetite for these lesser-known stories. When William Ewart MP first proposed the idea of the blue plaque in the House of Commons, in 1863, he apparently made an immediate impact on the public imagination. And today, open any *Time Out* and you will find guided walks taking place around the city, based on widely differing themes. The intrigue of the past attracts countless individuals interested in digging up such seemingly forgotten information.

The way we interpret a fragment of history is forever changing. It changes with each passing era, and with the individual who chooses to engage with it. Who should decide what is recorded? And where would they record it? We clearly would not wish for plaques on every street corner. Above all, the emerging narratives must not become incorporated into 'heritage'.

'The way we interpret a fragment of history is forever changing. It changes with each passing era and with the individual. Who would decide what is recorded? And where would they record it?'

The digital realm offers a promising answer. As long as it remains a place unmediated by 'authorities', the fragmented narratives found in blogs and on websites can play their part in the public's imagination. In the ether we are not restricted by what others choose to point out to us; and we can change history ourselves. The Museum of London set up a website – mapmylondon.com – based on this very premise. Here, anyone can write a memory onto a digital map. However, as with other unedited repositories of information on the web, much of its material comes across as random – a totally uninteresting medley of highly personal information. ('First night in London. Got lost. Refused to ask for help.') In this state, the stories are meaningless.

If they are to come alive and relate to society today, they need to be edited and curated, woven into something bigger than mere anecdotes. Not to say there aren't people who do this. Iain Sinclair is arguably one of the best known among those who crystallise a huge amount of urban knowledge into books that interest people worldwide. But even so, this wealth of history remains opaque, available only to those curious enough to pick up these books.

I'm beginning to wonder if maybe this is the way these urban stories should remain: sentenced to obscurity, emerging unexpectedly in disparate places. As London mayor Boris Johnson says: 'There are so many stories to tell, in so many different ways…' Whether we stumble across them by word of mouth, on council plaques, in poems, artworks, books or websites isn't important. What is important is that they should create unexpected shifts of attention that give us a new perspective on our city. They should intrigue us, as for a brief moment they deliver us from the fast flow of contemporary life, making us each aware that we are but one small part of a larger continuum.

ANNABEL FRASER IS AN EXHIBITION AND GRAPHIC DESIGNER. ANNABELFRASER.COM

THE
LONDON
DESIGN
FESTIVAL

2010

18–26
September
www.londondesignfestival.com

Soho

HENRY HEATH HAT FACTORY, HOLLEN STREET

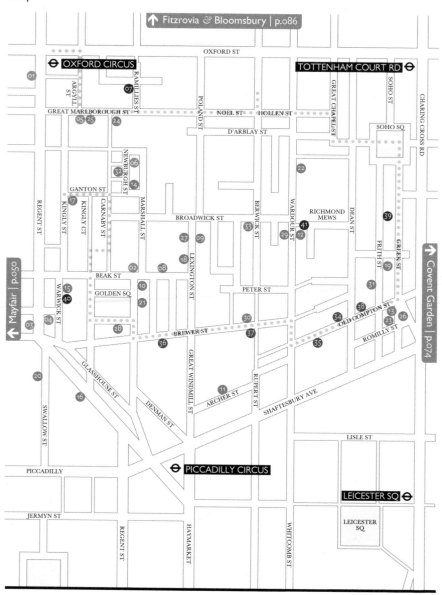

Soho

TAKE A WALK

*Michelle Alger**

After arriving at Oxford Circus tube, take the exit leading onto Argyll Street and you'll be facing the large Tudor-style building that is the iconic Liberty. Biased, I know, but in my opinion it is the most interesting store in the area, filled with delights ranging from high fashion through to luxury furniture.

Walking along Great Marlborough Street you'll pass the dress-fabric district. Be sure to check out the famous Cloth House stores on Berwick Street, with their lush fabrics and trims. Continue along Noel Street to Hollen Street and the imposing Henry Heath Hat Factory – another fragment of the old artisan Soho.

Snake through to Soho Square, with its mock-Tudor gatehouse and welcome green space in the heart of the metropolis. On the corner of Old Compton Street and Greek Street, visit Café Boheme and enjoy an afternoon Kir Royale and an atmosphere of Paris circa 1920. Next door is Soho House, where you can enjoy a terrific rooftop terrace if you know a friend with membership.

Continue down Old Compton Street past Patisserie Valerie, a must-visit for cakes and coffee. On Brewer Street, check out Madame Jojo's for burlesque dancing and kitsch cabaret and, a few doors further down, Soho's Original Bookshop, with its edgy collection of fashion and art titles (and a sneaky hidden sex shop downstairs). Carry on along Brewer Street to the Vintage Magazine Shop – great for silver-screen and comic-book fans. Continue in the same direction to Tommy Guns for a quick 'too cool for school' trim. Then do some celeb-spotting at Whole Foods.

Take a right into Lower James Street and catch a glimpse of the beautiful arches of lower Regent Street behind you. In Golden Square, stop by Nordic Bakery for coffee and Scandinavian treats before reaching Play Lounge for vinyl collectors on Beak Street. Cut through Kingly Court – a medley of vintage clothing, homewares and beauty boutiques – and re-emerge on Carnaby Street. Head left to howies, my favourite store on the street, selling unisex ethical clothing. Finally, on the corner of Ganton Street and Kingly Street, enjoy a glass of Manzanilla and tapas at Dehesa.

Buying manager for home and gift at Liberty (p.068) liberty.co.uk

01 APPLE STORE
- 235 REGENT STREET W1B 2EL
- 020 7153 9000
- APPLE.COM
- MON–SAT 9-9, SUN 12-6
- OXFORD CIRCUS

02 DO
- 47 BEAK STREET W1F 9SE
- 020 7494 9090
- DO-SHOP.COM
- MON–SAT 10-6.30, THU 10-8, SUN 12-6
- PICCADILLY CIRCUS/OXFORD CIRCUS

If you're a creative type, my bet is you're carrying an iPhone, you're listening to tunes on your iPod and a MacBook is perched on your desk. If you happen to be reading this, thank you for diverting your attention from one of Apple's fundamental tools for modern life.

With product sales ever buoyant, Apple's success must have something to do with the company's intuitively minimal signature style. The design team, headed up by Jonathan Ive, has worked tirelessly to make Apple products as easy as possible to use. By reducing the visual language to its essentials, technology no longer seems intimidating.

Flocks of people head to Apple's Regent Street flagship on a daily pilgrimage to get their fix of Apple-dom. The store is housed in a historic Edwardian building, which contrasts with the two-storey interior, dominated by glass, stainless-steel and cool stone.

On a Saturday afternoon the space is swarming with Apple groupies. Casual-looking staff hover nearby, ready to be summoned for help or assist with a sale. Head upstairs to the Genius Bar for technical help, or get free advice in the seminar space.

I'm an Apple user and I enjoy the gadgets on offer. But I don't much care for the devotee attitude that now goes along with that, and the sort of cultish 'coolness' in the swagger of most new customers. After theft, one suspects that the next biggest crime you could commit in the Apple Store would be the brandishing of a clunky PC laptop. Be warned.

Walking along Soho's Beak Street, I nearly missed this modest design shop with only a small neon sign to distinguish it. When I peered through the window, the long, narrow space lined with deep display shelving seemed to promise a treasure-trove of design. Venturing in, I was met with an affordable collection of tabletop creations, books and home accessories, with a smattering of furniture and lighting options.

Sourcing pieces from around the world is an ongoing task for the owner: enthusiastic former investment banker Andrew Ying, who set up shop in 2006. Playful products – such as the yellow Mattia Cimadoro cuckoo clock, multicoloured salt and pepper mills by Muuto and Lucinda Barnes's *Tierdrop* cake stand – contrast with affordable white crockery and simple cutlery and glassware. Very little in the way of furniture is offered, but the few choices, including some Moroso designs, seem rather isolated and peripheral to the smaller items.

In light of its buzzy central location, it strikes me as strange that Do doesn't, well, do more to shout about itself. On each visit it feels sparse and under-stocked and, by virtue of that, places too much focus on each piece. That approach can be effective, except the selection here isn't quite remarkable enough to pull it off. If I were the owner, I'd ditch the furniture and become a destination for well-edited contemporary accessories and gifts.

03 HABITAT

- 📌 121-123 REGENT STREET W1B 4TB
- ☎ 0844 499 1134
- ↖ HABITAT.CO.UK
- 🕐 MON-SAT 10-7, THU 10-8, SUN 12-6
- ⊖ PICCADILLY CIRCUS

04 IITTALA

- 📌 126 REGENT STREET W1B 5SD
- ☎ 020 7287 5600
- ↖ IITTALA.COM
- 🕐 MON-SAT 10-7, SUN 12-6
- ⊖ PICCADILLY CIRCUS

The brainchild of British design entrepreneur Terence Conran, Habitat began a revolution in everyday home furnishings when it opened its doors on Fulham Road back in 1964. Recognising changing consumer patterns during the Swinging Sixties, Conran sought to offer simple, functional, beautiful designs at affordable prices. Since then a lot has changed – not least that Habitat is now owned by Swedish giant IKEA. Nevertheless, it maintains its commitment to its original brand values with a collection of accessible interior furnishings and decorative items for all areas of the home.

Habitat's Regent Street flagship was built into the shell of a former Victorian cinema and sensitively transformed by former creative director Tom Dixon. The magnificent auditorium, vaulted plaster ceiling, Neo-Egyptian light fittings and original Wurlitzer organ all create a theatrical shopping ambience that sets up a striking contrast with Habitat's modern homewares. The simple displays showcase a wide range of Habitat's stable of offerings, updated seasonally with new designs from the Habitat in-house team.

Today Habitat operates across 38 locations in the UK. The stores seem to go through ups and downs, but on my recent visit the products and merchandising were coherent and confident. Perhaps this is a testament to the leadership of creative director Theo Williams.

Other London stores are located in Tottenham Court Road, King's Road, Finchley Road and Westfield shopping centre.

Since 1881, Finnish stalwart iittala has offered classic everyday glassware to a growing band of loyal customers around the world. Over the years the company has commissioned 20th-century design heros like Aino and Alvar Aalto, Kaj Franck and Tapio Wirkkala. Today iittala continues to work with leading designers who adhere to its vision of timeless, functional essentials. More recently, the company has subsumed producers Arabia and Hackman among others.

The 100-square-metre London iittala store is a physical manifestation of the brand's core philosophy: 'lasting design against throwawayism'. Walking in, you find yourself in a clean, open space dominated by colourful organic forms from the iittala catalogue. The glassware is arranged in harmonious groups, so the customer can explore the possibilities of mixing and matching different pieces. Featured together may be a *Kartio* pitcher by Kaj Franck, *Ote* drinking glasses by Aleksi Perälä and Aalto's iconic *Savoy* vase. Past the clean-lined shelving is a giant backlit montage of colourful glassware that dominates the back wall. On my visit it was arranged in the shape of an owl's face to mimic the *Taika* illustration by Klaus Haapaniemi.

Out of all of the myriad kitchenware available in London, I always come back to the confident simplicity of the iittala collections. I could quite happily kit out my home in iittala without running the risk of boredom.

05 LIBERTY

GREAT MARLBOROUGH STREET W1B 5AH

020 7734 1234

LIBERTY.CO.UK

MON-SAT 10-9, SUN 12-6

OXFORD CIRCUS

Walking down Argyll Street from Oxford Circus, you cannot miss this Tudor revival Arts and Crafts building: the striking timber-framed home of the historic Liberty department store. Its *raison d'etre* when it was founded in 1875 by Arthur Lasenby Liberty was to sell ornaments, fabrics and miscellaneous *objets d'art* from Japan and the Far East. But it soon developed its very own distinctive style and has evolved into one of London's favourite shopping destinations.

Intricately crafted interiors, wooden balconies, glass atriums and intimate staircases are all features of Liberty's impressive retail environment, against which the latest avant-garde fashions are displayed. Over the years Liberty has established powerful working relationships with leading British talents and has nurtured the exquisite craftsmanship and has grown in step with notable movements in design and fashion. The store regularly showcases new designers, celebrating the most exciting developments in fashion, accessories, beauty and home furnishings.

In the home department, which spans the building's top floor, contemporary furniture and lighting by the likes of Pieke Bergmans, Alexander Taylor, naughtone, Russell Pinch, Tom Dixon and Squint is displayed alongside stunning Arts and Crafts and Modernist pieces. Mixing the eras creates a richer and more diverse presentation than that of a one-brand concession. Be sure to peruse the stunning Liberty fabric archive on the third floor, lunch in the second floor café or rest your legs with Champagne and oysters in the basement bar.

06 LIFESTYLEBAZAAR	**07 THE PHOTOGRAPHER'S GALLERY**
10 NEWBURGH STREET W1F 7RN	16-18 RAMILLIES STREET W1F 7LW
020 7734 9970	0845 262 1618
LIFESTYLEBAZAAR.COM	PHOTONET.ORG.UK
MON-SAT 11-7, SUN 12-5	TUE-SAT 11-6, THU-FRI 11-8, SUN 12-6
OXFORD CIRCUS	OXFORD CIRCUS

Joining the plethora of lifestyle and fashion boutiques in the Carnaby Street 'village' is Lifestylebazaar, the creation of Laurent Nurisso and Christopher Curtis. The team has succeeded for more than a decade in supplying an eclectic selection of furniture, tableware and lighting, accompanied by other household items like coat hooks and candleholders with a twist.

Instead of pitching themselves at the high end of the market, the owners have gone for the young hipster base, with a focus on fun gifts brimming with character that don't break the bank. It is spread over two floors, with little space for much furniture; most of the daintier offerings are displayed collectively on white shelving or plinths. On my visit, a series of trays with bizarre portraits of bird-headed aristocrats by ibride caught my attention, as did the angular book shelving by Edition Compagnie. Among the smaller homewares, you can find affordable accessories and tableware from companies like Black & Blum, La Corbeille, JosephJoseph and Thelermont Hupton.

The store, layout and product displays are arresting, yet approachable to passers-by. Some of the content here is just too whimsical for me. And while it might elicit a smile from some, they seem to make too much of a one-liner statement to be truly practical. That said, Curtis and Nurisso have clearly identified an enthusiastic market, and progressed to the point that they have opened their second store, in London's East End (p.133).

If you're looking to escape the ghastly shopping thoroughfare that is Oxford Street, or you have half an hour to spare in the area, you would be best advised to pop in to the Photographer's Gallery for a quick fix of contemporary photography. The space is tucked away on a quiet side street, yet it can boast originals by some of the best and brightest in British photography hanging from its walls. Furthermore, there are no crowds here to obscure your view.

The gallery was the first independent collection in the UK devoted specifically to the medium of photography. Over the years it has nurtured generations of artists and succeeded at establishing photography as a more popular and accessible art form. It was the first gallery of its kind to display now-prominent names like Juergen Teller, Andreas Gursky, Irving Penn and Jacques-Henri Lartigue.

The gallery, now in a new space after moving from Great Newport Street, has a year-round program of exhibitions and educational events, with a wide range of photographic work permanently on display. There is also a print sales room and a specialist bookshop with an impressive range of hard-to-find titles, art books and cool postcards. A peaceful café on the first floor offers a nice alternative to the super-crowded cafés in the area.

Eat & Drink

08 ALPHABET BAR 61-63 BEAK STREET W1F 9SL
020 7439 2190 | ALPHABETBAR.COM

A quirky art bar in the heart of Soho. Full of character. Old car seating as furniture. Map of central London painted on the floor. Nice mix of local after-workers and cool kids.

09 ANDREW EDMUNDS 46 LEXINGTON ST W1F 0LW
020 7437 5708

British take on Modern European dining. Resembles a charming country cottage. Rustic wood furniture, cosy booths, dim lighting. Very small. Intimate, romantic mood. Great place for a date. Open conservatory in summer.

10 BOB BOB RICARD 1 UPPER JAMES STREET W1F 9DF
020 3145 1000 | BOBBOBRICARD.COM

All-day dining, upscale brasserie and cocktail bar. Special take on English comfort food. Oriental Express decor. Old-fashioned quirkiness. Art Deco fittings. Eclectic, ebullient and witty. You'll love it or think it's ridiculous.

11 BOCCA DI LUPO 12 ARCHER STREET W1D 7BB
020 7734 2223 | BOCCADILUPO.COM

Rustic Italian dishes reworked with designer flourishes. Dramatic light fittings, antique mirrors, marble-topped bar. Good vibe and loads of atmosphere.

12 BUSABA EATHAI 106-110 WARDOUR ST W1F 0RT
020 7255 8686 | BUSABA.COM

Delicious and excellent-value canteen-style Thai eating. Simple, modern surroundings. Communal tables encourage lively conversation. Convenient location. No booking allowed, so expect to queue at peak times.

13 CAFÉ BOHEME 13-17 OLD COMPTON ST W1D 5GQ
020 7734 0623 | CAFEBOHEME.CO.UK

Typical brasserie fare. An appealing Parisian boho vibe. Leather banquettes, brass fittings. Fun and buzzy. Live music on weekends. Open from 7:30AM until 3AM.

14 CANELA 1 NEWBURGH STREET W1F 7RB
020 7494 9980 | CANELACAFE.COM

Tiny Portuguese deli and café. Popular selection of traditional prepared meals and desserts. Affordable comfort food. Full of charm.

15 THE CLUB BAR & DINING 21-22 WARWICK ST
W1B 5NE | 020 7734 1002
THECLUBBARANDDINING.CO.UK

Typical Soho hangout. All-day dining in brasserie style on the ground floor. Moody basement bar. Exposed brickwork, leather booths, block-wood tables. Smart, yet laidback and fun.

16 COCOON 65 REGENT STREET W1B 4EA
020 7494 7600 | COCOON-RESTAURANTS.COM

Blurs the lines between restaurant, bar, cocktail lounge and nightclub. Great sushi and tasty fusion food. Futurist design. Egg-shaped seating, padded walls. Self-consciously trendy with surprisingly amiable staff.

17 DEHESA 25 GANTON STREET W1F 9BP
020 7494 4170 | DEHESA.CO.UK

Charcuterie and tapas bar. A delicious range of Spanish- and Italian-inspired sharing dishes. Beautiful decor, bay windows and a reclaimed-oak parquet floor. Great wine list. A fine tapas experience.

18 FERNANDEZ & WELLS 43 LEXINGTON ST W1F 9AL
020 7734 1546 | FERNANDEZANDWELLS.COM

Upmarket deli, charcuterie and cheese room. Can't miss it, with the butcher's block and whole leg of ham hanging in the window. Fresh, quality produce from the most reputable suppliers. Pop into the Fernandez & Wells sandwich and coffee shop around the corner (73 BEAK STREET, W1F 9SR, 020 7287 8124).

19 GARLIC & SHOTS 14 FRITH STREET W1D 4RD
020 7734 9505 | GARLICANDSHOTS.COM

One of London's most original bars. Garlic-flavoured food and drink. Hairy-biker appeal. Dark, quirky interior. Popular with Goths but an absolute must-go for everyone else.

20 GAUCHO 25 SWALLOW STREET W1B 4QR
020 7734 4040 | GAUCHORESTAURANTS.CO.UK

Some of the most succulent Argentinian steak in town. Four floors of dining. Decor dominated by cowhide upholsteries and black lacquer. If you can, get a table on the ground floor at the Cavas De Gaucho wine boutique, or on the top floor lounge with live jazz music.

21 GRAPHIC BAR 4 GOLDEN SQUARE W1F 9HT
020 7287 9241 | GRAPHICBAR.COM

A slick, summery cocktail bar overlooking one of the most beautiful squares in Soho. Vibrant and seductive environment. Signature mix of chocolate-brown, gold and bronze shades. Great bar to unwind in.

22 INAMO 134-136 WARDOUR STREET W1F 8ZP
020 7851 7051 | INAMO-RESTAURANT.COM

The most technologically advanced restaurant in the city. Designed by London-based studio Blacksheep. Interactive projections on tables. Computerised menus. Kitchen webcam. Funky, futuristic furniture. Modern pan-Asian menu. Fun for the experience.

23 KETTNERS 29 ROMILLY STREET W1D 5HP
020 7734 6112 | KETTNERS.COM

Modern French brasserie and much-loved Champagne bar. One of London's oldest restaurants recently revamped by Studioilse. Grand, Belle Epoque interiors. Buzzy, convivial atmosphere.

24   LEON 35 GREAT MARLBOROUGH STREET W1F 7JE
020 7437 5280 | LEONRESTAURANTS.CO.UK

A fast-food joint with a difference. Healthy, seasonal and very tasty food. Great for takeaway lunch but open in the evening with a wide selection of wines.

25   LIBERTY CHAMPAGNE AND OYSTER BAR
GREAT MARLBOROUGH STREET W1B 5AH
020 7734 1234 | LIBERTY.CO.UK

Decadent seafood and champagne bar in a former Edwardian basement storeroom. White marble-topped horseshoe bar. An individual edge with a sprinkle of English eccentricity.

26   MAISON BERTAUX 28 GREEK STREET W1D 5DQ
020 7437 6007

A taste of rural France. Established in 1871. Deli, patisserie, tea room and, believe it or not, fashion boutique – all under one roof. Old bentwood tables and chairs. Cramped and kitsch. Legendary.

27   MRS MARENGO'S 53 LEXINGTON STREET W1F 9AS
020 7287 2544 | MRSMARENGOS.CO.UK

Charming little vegetarian eat-in on a chic Soho street. Does a very good takeaway. Impossibly tempting cakes and desserts. Pop in for a hearty breakfast.

28   NORDIC BAKERY 14A GOLDEN SQUARE W1F 9JG
020 3230 1077 | NORDICBAKERY.COM

Original Helsinki café. Classic Scandinavian fare. Clean, simple decor. Quiet and contemplative.

29   PRINCI 135 WARDOUR STREET W1F 0UT
020 7478 8888 | PRINCI.CO.UK

Authentic Italian bakery turned canteen-style eaterie. Selection of fresh breads, pastries and pasta. Designed by Claudio Silvestrin. Stone floors, bronze fittings. One long, narrow central table with stools. Buzzing from morning till night.

30   RANDALL & AUBIN 16 BREWER STREET W1F 0SQ
020 7287 4447 | RANDALLANDAUBIN.COM

Fresh seafood and Champagne. Tiny former butchers shop. Booths for two and central communal tables. Very small but very popular. Expect to queue.

31   RONNIE SCOTT'S 47 FRITH STREET W1D 4HT
020 7439 0747 | RONNIESCOTTS.CO.UK

One of London's best and most famous jazz bars. Smoky and dark, as a jazz bar should be. American-influenced menu available. Packed night after night.

32   LA TROUVAILLE 12A NEWBURGH STREET W1F 7RR
020 7287 8488 | LATROUVAILLE.CO.UK

Inventive take on French classics with well chosen list of some of France's most interesting wines. Small, pale, light dining room upstairs. Ground-floor wine bar. Laidback charm.

33   YAUATCHA 15-17 BROADWICK STREET W1F 0DL
020 7494 8888 | YAUATCHA.COM

Trendy all-day (and night) dim sum restaurant. A chic, modern take on the oriental tea-house theme. Sophisticated underground feel. Atmosphere always buzzing.

● *Indulge*

34   ALGERIAN COFFEE STORES 52 OLD COMPTON ST
W1D 4PB | 020 7437 2480 | ALGCOFFEE.CO.UK

Large variety of coffee blends and teas from around the world. Dating back to 1887. Original fixtures, including rustic wooden shelving and counters.

35   I CAMISA & SON 61 OLD COMPTON ST W1D 6HS
020 7437 7610

A superb Italian delicatessen. Homemade pastas and pork sausages.

36   MRS KIBBLE'S OLDE SWEET SHOPPE
57A BREWER STREET W1F 9UL | 020 7734 6633

Unadulterated, candy-filled fun. Crammed full of old-fashioned sugary sweets.

37   SNOG 9 BREWER ST W1F 0RG | 020 7494 3301
IFANCYASNOG.COM

Delicious frozen yogurt. Healthier alternative to ice cream. Bright and cheerful interior designed by Cinimod Studio.

38   VINTAGE HOUSE 42 OLD COMPTON STREET
W1D 4LR | 020 7437 2592
FREESPACE.VIRGIN.NET/VINTAGEHOUSE.CO

Premier London malt whisky retailer. Family-run business. Stocks more than 1,450 malts, 200 rums and 100 tequilas and Bordeaux wines.

● *Sleep*

39   HAZLITT'S 6 FRITH STREET W1D 3JA
020 7434 1771 | HAZLITTSHOTEL.CO.UK

Period charm with 21st-century comfort. Georgian panelling, cavernous fireplaces and gothic screens. Particularly popular with artists and writers. Step back in time.

40   SANCTUM SOHO HOTEL 20 WARWICK ST W1B 5NF
020 7292 6100 | SANCTUMSOHO.COM

An arty, bohemian hideaway. Edgy glamour and individual look. Room decor varies from baroque fantasy to glitzy mirrored glamour – whatever your fancy. Roof garden with outdoor jacuzzi. Underground 45-seat cinema. Comfort, style and sophistication.

41   THE SOHO HOTEL 4 RICHMOND MEWS W1D 3DH
020 7559 3000 | FIRMDALE.COM

Stylish and peaceful townhouse hotel. Modern English style. Luxurious granite and oak design. Expensive but deluxe.

THORSTEN
VAN
ELTEN

www.thorstenvanelten.com

Covent Garden

FREEMASON'S HALL, GREAT QUEEN STREET

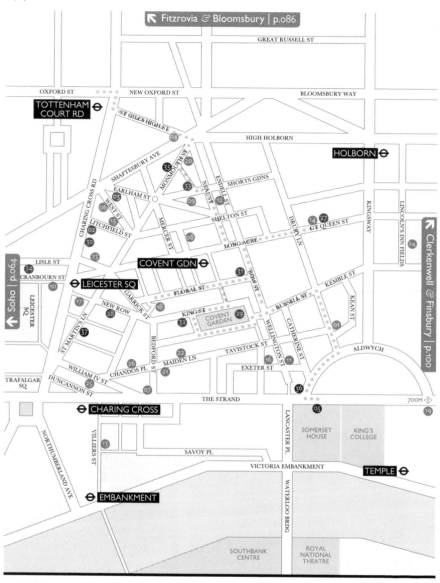

Fitzrovia & Bloomsbury | p.086

Soho | p.064

Clerkenwell & Finsbury | p.100

● Design galleries & institutions
● Design shops & C20th vintage
● Design bookshops

● Eat & Drink
● Indulge
● Sleep
(pp.080-081)

●●● Take a walk route

01	ARAM
02	KOENIG BOOKS
03	MAGMA
04	MOLTENI & C DADA
05	**SOMERSET HOUSE**

Covent Garden

TAKE A WALK
*Kati Price**

Start off at Tottenham Court Road, where you can't miss Centrepoint, one of London's first skyscrapers, which has a fascinating and controversial history.

Wander down St Giles High Street, cross over into Monmouth Street and pop into Miss Lala's Boudoir for luxury lingerie, then into Orla Kiely for some of her trademark patterned bags and accessories. Keep an eye out for a passageway that leads you into the hippie oasis of Neal's Yard and emerge onto Short's Gardens, where you can sample some 200 cheeses at the world-famous Neal's Yard Dairy.

After exploring Neal Street, bear left onto Long Acre and walk over to Great Queen Street for some robust British fare, taking in the Art Deco Freemason's Hall opposite – it serves as the headquarters of the United Grand Lodge of England.

Head back down Long Acre and bear left into Bow Street, which is dominated by the impressive façade of the Royal Opera House. As you turn into Floral Street, look up and you'll spot the twisting glass *Bridge of Aspirations*, designed by architects Wilkinson Eyre, which connects the Royal Ballet School with the Opera House.

Pick up some treats at Kastner & Ovens as you stroll down Floral Street en route to the Paul Smith store. As Floral Street ends you'll find Covent Garden's oldest pub, the Lamb & Flag. After a quick pint, head down James Street into the Piazza, the heart of Covent Garden, designed by Inigo Jones in the 17th century. Formerly a vegetable market, the space now hosts lots of craft and food stalls, boutiques and street entertainers.

After a refreshing frozen yoghurt at Yu-foria, visit the London Transport Museum or head down Russell Street to Drury Lane and Aram, which, in the 60s, first brought furniture by the likes of Marcel Breuer and Le Corbusier to the UK.

If you're feeling thirsty, grab a seat at the brilliant Lobby Bar at One Aldwych or head underground to CellarDoor, where you'll discover drag queens and cabaret crooners in this former Gents toilet. Cross over the Strand and finish your tour at Somerset House – a spectacular spot for ice skating in winter or al fresco drinks and music on the River Terrace in summer.

Marketing and content manager at Design Council designcouncil.org.uk

01 ARAM

110 DRURY LANE WC2B 5SG

020 7557 7557

ARAM.CO.UK

MON-SAT 10-6, THU 10-7

COVENT GARDEN

It was 1964 on London's King's Road when Zeev Aram opened his first showroom introducing an altogether new and striking vocabulary of furniture to shocked passers-by. At the time, acceptance of modern design was only in its infancy in this country and Aram was taking a punt that it might catch on. Many considered the work of Castiglioni, Breuer and Le Corbusier to be too clinical but, with patience, an interest in this modern vernacular did emerge. In 1973 the company moved to the Aldwych end of Covent Garden with a focus on the contract market.

A turn-of-the-millennium opportunity arose when the old fruit and vegetable warehouse next door went up for sale, which, in 2002, enabled Aram to expand into a five-floor emporium of more than 1,800-square-metres. The ensuing retail destination, with its wraparound corner location and raw-industrial feel, has become somewhat of an institution with plenty of space dedicated to leading furniture and lighting brands such as Artek, Alias, Cassina, Artemide, Flos, Vitra, Fritz Hansen, Interlubke, Knoll, Flexform, Montana and USM. It is worth pointing out to those die-hard fans out there that Aram holds the worldwide license for the designs of Bauhaus legend Eileen Gray.

It is my impression that the emporium could be accessorised to feel more shop-like, rather than an unembellished showroom with single-brand displays. For something more subversive, it is worth checking out the Aram Gallery on the top floor, which is dedicated to a changing schedule of exhibitions showcasing exciting concepts and experiments from emerging designers.

02 KOENIG BOOKS

- 80 CHARING CROSS ROAD WC2H 0BF
- 020 7240 8190
- KOENIGBOOKS.CO.UK
- MON-SAT 10-8, THU 10-9, SUN 1-8
- LEICESTER SQUARE

03 MAGMA

- 8 EARLHAM STREET WC2H 9RY
- 020 7240 8498
- MAGMABOOKS.COM
- MON-SAT 10-7, SUN 12-6
- LEICESTER SQUARE

It's worth plowing through the tourists swarms in Leicester Square to get to busy Charing Cross Road, where you'll find a variety of specialists bookshops, including this little gem. Here, the second London branch of Walther Koenig Books Ltd – Germany's most established and reputable bookshop of this genre – builds on its established presence at the Serpentine Gallery (p.019).

The shop is stylishly designed in black, which forms a simple backdrop to the vibrant book and magazine covers. The imperceptibly 'designed' visual identity by the London-based studio YES gives it a confident presence on this street corner. The small but dense shop is piled high with international books on modern and contemporary art, art theory, photography, design and architecture, with complementing magazine titles. You will find anything from the *Documents Of Contemporary Art* series and the latest popular art-market biographies to an impressive array of philosophy texts and less-common titles such as a canary-yellow-cotton-covered publication dedicated to T-shirt design.

Koenig Books is a place that carries enough interesting titles to encourage anyone to happily spend a small fortune. These sort of books often don't come cheap – £50 per tome is commonplace. Nevertheless, this is clearly a business committed to supplying a well-edited range of quality publications.

For anyone with a serious interest in art and design, Magma in London's Covent Garden is something of a Mecca. Not so much a regular bookshop as a thriving micro-industry of printed matter, this is the original Magma store, now a decade old, which soon spawned a larger counterpart in Clerkenwell (p.103).

Magma has come to occupy a somewhat unique status in London's contemporary design world. Based on a rare combination of good buying policy, a layout conducive to browsing and discovery, plus informed friendly service, it has become a regular hangout for all sorts of creative types. It is one of the best places to go for the latest design, architecture and photography titles, layout and typography textbooks and cutting-edge industry magazines, all displayed from floor to ceiling in this tiny shop. A quick visit may be possible here, but you could easily lose a whole afternoon, ending up with a hefty purchase of global publications.

Expanding its brand, Magma also has its own multi-purpose product shop only a few doors up the road at 16 Earlham Street. Designed by architects Julie Blum and Nikki Blustin, the space complements its sister with a range of graphic stationery, gift accessories, cultish games and toys and various eco-products.

04 MOLTENI & C DADA
199 SHAFTESBURY AVENUE WC2H 8JR
020 7631 2345
MOLTENI.IT
MON-FRI 9-5.30, SAT 10-5
TOTTENHAM COURT ROAD

Established Italian furniture producer Molteni & C opened this 400-square-metre flagship on a prominent Covent Garden corner in 2008, introducing the West End to its slick domestic creations designed by a roster of international stars. To the passing traffic, nine immense glass windows provide an excellent view of the store's interior. You'll spy a vast selection of the company's table, chair, sofa, shelving-system, bed and wardrobe collections, with plenty of space also given over to the slick kitchen designs from sister company Dada.

Visitors are welcomed by a friendly member of staff. Opting to browse alone, I was surprised to be presented with what felt like quite a limited selection of designs. I know that a certain Minimalist aesthetic is characteristic of this brand but I can't help feeling that a few more flourishes could be added to the displays to create a softer, less styled finish.

That said, as it stands, the formalism of the space focuses one's eyes on the products at hand. The confident, angular and rather masculine *Diamond* table by Patricia Urquiola softened by her padded *Glove* chair caught my attention, as did Jean Nouvel's slender anchored *Graduate* shelving. The no-nonsense high-end Dada kitchens designed by the likes of Foster and Partners, Hannes Wettstein and Ferruccio Laviani are worth exploring for their tactile materials and superb finishes.

Unquestionable quality, clean lines and technical finesse characterise this company's products, even if the displays could do with some more warmth.

 SOMERSET HOUSE

STRAND WC2R 1LA

020 7845 4600

SOMERSETHOUSE.ORG.UK

DAILY 10-6

COVENT GARDEN/CHARING CROSS

You can enjoy a year-round programme of music, performance art, even ice skating in the shadow of Somerset House's imposing neoclassical façade. Or you can head past the arches commissioned by King George III and engage in culture of another kind. Somerset House has hosted its share of respected learned societies, including the Royal Academy. And until recently it was home to two of the world's most important collections of art and decorative arts: the Gilbert Collection, now residing at the v&a (p.021), and the Hermitage Rooms.

Now there are the Embankment Galleries, 750-square-metres of exhibition space on the bank of the Thames. A dramatic steel-and-glass feature staircase, hard-stone floor and light walls introduce a more contemporary element to this historical space and offer a fitting backdrop for the roster of distinctive cross-disciplinary exhibitions. The programme – which focuses on a broad spectrum of contemporary arts, from fashion and architecture to design and photography, launched two years ago with the *Skin + Bones: Parallel Practice in Fashion and Architecture* exhibition, featuring 50 of the world's leading fashion designers and architects, including Vivienne Westwood, Alexander McQueen, Frank Gehry and Zaha Hadid.

The view from the entrance, with its expansive courtyard hiding playful fountains, completes the experience. This is not only one of London's architectural gems but also an important centre for the visual arts, complete with its own restaurant and outstanding views along the Thames.

● *Eat & Drink*

06   L'ATELIER DE JOEL ROBUCHON
13-15 WEST STREET WC2H 9NE
020 7010 8600 | JOEL-ROBUCHON.COM
A Japanese-styled eatery offering fanciful French
dishes. The decor is opulent and sumptuous.
A Japanese red-and-black-lacquer theme runs
throughout. A reasonably priced, welcoming
high-end experience.

07   BEDFORD & STRAND   1A BEDFORD ST WC2E 9HH
020 7836 3033 | BEDFORD-STRAND.COM
Unconventional wine bar. Black and white tiles,
simple furniture. One of few non-touristy places
in this busy area. Trad French-bistro food.

08   CAFÉ PACIFICO   5 LANGLEY STREET WC2H 9JA
020 7379 7728 | CAFEPACIFICO-LAPERLA.COM
Tex-Mex food since 1982. Typical regional dishes.
Old-school Mexican cantina. Old-fashioned
Spanish posters, cheerfully painted walls. Busy at
lunchtime and weekends.

09   CANELA   33 EARLHAM STREET WC2H 9LS
020 7240 6926 | CANELACAFE.COM
Portuguese/Brazilian deli and café. Freshly
prepared meals alongside regional delicacies.
Cool, sparse interior. A few tables outside. Low-
key, simple and relaxed surroundings.

10   CORK & BOTTLE   44-46 CRANBOURN ST WC2H 7AN
020 7734 7807 | CORKANDBOTTLE.NET
Established in 1971. Popular and timeless gem. A
relaxed place to enjoy a good glass of wine and
a slab of homemade quiche at any time of day.
Expect it to be packed with wine lovers.

11   CHRISTOPHER'S MARTINI BAR   18 WELLINGTON ST
WC2E 7DD | 020 7240 4222
CHRISTOPHERSGRILL.COM
Long, narrow bar at Christopher's American
Bar & Grill. Dark woods. Mellow, laidback
atmosphere. Popular with theatre-goers.

12   CROSS KEYS   31 ENDELL STREET WC2H 9EB
020 7836 5185
An old man's pub. Hidden behind baskets and
pots of tumbling foliage. Over-the-top interior,
with walls covered in theatre-, film- or music-
related paintings, photographs and posters.
Copper pots, kettles, scuttles, musical instruments
hanging from the ceiling. Unusual and charming.

13   GORDON'S WINE BAR   47 VILLIERS ST WC2N 6NE
020 7930 1408 | GORDONSWINEBAR.COM
London's oldest wine bar, circa 1890, and one
of central London's hidden gems. Rickety room
plastered with old newspaper cuttings and dusty
wine bottles. Delicious homemade food and
cheeses. Always crowded. Friendly staff.

14   GREAT QUEEN STREET   32 GREAT QUEEN STREET
WC2B 5AA | 020 7242 0622

Hidden behind a nameless black frontage
at No.32. A daily-changing menu of hearty
British fare. Long, narrow room. Casual,
rustic decor. Dark maroon walls, understated
furniture, Victorian lampshades. Unfussy and
unpretentious. A regular haunt not only for those
who live and work in the area.

15   THE IVY   1-5 WEST STREET WC2H 9NQ
020 7836 4751 | THE-IVY.CO.UK
The It restaurant of the past years. Food of
a traditional British variety but done to an
unusual standard. Above all, a great ambience.
Simple, yet elegant feel. Pricey but certainly an
experience. Go there to feel famous.

16   JOE ALLEN   13 EXETER STREET WC2E 7DT
020 7836 0651 | JOEALLEN.CO.UK
Traditional American menu with a warm,
underground atmosphere. Friendly atmosphere.
Great for brunch or a laidback post-theatre meal.
Live jazz on some evenings.

17   J SHEEKEY   28-32 ST MARTIN'S COURT WC2N 4AL
020 7240 2565 | J-SHEEKEY.CO.UK
A legendary oyster bar combine with spanking
bivalve bistro. Art-Deco mini-palace. Smoky
mirrors with orange sconces, monochrome
photos of faded actors, Orient Express like table
lamps. Glamorous, chic and charming enough to
almost forget about the great food.

18   LAMB & FLAG   33 ROSE STREET WC2E 9EB
020 7497 9504
Charles Dickens once frequented this place,
one of the oldest pubs in town. Low beams,
wood panelling and bare pine floorboards.
Unabashedly traditional and full of character.

19   LUTYENS RESTAURANT   85 FLEET STREET EC4Y 1AE
020 7583 8385 | LUTYENS-RESTAURANT.COM
The latest venture from Sir Terence Conran.
Housed in the former Reuters building.
Restaurant serves French food with Irish
influences and includes a crustacean and sushi
bar. The ground floor bar features a charcuterie
counter. Interiors in fresh green palette.

20   MONMOUTH COFFEE COMPANY
27 MONMOUTH STREET WC2H 9EU | 020 7379 3516
MONMOUTHCOFFEE.CO.UK
A small, traditional coffee house, roasting and
retailing coffee from 1978. Sampling room.
Tiny seating area that looks as if it's been
carved out of a block of wood. Small and
personal. Very popular. A range of pastries
and cakes from Villandry and Paul. All
available to stay or take away.

21   PORTERHOUSE   21-22 MAIDEN LANE WC2E 7NA
020 7379 7917 | PORTERHOUSEBREWCO.COM
Genuine Irish Brewery in the heart of Covent
Garden. A huge range of different porters and

stouts from around the world. It's easy to get lost in this large, multi-level space. Gets very busy in the evenings and on weekends. Great outdoor space too.

22 RULES 32 MAIDEN LANE WC2E 7LB
020 7836 5314 | RULES.CO.UK

The oldest restaurant in London, dating back to 1789. Burgundy leather seating and walls decorated with old cartoons. A fittingly traditional British menu. Fish and chips served the old fashioned way, in newspaper.

23 SALVADOR & AMANDA
8 GREAT NEWPORT ST WC2H 7JA | 020 7240 1551
SALVADORANDAMANDA.COM

Classic Spanish tapas. Authentically Spanish feel. Scarlet walls, dark woods, posters from Spanish movies adorning the walls. Atmospheric and lively with often noisy energetic crowd and loud Spanish music.

24 THE TERRACE LINCOLN'S INN FIELDS WC2A 3LJ
020 7430 1234 | THETERRACE-RESTAURANT.COM

Picturesque park setting. Outdoor terrace. Modern British food with Carribbean twist. Recommended if you like a homely, filling meal at a good price.

25 TERROIRS 5 WILLIAM IV STREET WC2N 4DW
020 7036 0660 | TERROIRSWINEBAR.COM

A new take on the classic Parisian artisan wine bar. Offers 'natural' wines, those made from relatively small quantities of handpicked grapes. Noisy, informal and joyful place. Also great charcuterie.

26 WAHACA 66 CHANDOS PLACE WC2N 4HG
020 7240 1883 | WAHACA.CO.UK

Mexican market eating. Simple menu. Quality ingredients. Honest food to share with others. Light wood interior decorated with tomatillo cans dotted with bottle tops, wooden crates packed with fruit, and tubs of chilli plants. Fun, buzzy atmosphere.

● Indulge

27 BLOOMSBURY FLOWERS
29 GREAT QUEEN ST WC2B 5BB | 020 7242 2840
BLOOMSBURYFLOWERS.CO.UK

Flowers to impress. Classic hand-tied posies and extra-special individually designed bouquets.

28 THE DRURY TEA & COFFEE CO 3 NEW ROW
WC2N 4LH | 020 7836 1960 | DRURY.UK.COM

Old-school independent specialist shop. Teas and coffees from around the world. Check out the multicoloured ceramic tea pots.

29 ELLA'S BAKEHOUSE 20A COVENT GARDEN PIAZZA
WC2E 8RB | ELLASBAKEHOUSE.COM

New retro bakery from the former face of

Versace turned patisserie chef, Lorraine Pascale. Reputed for the delicious, colourful cupcakes.

30 G SMITH & SONS 74 CHARING CROSS ROAD
WC2H 0BG | 020 7836 7422

Traditional tobacconists, selling most brands of cigarettes, rolling and pipe tobacco, snuff and snuff boxes. Opened in 1869 as Charing Cross Road's first shop.

31 KASTNER & OVENS 52 FLORAL STREET WC2E 9DA
020 7836 2700

Café and food shop. A handy spot to grab a tasty lunch. Buffet-style tables. Two hot dishes a day and fresh home-baked pastries and tarts.

32 MUFFINSKI'S 5 KING STREET WC2E 8HN
020 7379 1525 | MUFFINSKIS.CO.UK

Freshly baked organic muffins. In summer they also serve delicious frozen yoghurt. Irresistible.

33 NEAL'S YARD DAIRY 17 SHORTS GDNS WC2H 9AT
020 7240 5700 | NEALSYARDDAIRY.CO.UK

Farm cheeses from the British Isles. Formerly a cheesemaker, now London's foremost cheese retailer.

34 SEE WOO HONG 18-20 LISLE STREET WC2H 7BE
020 7439 8325 | SEEWOO.COM

One of the most highly recommended South East Asian supermarkets in London. A large selection of ingredients and fresh spices, fruit and vegetables.

● Sleep

35 COVENT GARDEN HOTEL 10 MONMOUTH STREET
WC2H 9HB | 020 7806 1000 | FIRMDALE.COM

Former hospital converted into a charming boutique hotel. A modern update on traditional English decor. Antique tapestries and paisley fabrics. Charming, laid back, home-from-home atmosphere. Great location in the heart of the West End.

36 ONE ALDWYCH ONE ALDWYCH WC2B 4RH
020 7300 0500 | ONEALDWYCH.COM

Contemporary-luxe interiors behind the hotel's signature Edwardian facade. Glamorous accommodation with immaculate, five-star service and many more bells and whistles. Popular Lobby Bar and two acclaimed restaurants, Axis and Indigo.

37 ST MARTINS LANE 45 ST MARTIN'S LANE
WC2N 4HX | 020 7300 5500
STMARTINSLANE.COM

Daring reinvention of the urban 'resort'. Smart, high-class and sophisticated. Eclectic mix of Philippe Starck-designed furniture and baroque-to-modern influences. Impressive, theatrical lobby. Fine dining at the Asia de Cuba restaurant and a hip nightlife scene at the Light Bar.

As consumer demand intensifies we shoppers are becoming more fickle. So how do retailers adapt? TIM GREENHALGH on the interactive future of retail

RETAIL EVOLUTION

There was a time when shopping was a rather simple affair. More often than not it was as much a chance to catch up on the local gossip as the need to stock the pantry. Your local community defined your retail experience and you only travelled into town when you needed to do a 'big shop' (usually for a special occasion) at the grand Victorian department store.

Today the definition of a big shop is far less tantalising – usually comprising a trip out of town to buy stuff for your stylish IKEA cupboards and American-style fridge-freezer. While you're at it, you might also pick up your prescriptions, get something to wear and find a book to read, all from the same one-stop shop. Your best chance of hearing a bit of gossip is picking up a copy of *Chat* magazine.

It seemed for a while that words like 'simple', 'special' and 'community' had all but disappeared from our retail vocabulary. To be replaced by 'scale', 'commodity' and 'roll-out'. Yes, there have been some spectacular retail concepts to emerge in recent times, from the first Nike Town to Selfridges, which has redefined the department store. Mr Jobs brought us his Apple stores – giant, gorgeous spaces filled with exciting, gorgeous products you're allowed to try in-store (known as 'playtail'). Interestingly, a chap in New York actually wrote an entire book on a laptop in the Apple store. Every day he took in a memory stick and was never asked to leave. Alas, I used to get shouted at for taking a sweet out of the Woolworths pick 'n' mix.

Things could be changing as the real and virtual worlds collide. The new generation of 'no-brow' (neither highbrow nor lowbrow) consumers are as happy buying a £1.99 T-shirt as they are treating themselves to a new Gucci watch. Buying off eBay is often a badge of honour these days ('I only bid £3.20 for this jacket – cool, innit!'), and paying considerably more at a farmers market is the new Saturday-morning institution. So

'The new generation of "no-brow" consumers are as happy buying a £1.99 T-shirt as they are treating themselves to a new Gucci watch'

we live in a world where discount sits alongside luxury, where the online world is as accessible as Tom's organic-sausage stall.

This convergence allows us to create a shopping atmosphere that both works for us and is increasingly defined by us. So where could this be going? Well, consumers expect shopping to become more interactive and customised. In Tokyo, more than 40,000 buildings are 'tagged' electronically, so mobile-phone users can pick up promotions simply by pointing in their direction. In New York 'kidchens', families can select ingredients, then cook a meal together guided by a professional chef.

Many hope that local retailers will come back in style. In the meantime, the Internet is the new community. Twangu is a term that describes mass-buying or 'net-haggling', whereby large groups sign up to buy a particular product, then approach the manufacturer directly to swing a bulk bargain.

Finally, there is 'freetail'. The Internet has taught us to expect a lot for nothing. There are already restaurants in London that operate on a 'pay what you think it's worth' system. And we will increasingly see 'try before you buy' stores, where you can experience products before reaching for your wallet.

Retailers and brands will look for new ways of keeping their offers exciting – even on a local level. Did you hear the story of a chap in North London who had a kitchen-appliance shop with the same name as a well-known Knightsbridge department store? After getting a call from an irate lawyer he changed the name to Sell Fridges.

Long live the entrepreneurial spirit. I'm looking forward to the sell_fridges.com interactive website, ringtone and iPhone app.

TIM GREENHALGH IS CHIEF CREATIVE OFFICER AT RETAIL DESIGN AGENCY FITCH. FITCH.COM

HANNAH MARTIN LONDON

REDEFINING LUXURY JEWELLERY

Fitzrovia & Bloomsbury

Design galleries & institutions
Design shops & C20th vintage
Design bookshops

Eat & Drink
Indulge
Sleep
(pp.094-095)

● ● ● *Take a walk route*

Fitzrovia & Bloomsbury

TAKE A WALK

Thorsten van Elten *

Walk down Warren Street and turn left into Fitzroy Square, the heart of Fitzrovia and London's only square designed by Neoclassical architect Robert Adam with fantastic views of the BT Tower through the trees. Turn right and take Conway Street back onto Warren Street. There is a beautiful, old blue-tiled dairy on the corner, which is now an Italian café. Keep walking until the end and turn left into Cleveland Street, then right into Carburton Street, which will take you into Great Portland Street. Turn left, and at No.109 is one of my all-time favourite shops in London: the Aquatic Design Centre, where they have amazing tanks of fish and very knowledgeable (although sometimes a bit grumpy) staff.

Bear left into Langham Street, which turns into Foley Street. On the corner with Cleveland Street is the King & Queen Pub, which has an open fire in the winter and is one of the nicest pubs in the area. Keep walking and turn right into Howland Street, then take the second right into Whitfield Street and the cute Pollock's Toy Museum and toyshop. Keep walking, crossing Goodge Street, until you see Colville Place on your right, a little stone-flagged pedestrian street with lovely 18th-century houses. This will lead you to the restaurants and galleries of Charlotte Street. Turn left. If it's a nice day, have a pint outside the Fitzroy Tavern. It's perfect for outdoor drinking, not so great inside.

Always worth checking out is the Contemporary Applied Arts gallery and shop in Percy Street. Then walk down to the end of Rathbone Place and turn left into Oxford Street and again into Hanway Street, an old lane cutting behind the major crossroads of Tottenham Court Road and Oxford Street. Once you get used to the smell, you'll find it's home to some cool second-hand record shops, flamenco bars and the fantastic Bradley's Spanish Bar, which is charmingly shabby and devoid of pretension.

Producer of design-led furniture and home accessories
thorstenvanelten.com

01 ARTEMIDE
- 106 GREAT RUSSELL STREET WC1B 3NB
- 020 7631 5200
- ARTEMIDE.COM
- TUE–FRI 10–1, 1.30–6, THU 11–7, SAT 10–5
- TOTTENHAM COURT ROAD

02 THE BUILDING CENTRE
- STORE STREET WC1E 7BT
- 020 7692 4000
- BUILDINGCENTRE.CO.UK
- MON–FRI 9.30–6, SAT 10–5
- GOODGE STREET

For decades the Artemide Group has been at the forefront of the international lighting world, producing contemporary lighting solutions and innovations for domestic and professional applications. Founded in Milan by Ernesto Gismondi, Artemide has grown to a considerable size and has developed an international distribution network and introduced own-brand showrooms to most of the world's key cities, including London.

Having moved from the company's impressive premises on Great Portland Street in 2006, the current showroom is now located in a small townhouse off the busy Tottenham Court Road. The space feels cramped, and, for a company that takes pride in its Italian manufacturing quality and innovation, I don't feel their London presence is significant enough to demonstrate the company's full potential.

After all, Artemide has commissioned many leading designers over the years and, along the way, has produced several design classics, such as the *Eclisse* table lamp by Vico Magistretti, the *Tizio* desk lamp by Richard Sapper and the *Tolomeo* series by Michele De Lucchi. More recent collaborations with star designers like Ross Lovegrove, Karim Rashid and Zaha Hadid have shown flair but verge on being over-the-top.

This showroom is primarily targeted at the trade, but the general public should not be deterred from visiting one of the world's finest leaders in lighting.

Established in 1931, the Building Centre is a permanent exhibition and source of information for the construction industry, covering all aspects of architecture and design, planning, home improvement and self-build. Open both to the public and construction professionals, this is kind of a permanent trade show where you can find some of the latest innovations in building materials and a showcase of today's architectural and engineering trends. The space really took off in 2005, with the building of a 1:1,500 scale model of central London, now on permanent display; it highlights all the city's recent and proposed planning submissions, including the Olympic Park.

Today the centre hosts many important events, building launches, models and architectural displays – as well as temporary exhibitions devoted to different aspects of London planning, like *Underground: London's Hidden Infrastructure*; *Digital Cities: London's Future*; and the architecture-meets-agriculture *London Yields* exhibition, to name a few. Its sphere of business also includes a specialist bookshop, small café, market research facilities and the Information Centre, which offers advice and consultation services for anyone wanting to undertake a housing project.

The centre remains fairly unknown to the general public. But as the city and its residents grow to consider local social, economic and ecological issues, it is likely to become a more popular reference point, and not only for design professionals. It is totally free and worth a visit.

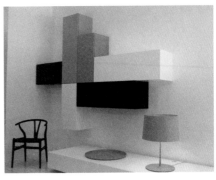

⓸ CONTEMPORARY APPLIED ARTS
- 📍 2 PERCY STREET W1T 1DD
- ✆ 020 7436 2344
- ↘ CAA.ORG.UK
- ⏱ MON–SAT 10–6
- ⊖ TOTTENHAM COURT ROAD

⓸ GEOFFREY DRAYTON
- 📍 85 HAMPSTEAD ROAD NW1 2PL
- ✆ 020 7387 5840
- ↘ GEOFFREYDRAYTON.COM
- ⏱ MON–SAT 10–6
- ⊖ WARREN STREET

The CAA is London's largest applied-arts gallery specialising in the exhibition and sale of, well, contemporary applied arts. It was founded after the Second World War as the Crafts Council of Great Britain with the objective to promote and champion British handicraft. Today the gallery represents more than 300 of its up-and-coming and established members, working across the disciplines of ceramics, glass, jewellery, metal, silver, textiles and wood.

The CAA has been at its current central location on Percy Street since 1995. The all-glass frontage gives passers-by a good view from the street into the airy split-level gallery. Welcomed at entry, visitors are invited to go downstairs to view uncluttered displays of some members' contemporary British craft, accompanied by a choice of topical books and magazines. The bright gallery on the raised ground level plays host to a changing programme of solo, mixed or themed exhibitions, often of external curation.

On sale is a range of handmade collectibles, some practical, some not so practical, ranging in price from affordable to moderate. Several of the CAA's big hitters are represented here. But my more functionalist tendencies steer me away from the more crafty, non-functional pieces. Instead, I'm apt to favour Gareth Neal's layered *Anne Table*, Michael Ruh's colourful glass vases, and David Clarke's distorted and playful vessels.

Geoffrey Drayton has been a mainstay of London design retailing for generations. He opened his first store in 1962 in Walthamstow and was one of the very first in the city to focus on Scandinavian furniture and lighting. He has since steadily grown his business to include a leading lineup of top European manufacturers.

The newly expanded store at the top end of Tottenham Court Road resides in a rather disjointed retail plaza. It is certainly worth a visit should you be considering some cutting-edge furniture and lighting in your home. The knowledgeable staff will tailor their suggestions to your particular needs, delving into their vast list of suppliers should you be looking for specifics. This list is comprehensive and includes leading brands such as Magis, Knoll, Vitra, Kartell, Ycami, B&B Italia and Zanotta, as well as lighting manufacturers Artemide, Flos, Luceplan, and Ingo Maurer. Classic and cutting-edge furniture produced by Cassina is prominent here, as Geoffrey Drayton is the oldest established retailer of their designs in Britain, stocking it for more than three decades.

There is a lot of choice to be had in the shop, and it can feel overcrowded at times. But don't be put off by this – it is all somehow part of the charm. Indeed, there are no pretensions here nor signs of designer showmanship. As obvious as it sounds, the emphasis remains much more focused on the quality of the product. Something to be thankful for.

06 HEAL'S

- 196 TOTTENHAM COURT ROAD W1T 7QL
- 020 7636 1666
- HEALS.CO.UK
- M-W 10-6, TH 10-8, FR 10-6.30, SA 9.30-6.30, SU 12-6
- GOODGE STREET

07 LIGNE ROSET WEST END

- 23-25 MORTIMER STREET W1T 3JE
- 020 7323 1248
- LIGNE-ROSET-WESTEND.CO.UK
- MON-SAT 10-6, THURS 10-8, SUN 12-5
- GOODGE STREET

This family-run bed-making business established by John Harris Heal recently celebrated its 200th birthday. Since its inception, Heal's has developed a distinctive reputation for innovation in domestic furnishings. The retailer operates out of an iconic, purpose-built showroom on Tottenham Court Road – one of London's largest and, to this day, considered a landmark in shop architecture.

The founder's original vision was a retailer that worked with the most skilled designers and craftsmen of the day to create furniture that is comfortable, beautiful and affordable. Thus, over the years Heal's has attracted influential 20th-century greats such as Mies van der Rohe, Marcel Breuer and Robin and Lucienne Day, to more recent collaborators like Tom Dixon, Matthew Hilton and Orla Kiely. Each year it also seeks out new and undiscovered talent – under the tag *Heal's Discovers* – helping emerging designers to make the transition from idea to reality. As a result, customers have the opportunity to invest in British design from talents like Russell Pinch, John Reeves and Alex Hellum.

Despite these occasional introductions, the sizable store doesn't seem to embody the energy for which the founder would have presumably strived – particularly in the rather conservative furniture department. That said, this is a reliable destination for useful gifts. And, should you tire, have a bite in the in-house Heal's restaurant.

The French interiors brand Ligne Roset has blossomed over the past five years and developed a new-found confidence in its own design direction. The family-run manufacturer seems to have made a strategic shift from 'modern' to 'contemporary' design and has commissioned a team of industry stars to reinforce that shift. Primarily, it manufactures quality furniture but, unlike many of its Italian counterparts, it also includes lighting and home accessories for a well-rounded offering.

The Ligne Roset catalogue is vast, which means that what you see in this two-storey showroom is a representative selection, the contents of which change regularly. Floor-to-ceiling glass windows give the wares – usually the new or notable collections – plenty of visibility from the street. Personally, I don't buy into all the designs here; I feel that some of them don't possess a real timelessness. That said, I make plenty of exceptions. My particular favourite is the strikingly angular *Facett* armchair and settee by the illustrious French brothers Erwan and Ronan Bouroullec.

Ligne Roset works almost exclusively with French designers, including Arik Levy, Inga Sempé, François Bauchet and the late Pierre Paulin, along with long-time collaborators Pascal Mourgue, Eric Jourdan, Peter Maly and Didiez Gomez (I particularly recommend his designs if you're looking for a comfortable sofa). The results are strong and this brand can be proud of its progression since its humble beginnings in 1860, when Antoine Roset founded the business producing walking sticks and umbrellas.

68 MINOTTI LONDON BY EUROPEAN DESIGN CENTRE
- 77 MARGARET STREET W1W 8SY
- 020 7323 3233
- EDCPLC.CO.UK
- MON–FRI 9-6, SAT 10-5, SUN 12-5
- OXFORD CIRCUS

09 MUJI
- UNIT 4/5, 6-17 TOTTENHAM COURT ROAD W1 9DP
- 020 7436 1779
- MUJI.CO.UK
- MON–SAT 10-8, SUN 12-6
- TOTTENHAM COURT ROAD

This is Minotti's first London showroom and a new kid on the block here in Fitzrovia. The store is run by its local partner of 15 years, the European Design Centre, in a historical building on Margaret Street, where this Italian thoroughbred has space to present its entire range of contemporary living, dining and bedroom furniture. The family-run brand has become well known for its modern sofas and armchairs, tables and coffee tables, beds, sideboards, bookcases and rugs, with the recent addition of textiles.

The showroom is divided into several sections by large mirrored walls, which take you on a path through the different living environments: daytime, dining, nighttime. From chic living-room armchairs and sofas to bedroom and dining solutions, you get to experience Minotti's signature 'classic meets modern' style in mono-brand, room-set scenarios. This typically slick presentation is what one has come to expect from so many high-end Italian furniture brands and would benefit from some more characterful interjections. That said, the quality of design and production is flawless and can be fully scrutinised in this no-nonsense environment.

Driving or walking past the shop, you will be impressed by the large front windows, raised to offer a better view of the products from the outside. Venture inside, where you can expect professional and efficient service from the European Design Centre team, which also represents a number of other European furniture and lighting brands.

This year Muji, the Minimalist Japanese super-retailer, celebrates three decades as a high-street staple. In 1991, the first European store was opened in London as a concession at the back of Liberty. Today there are 15 stores in the UK and nine in London alone. The company's line of sleek, no-nonsense, good-quality (though low-priced) products for the home now attracts a cultish international following.

The company doesn't officially credit the designers with whom it works, but Muji has commissioned some internationally established talents – Naoto Fukusawa, Sam Hecht and the Azumis, among others. With their truly Japanese aesthetic they have created some quiet classics: clean, minimal, functional objects that are likely to outlive shifting trends.

Occasionally Muji participates in design collaborations with other companies. The latest is a collection of chairs, dining tables and desks designed and manufactured in association with the classic German furniture-maker Thonet. The line is a sensitive reinterpretation of two of Thonet's iconic designs – the 150-year-old *No.14* bentwood chair has been reworked by James Irvine, and the tubular-steel furniture created by members of the Bauhaus group in the 1920s has been reinvigorated by Konstantin Grcic.

From household furniture, storage and kitchenware to accessories, stationery and clothing, Muji distinguishes itself with its minimal, practical designs, good value for money and its 'no brand' policy. It is ironic that, despite this original modesty, the company has now become a widely recognised brand.

10 RD FRANKS

5 WINSLEY STREET W1W 8HG

020 7636 1244

RDFRANKS.CO.UK

MON-FRI 9-6

OXFORD CIRCUS

11 RIBA

66 PORTLAND PLACE W1B 1AD

020 7580 5533

ARCHITECTURE.COM

MON-SAT 9-5, TUE 9-9

GREAT PORTLAND STREET

One of London's oldest specialist book stores, RD Franks has offered a diverse range of fashion books, magazines and trend-forecasting services since 1877. The store recently moved from its longtime location near Oxford Circus to a new space around the corner, set apart from the hustle and bustle of Oxford Street. The bookshop carries a comprehensive range of international fashion magazines and stocks books about fashion and textile design, fashion history, fashion photography, colour theory and pattern cutting. There is also a good number of fashion city guides and a section devoted to fashion figure templates, pattern blocks and dress stands.

Clearly fashion is the prime focus here, which is handy for students of the nearby London College of Fashion. But there is the added surprise of a thorough range of interior design books, titles on graphic design and stands weighted with glossy design and architecture magazines from around the world. Whether you are looking for the latest release from a specific publisher, or you are just passing by en route to the tube, RD Franks is a perfect escape from the madness of the West End.

The Royal Institute of British Architects (RIBA) is the UK's body for architecture, education and professional support. From its 1930s headquarters on this grand London boulevard, RIBA supports more than 40,500 members worldwide in the form of training, publishing, information services and events. The organisation promotes and champions excellence in the architectural profession and helps increase the benefits of good architecture on society. Should you be searching for the right architect, RIBA will help you find one.

To reinforce its mission, RIBA has teamed up with a variety of internationally respected arts institutions in recent years. In 2005, RIBA partnered with the V&A (p.021) to bring together the resources and expertise of each institution in a new programme of temporary exhibitions – at both locations and on tour. More recently, RIBA collaborated with the Barbican Art Gallery (p.102) on the presentation of *Le Corbusier – The Art of Architecture*, the first major Le Corbusier survey in London in more than 20 years.

Owned and operated by the institute, the RIBA bookshop is a key source for all the latest books, contracts and forms on architecture, design and construction. One of a family of six bookshops located across the UK, the flagship in these headquarters is a relaxed environment that is well equipped for servicing an ever increasing interest in architecture and design. To make your visit complete, you can enjoy an afternoon tea at the all-day café-bar designed by Azman Architects, or feast at the RIBA restaurant, with its tasty lunch menu.

12 WELLCOME COLLECTION

183 EUSTON ROAD NW1 2BE

020 7611 2222

WELLCOMECOLLECTION.ORG

TUE-SAT 10-6, THU 10-10, SUN 11-6

EUSTON STATION

The mission of the Wellcome Trust? To promote research to improve human and animal health. Thus is the legacy of its founder, pharmaceutical entrepreneur Sir Henry Solomon Wellcome. He had a passionate interest in medicine and its history, which led him to collect more than one million artefacts from around the world.

So, I hear you say, *why would it feature in a design guide?* Well, enter and you'll sense a refreshing shift away from the uber-consumption of nearby Tottenham Court Road towards a more pragmatic, potentially life-saving area of product design: healthcare. It is within the three galleries of the Wellcome Collection, a £30-million attraction in an imposing mansion on Euston Road, where one can view a thought-provoking range of works in this genre.

Bridging the worlds of art, science and history, subjects range from the bizarre to the beautiful, the ancient to the futuristic. One's attention is drawn towards the weird and wonderful design solutions that have been used over time to aid or repair our bodies and minds – from diagnostic dolls, Japanese sex aids and amputation saws to prosthetic limbs, forceps and DNA-sequencing robots. These objects at once expose mankind's primitive past while reminding us just how resourceful we can be. It is a wake-up call, reminding us where our priorities should remain, and where designers would be wise to focus their energies.

The Wellcome Collection hosts a schedule of temporary exhibitions and lectures and houses a library, conference centre, bookshop and branch of the chic Peyton & Byrne café.

● Eat & Drink

13 ARTESIAN THE LANGHAM, 1C PORTLAND PL W1B 1JA
020 7636 1000 | ARTESIAN-BAR.CO.UK

One of London's most glamorous hotel cocktail bars. Designed by David Collins Studio. Opulent decor summed up as Victoriana meets the Orient. Lilac marble-topped bar, timber chandeliers, glossy resin tables. Nice for breakfast, afternoon tea or evening cocktails.

14 BAM BOU 1 PERCY STREET W1T 1DB
020 7323 9130 | BAM-BOU.CO.UK

Elegant French-Vietnamese restaurant in a sprawling Georgian townhouse. Decor is a mix of Vietnamese simplicity and tarnished French opulence. Lacquered floors, plush antique furniture, gilt mirrors.

15 BOURNE & HOLLINGSWORTH
28 RATHBONE PLACE W1T 1JF | 020 7636 8228
BOURNEANDHOLLINGSWORTH.COM

Not so much a bar as a reproduction of your granny's sitting room, in a good way. Old fireplace, flowery wallpaper, postwar classics and fine bone china – in which your drink may be served, as per the Prohibition theme. Small, but a fairy-tale spot for a laidback night out.

16 BUSABA EATHAI 22 STORE STREET WC1E 7DF
020 7299 7900 | BUSABA.COM

Authentic modern Thai. Affordable. Chic wood panelling. Floor-to-ceiling windows. Communal tables, buzzy atmosphere. Try the squid side.

17 CHEZ GERARD 8 CHARLOTTE STREET W1T 2LS
020 7636 4975 | CHEZGERARD.COM

A French dining institution. Reminiscent of a classic 1930s Parisian brasserie. Gourmet Gallic menu. Trademark white tiles with royal-blue trimmings.Comfortable in the extreme – it lends itself naturally to West End pre-theatre dining. Ideal for a discreet working lunch.

18 ELENA'S L'ETOILE 30 CHARLOTTE STREET W1T 2NG
020 7636 7189 | ELENASLETOILE.CO.UK

Old-fashioned French resto, circa 1896. Authentic French bistro – white tablecloths, embossed wallpaper, red-velvet upholstery, silver drinks trolley. Charming old-world glamour.

19 FINO 33 CHARLOTTE STREET W1T 1RR
020 7813 8010 | FINORESTAURANT.COM

Authentic Spanish tapas served in a formal environment. Surprisingly bright and airy for a basement. Minimalist light-brown decor. You can also choose to eat at the bar. Big portions and good value for money.

20 HAKKASAN 8 HANWAY PLACE W1T 1HD
020 7927 7000 | HAKKASAN.COM

A high-class Oriental-fusion restaurant. Charcoal-grey walls, dark wood panelling, decadent red lighting, like something out of James Bond. Sexy, dramatic and, yes, expensive. But worth the experience.

21 LANTANA 13 CHARLOTTE PLACE W1T 1SN
020 7637 3347 | LANTANACAFE.CO.UK

A new independent café serving quality, no-nonsense food and proper coffee. Try their super-salads. The airy space is ideal for a quiet breakfast or lunch. Eat in or takeaway. Difficult to get a seat during lunchtime, so visit off-peak.

22 LA PERLA 11 CHARLOTTE STREET W1T 1RQ
020 7436 1744 | CAFEPACIFICO-LAPERLA.COM

Classic Mexican tapas bar and dining room. Lively, entertaining atmosphere. Modern Mexican murals, paintings and graphics. Atmospheric, friendly and relaxed. Great selection of Mexican beers and tequilas.

23 MEALS AT HEAL'S THE HEAL'S BUILDING,
196 TOTTENHAM COURT ROAD W1T 7LQ
020 7580 2522 | MEALS-RESTAURANT.CO.UK

A casual brasserie, the brainchild of chef/restaurateur Oliver Peyton. Decidedly childlike interior. Pale oak, white-painted chairs and pastel colours. A great place for a leisurely break from shopping. Freshly baked bread and all-day breakfast at weekends.

24 NEWMAN ARMS 23 RATHBONE STREET W1T 1NG
020 7636 1127 | NEWMANARMS.CO.UK

A friendly, old-fashioned little boozer with a pie room upstairs. George Orwell's local hangout. Set in a cosy, traditional Northern England dining room. The place is small, so it may be worth making a reservation.

25 OOZE RISOTTERIA 62 GOODGE STREET W1T 4NE
020 7436 9444 | OOZE.BIZ

Inspired by food of Northern Italy. Specialises in authentically produced risotto and other Italian classics. Best seasonal ingredients. Café-style ambience. Surprisingly low prices. Small shop at the front selling mainly Italian produce.

26 PIED À TERRE 34 CHARLOTTE STREET W1T 2NH
020 7636 1178 | PIED-A-TERRE.CO.UK

The finest contemporary French cuisine in the neighbourhood. Muted, intimate space with smooth curves, indulgent soft chairs and big mirrors. Formal and serious. A venue to explore accomplished, memorable cooking.

27 PHO 3 GREAT TITCHFIELD STREET W1W 8AX
020 7436 0111 | PHOCAFE.CO.UK

Great value, deliciously healthy and authentically prepared Vietnamese food. Menu consists of variations on a couple of simple, tasty standbys. Generous portions are sensibly priced. Clean, simple interiors. Small and informal – ultimately a minimalist affair. Remarkably fast and efficient service at any hour.

28 RIBA CAFÉ AND RESTAURANT 66 PORTLAND PLACE W1B 1AD | 020 7631 0467 | ARCHITECTURE.COM
Inventive Modern European menu on the first floor of this 1930s building. Grand open space with high ceilings and big windows. Modern, sophisticated atmosphere. In summer, enjoy lunch on the sunny terrace.

29 ROKA 37 CHARLOTTE STREET W1T 1RR 020 7580 6464 | ROKARESTAURANT.COM
Modern Japanese cuisine in a stylish, funky setting. Warm and elegant room constructed in smooth woods and dominated by a centrally located sushi bar and robata grill. An expensive but impressive place with a separate, stylish basement bar, Shochu Lounge.

30 SALT YARD 54 GOODGE STREET W1T 4NA 020 7637 0657 | SALTYARD.CO.UK
Charcuterie bar and restaurant. Modern tapas inspired by Spain and Italy. Complemented by cheese boards and a wide selection of wines and sherries. Vibrant, sophisticated with contemporary edge. Smart, yet relaxed. Book ahead, and try to secure an upstairs table.

31 SQUAT & GOBBLE 69 CHARLOTTE STREET W1T 4PJ 020 7580 5338 | SQUATANDGOBBLE.CO.UK
Wholesome continental food. A superb café / deli for breakfast and lunchtime. Diverse, cosmopolitan feel. Clean decor. Wholesome food served in large portions and at good prices. Polite, prompt service – even during the lunch-hour rush. All-year-round outdoor seating.

32 SIAM CENTRAL 14 CHARLOTTE STREET W1T 2LX 020 7436 7460
Thai tapas restaurant with take-away and an express lunch menu. Usual traditional favourites. Low-key, no-nonsense atmosphere. Simple, modern decor. Buzzy, welcoming and cosy. Perfect for a lunchtime meeting or leisurely evening meal. Tasty food, very well priced. Often packed.

33 TSUNAMI 93 CHARLOTTE STREET W1T 4PY 020 7637 0050 | TSUNAMIRESTAURANT.CO.UK
Traditional Japanese food at reasonable prices. Small but comfortable. Cool, contemporary interior. Sleek banquette seating. Delicate floral motifs on the walls. Ideal setting for laidback lunches and intimate pre-theatre dinners.

34 VANILLA 131 GREAT TITCHFIELD STREET W1W 5BB 020 3008 7763 | VANILLALONDON.CO.UK
Small, attractive bar. Discreet – you must ring a buzzer to be allowed in. Clean, understated glamour. An unusual mix of upmarket glam. And in this part of town, great value for money.

35 VILLANDRY 170 GREAT PORTLAND ST W1W 5QB 020 7631 3131 | VILLANDRY.COM
French restaurant, bar and foodstore.

A respected culinary institution celebrated for its gourmet heritage. A gem, bursting with excellent produce and eat-me foods. Gorgeous smells waft through the high-ceilinged spaces all day long. Buzzy, and ideal for a relaxing glass of wine and a snack.

● *Indulge*

36 CHIVERS 43-45 CHARLOTTE STREET W1T 1RS 020 7580 7595 | CHIVERSFLOWERS.CO.UK
A popular neighbourhood florist with a 40-year tradition.

37 PEYTON AND BYRNE AT HEAL'S 196 TOTTENHAM COURT ROAD W1T 7LQ 020 7580 3451 | PEYTONANDBYRNE.COM
Cakes and cupcakes of the British variety. Traditional, old-fashioned with a twist. Space designed by FAT.

38 VILLANDRY 170 GREAT PORTLAND ST W1W 5QB 020 7631 3131 | VILLANDRY.COM
Seasonal, artisanal products from independent and regional producers. Deli and rotisserie. Salad and sandwich bar for food to go.

● *Sleep*

39 CHARLOTTE STREET HOTEL 15-17 CHARLOTTE STREET W1T 1RJ | 020 7806 2000 CHARLOTTESTREETHOTEL.COM
Charmingly stylish destination for witty repartee. Bustling neighbourhood feel. Original period features fused with avant-garde contemporary style. The Oscar restaurant and bar is particularly great in summer when big windows open onto the street. Luxury accommodation for discerning visitors.

40 MYHOTEL BLOOMSBURY 11-13 BAYLEY STREET WC1B 3HD | 020 3004 6000 | MYHOTELS.COM
Designed with contemporary eclecticism in mind. Stylish and modern. Cutting-edge East-meets-West design by Conran & Partners. Relax at the 24/7 mybar and dine at the YO! Sushi hotel restaurant. Upmarket prices, high value on service and guest satisfaction.

41 SANDERSON 50 BERNERS STREET W1T 3NG 020 7300 1400 | SANDERSONLONDON.COM
A hotel experience with a difference. Elegant oasis in the heart of the city. Classic modern hotel that celebrates glamour, extravagance and style. Interiors by Phillippe Starck. Lavish, sleek and ultramodern. Slip onto a barstool and sip a wonderful cocktail at Starck's iconic Long Bar. Try the delicious British-Malaysian menu at the Suka restaurant or sit at the outdoor garden restaurant. A truly special treat.

Are home-grown furniture producers really spurring growth at home? Yes, says JOHN MILLER – British brands are the crucial link between the old-guard manufacturers and the Young Turk designers

BUY BRITISH?

The profile of British furniture manufacturers has risen recently. This may have much to do with the low value of the pound, which has made British products more competitive than they have been for years. Not to mention the credit-crunch tendency to buy local and the recent movement to promote sustainability. Still, a product is more appealing not only if it is well made, but if it has a good story behind it – a provenance that lends it greater emotional value. And British products have that.

Today, many 'old guard' design shops – The Conran Shop, Liberty and the General Trading Company, to name a few – deliver a 'buy British' message. Add to this the brash newcomers, all of whom have flaunted their Britishness to some extent: Modus, Established & Sons, naughtone, Decode and MARK (the last two even hype a specific location – London and Cornwall respectively). The Brits are highly noticeable in Milan and other overseas design fairs, where they tend to cluster together. And the design press obliges by publishing their own guides offering visitors an almost exclusively British experience abroad.

In a global economy, why is it important that home-grown firms succeed? Is there really any great benefit in buying local? In answering this, it is worth looking at how the industry works. All these new firms are based on the Italian model of networked production. They don't own their own factories, nor do they make everything under one roof. Instead, they rely on relationships with suppliers they call upon when they require a specific skill. This offers greater design freedom; 'keeping the factory busy' becomes irrelevant, so designers need not be constrained by in-house demands.

This approach means that, apart from a few pockets of excellence (Hitch Mylius's upholstery and Trannon's bent ash are good examples), we don't have a particular British inclination. Not like the Scandinavians, who are associated with bentwood, or the

'If we want to have a diverse and sustainable economy employing skilled people in a variety of trades, we need to have the British brands to support it'

Germans, who are recognised engineers. It also means that the sector relies on access to a range of specialist suppliers. In the UK, these are usually small, enthusiast-run firms that often cater to many different brands. The small number and small size of these suppliers means it's a fairly fragile network – and one reliant on design, particularly as the old model of mass-production all but disappears.

So, yes, if we want to have a diverse and sustainable economy employing skilled people in a variety of trades, we need to have the British brands to support it.

Along with skilled suppliers, there is a second crucial community that UK brands support: the designers themselves. While British designers work everywhere in the world, British manufacturers tend to hire local talent. UK companies like SCP, Allermuir and Hitch Mylius have been instrumental in spotting talent and developing the abilities of generations of designers – most of who go on to international success. Having been involved in this process many times, it is hard to see how any designer could polish his skills without direct access to a local manufacturer. The difference between a good design graduate and a good designer is the experience of working hands-on with people who make things.

It would not stretch the point too far to say that London's preeminence as a design capital is dependent on the existence of a design-facing UK manufacturing sector that is willing to innovate. In short, we need the Brit brands. But their ability to grow beyond the current 'buy British' boost will depend on how well the industry as a whole can develop excellent sustainable products and communicate their advantages to consumers.

JOHN MILLER IS DIRECTOR OF THE SCHOOL OF DESIGN AT UNIVERSITY COLLEGE FALMOUTH AND A DIRECTOR OF MARK. MARKPRODUCT.COM

Clerkenwell & Finsbury

ST JOHN'S GATE, ST JOHN'S SQUARE

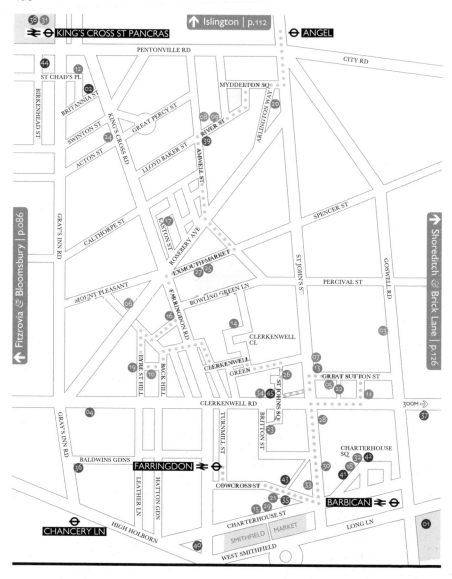

Islington | p.112

Fitzrovia & Bloomsbury | p.086

Shoreditch & Brick Lane | p.126

- Design galleries & institutions
- Design shops & C20th vintage
- Design bookshops

- Eat & Drink
- Indulge
- Sleep
  (pp.108-109)

••• Take a walk route

01 BARBICAN ART GALLERY
02 GAGOSIAN GALLERY
03 KNOLL
04 MAGMA
05 MODUS
06 MOROSO
07 PF GROUP
08 TIMOROUS BEASTIES
09 TWENTYTWENTYONE
10 VIADUCT
11 VITRA

Clerkenwell & Finsbury

TAKE A WALK
*Michael Sodeau**

Starting at Angel tube, wend your way past Myddelton Square to twentytwentyone's design showroom, where you'll find vintage and contemporary classics. At the end of River Street is the Unpackaged deli, which does what it says on the period shopfront – namely *not* package your purchases. A few doors up Amwell Street is Timorous Beasties, with its subversive fabrics and wallpapers. Amwell meets Rosebery Avenue at the old Art Nouveau-inspired Finsbury Town Hall (now a performing-arts school). From here you can spot Exmouth Market, which is peppered with restaurants and cafés, including Medcalf and the famous Moro. Market stalls that open at lunchtime produce a heady mix of exotic aromas; don't miss Moro's stall, with its shredded spiced lamb. Halfway down Exmouth Market you'll hear cries from Café Kick as another foosball goal is conceded.

Around the corner on Farringdon Road is London's original gastropub, the Eagle, offering tasty daily menus. A few doors up is Gazzano's premier Italian deli, making some of London's best handmade pasta and gnocchi, homemade pesto and delicious pork and fennel sausages. In the streets behind, discover furniture showroom Viaduct, with its sizable selection of contemporary designs. Avoiding Clerkenwell Road, head to Clerkenwell Green and catch a glimpse of the 1792 St. James's Church from the Three Kings pub on Clerkenwell Close. If you're hungry, check out the Modern Pantry or The Zetter hotel. Straight over Clerkenwell Road you'll see St John's Gate – one of the few tangible remains from Clerkenwell's monastic past.

Walk along Albemarle Way to St John Street. To your left is the new Poltrona Frau furniture showroom; straight ahead is Great Sutton Street and the new shop from British furniture manufacturer Modus. Turn right into Berry Street to join Clerkenwell Road, where you'll find the Vitra showroom for design classics and Bulthaup for striking kitchens. Nestled next to the Wyvern artisan bookbinders is the small and ever-so-yellow Watch Service Centre for watch fanatics. But if it's fine bread you want, you have to hit St John restaurant. While you're there, pick up a tub of Trotter Gear, or pull up a chair with a bowl of warm chestnuts and a nice glass of wine.

Designer and founder of Michael Sodeau Partnership
michaelsodeau.com

01 BARBICAN ART GALLERY

- SILK STREET EC2Y 8DS
- 020 7638 4141
- BARBICAN.ORG.UK
- MON, FRI, SAT, SUN 11-8, TUE-WED 11-6, THU 11-10
- BARBICAN/MOORGATE

02 GAGOSIAN GALLERY

- 6-24 BRITANNIA STREET WC1X 9JD
- 020 7841 9960
- GAGOSIAN.COM
- TUE-SAT 10-6
- KING'S CROSS ST PANCRAS

Since its launch in 1982, the Barbican Art Gallery has staged major shows by leading international figures – more recently the world-renowned architect Le Corbusier, controversial Dutch fashion designers Victor & Rolf and Turner Prize-winners Jeremy Deller and Grayson Perry.

The main gallery shows a variety of design, architecture, fine art, fashion and photography, while a smaller horseshoe-shaped gallery, the Curve, houses experimental works better suited to its distinctive architecture. The surrounding Barbican Centre is one of the largest multi-arts centres in Europe, with two theatres, three cinemas, a concert hall and exhibition halls, as well as a public library, conference suites and three restaurants.

Erected in an area that was badly bombed during the First World War, the centre was designed by Modernist trio Chamberlin, Powell and Bon in the Brutalist style that has always sparked controversy and divided opinion. Recently the centre underwent a significant refurbishment by architects Allford Hall Monaghan Morris, which reinforced the essential qualities of the original building, improved circulation and added some interesting features – like an internal bridge and a new grand route with main entrances at each end.

Once voted 'London ugliest building', the Barbican Centre is now considered an architectural icon that attracts world-class performances and visual art in the heart of the City of London.

One of many galleries owned by art mogul Larry Gagosian, this Britannia Street location is London's largest; his other, smaller space is in Mayfair (p.055). Located in a converted police garage near King's Cross station – rather unfamiliar territory on the usual gallery circuit – the Gagosian has been a healthy addition to London's art scene and a welcome asset for the regenerating area.

Come off the quiet street, past the burly security guards, and the contemporary grandeur of the gallery is immediately apparent. Under the watchful eye of Caruso St John Architects, the rooms have been transformed into an impressive vision of light and space. The gallery boasts large, minimal, bright spaces – one main gallery and two adjoining smaller exhibition rooms – ideal for exhibiting large-scale and often very heavy works and installations, like monumental sculptures by Richard Serra, Rachel Whiteread, Hiroshi Sugimoto, and some of Jeff Koons's signature creations.

Because of its location near a busy commuter thoroughfare, the gallery is generally quieter than some of its West End counterparts. Arrive off-peak and you may have the place to yourself, so you can fully appreciate the clean spaces and absorb the artworks at your leisure. This is a stellar venue and worth a visit for anyone interested in the contemporary art form.

03 KNOLL
🏷 91 GOSWELL ROAD EC1V 7EX
📞 020 7236 6655
↖ KNOLL-INT.COM
🕐 MON-FRI 9-5.30
⊖ BARBICAN

04 MAGMA
🏷 117-119 CLERKENWELL ROAD EC1R 5BY
📞 020 7242 9503
↖ MAGMABOOKS.COM
🕐 MON-SAT 10-7
⊖ FARRINGDON

Knoll is a leading legacy of the Modernist furniture movement in America. The company was founded before the Second World War by Hans Knoll, who had the simple vision that modern architects would need modern furniture to make their buildings livable. During the war he met Florence Schust, who later became his partner in life and business and played an instrumental role in the company's development. Florence followed the Bauhaus school of thought and sought to combine design excellence with material honesty, technological innovation and mass production. Together the couple made it their mission to nurture and champion the most talented designers of their time. Knoll quickly defined the look and feel of modern interiors in the mid 20th century.

Today the brand's global reach extends to this voluminous Clerkenwell showroom, designed by Lissoni Associates to showcase one of the largest Knoll collections in Europe. While office systems represent a huge portion of their turnover, it is the KnollStudio collection that induces the most excitement. My particular favourites include the Mies van der Rohe *Barcelona Chair*; the *Tulip chair* and table by Eero Saarinen; the *Diamond Chair* by Harry Bertoia; and the *Platner* tables and chairs by Warren Platner. Also on display are new collections from Ross Lovegrove and Cini Boeri.

Knoll was just adding the final touches to this showroom at the time of going to press. But there was every indication it would adhere to the principles of its founding couple.

Magma is a reference point for all design types, principally stocking a choice selection of the latest books on design, architecture, art, photography, fashion and style. This time on a busy Clerkenwell street, the slightly larger yet younger sibling of the Covent Garden original (p.077) is more than just a bookshop. It is a kind of starting point for small design-related items – from stationery and cards to home accessories, games and toys. Along with a handful of cultish-cool objects, the store stocks items for its design-hungry clientele.

The owners seem to understand that most customers don't come into Magma with a particular purchase in mind but rather pop in to browse through the latest titles relating to their craft. The clever space management succeeds at cramming a lot in without mess and the displays entice you to pick up a publication and explore. This is a great place to buy a coffee-table book, a niche magazine or a small, cheerful present. You can easily spend an hour simply discovering, and if you need help, the staff can steer you towards suitable publications.

05 MODUS

- 28-29 GREAT SUTTON STREET EC1V ODS
- 01460 258 590
- MODUSFURNITURE.CO.UK
- MON-FRI 10-6
- FARRINGDON

06 MOROSO

- 7-15 ROSEBERY AVENUE, EC1R 4SP
- 020 3328 3560
- MOROSO.CO.UK
- MON-FRI 9-5
- FARRINGDON

There aren't many good-quality, contemporary furniture brands in the UK, but of those that exist, Modus is one. Founded in 2000 by Jon Powell and Ed Richardson, Modus has steadily established itself with a product range geared towards the contract market. In many cases, though, it is suitable for domestic interiors.

From the start Modus chose its partners shrewdly, collaborating with leading designers on commercially viable collections of tables, chairs, sofas, stools, benches and storage. The emphasis here is on British talent, young and acclaimed: think Simon Pengelly, Michael Sodeau, Sam Johnson, Ed Carpenter, Morph, Jonathan Prestwich, Paolo Notaro, Michael Marriott and PearsonLloyd. Recently the list has grown to include international names like Stephen Burks, Christophe Pillet, Claesson Koivisto Rune, Patrick Norguet and Monica Förster.

As for the designs, expect clean-lined, functional pieces that are unlikely to date. The *Float* sofa by Michael Sodeau sits elegantly on slender metal legs; a polyester knit cover stretches over a graphic steel frame in Jonathan Prestwich's *OS* chair; simple standalone *Parallel* shelving by Stephen Burks commands the same light and understated visual language as Paolo Notaro's *Trim* table range.

The new Modus showroom was on the cusp of opening as we went to press. But as it is designed under the watchful eye of Michael Sodeau Partnership, I expect this to be a welcome addition to Clerkenwell's design scene.

Moroso is a family-run Italian furniture manufacturer of genuine verve that is unrivalled by most other high-end furniture brands. Under the creative direction of the energetic visionary Patrizia Moroso, the company boasts a tremendous diversity across its collections. Designers are given the space for expression and the freedom to challenge forms, materials, structures and techniques without prescribed outcomes. Influences are global; designers include Ron Arad, Tord Boontje, Stefan Diez, Konstantin Grcic, Alfredo Häberli, Doshi Levien, Marcel Wanders, Stephen Burks, Tokujin Yoshioka and Patricia Urquiola.

Moroso's presence in London grew significantly in September 2009 with the opening of an immense Urquiola-designed showroom, shared with lighting brand Flos. Vibrant window displays dazzle at floor level, but it is only on entry that one gets a glimpse into the mammoth high-ceilinged basement space. Venture down and the room opens to reveal a vast layout of contract and domestic furniture.

Throughout the showroom, Moroso designs are given the space to breathe, and pieces don't battle for your attention. Staff are well versed in the products and happy to provide background and history for each. This goes some way to explaining why the design community considers Moroso to be one of the most trailblazing Italian furniture producers.

 PF GROUP
- 150 ST JOHN STREET EC1V 4UD
- 020 7600 0600
- POLTRONAFRAU.IT
- MON-FRI 9-5
- FARRINGDON

68 TIMOROUS BEASTIES
- 46 AMWELL STREET EC1R 1XS
- 020 7833 5010
- TIMOROUSBEASTIES.COM
- MON-THU 10-6, FRI 10-5, SAT 11-4
- ANGEL

The latest addition to the lively Clerkenwell design landscape is this 650-square-metre showroom dedicated to the furniture brands of the Poltrona Frau Group. Don't be put off by the corporate name – this Italian holding company controls some of Europe's leading contemporary furniture brands: Cappellini, Cassina, Alias, Gebrüder Thonet Vienna, Gufram, Nemo and, of course, Poltrona Frau itself.

The showroom occupies two floors of an ex-industrial, Grade II-listed building. Retaining the character of the original industrial shell, the immense space was transformed by Universal Design Studio to provide a calming backdrop against which the furniture can be viewed. At the time of going to press, the layout was going through a final finessing before the launch, with each brand allocated a well defined home on the ground floor.

Highlights include my favourite lounge chair, *Low Pad* by Jasper Morrison for Cappellini; the retro-modern *Kennedee* sofa by Jean-Marie Massaud for Poltrona Frau; the classic Le Corbusier designs from Cassina's *I Maestri* collection; as well as the angular *Stabiles* oval-topped table by Alfredo Häberli for Alias.

Dropped through the middle of the ground floor is a monumental staircase in matt-black steel with chunky oak-slab stair treads. This feature draws your attention to the basement level, where meetings are held along with more furniture displays and information about the group's contract projects.

Noted for its surreal and provocative textiles and wallpapers, the design studio Timorous Beasties was founded in Glasgow in 1990 by Alistair McAuley and Paul Simmons, shortly after they studied together at the Glasgow School of Art. By depicting uncompromisingly contemporary images on heritage fabrics and wallpapers, Timorous Beasties defined its very own design style: Victorian grandeur subverted with modern undertones and humour.

Following the company's initial success and widespread recognition, the pair opened their London showroom in 2007 to complement their Glasgow space. What may outwardly appear to be an unprepossessing fabric shop among other independent traders on Amwell Street is really a wild boutique carrying the duo's entire collection of wallpapers and hand-printed fabrics.

The pristine interior provides a calming backdrop to the otherwise sumptuously colourful and playfully patterned large-scale designs. Upstairs, the fabrics – including the critical favourites *London Toile* and *Devil Damask Lace* – hang like banners from the ceiling and offer a sense of scale to the designs. In the tiny basement, the wallpapers are similarly hung in a space used for meetings with clients.

The store is small and homely – indeed, you even have to pass through a kitchen on your way to the wallpaper room. With only one shop assistant who is helpful and knowledgeable, this is a charming space to pop into if you are refurbishing your home or looking for an accent addition to your existing interior.

09 TWENTYTWENTYONE SHOWROOM

- 18C RIVER STREET EC1R 1XN
- 020 7837 1900
- TWENTYTWENTYONE.COM
- MON-SAT 9.30-5.30
- ANGEL

10 VIADUCT

- 1-10 SUMMERS STREET EC1R 5BD
- 020 7278 8456
- VIADUCT.CO.UK
- MON-FRI 9.30-6; SAT 10.30-4
- FARRINGDON

The big sister to twentytwentyone's Upper Street shop (p.119), this showroom hidden in a former warehouse on a residential street plays host to a well-edited selection of vintage and contemporary furniture and lighting from design-world leaders. The company was set up in 1993 by Simon Alderson and Tony Cunningham, who started out selling 20th-century originals before expanding to include contemporary design. In this tranquil space, you can browse among iconic 20th-century classics from the likes of Le Corbusier, Panton, Eames, Wegner and Kjaerholm, alongside the classics of tomorrow from Morrison, Arad, Barber Osgerby, Dixon, Urquiola, Newson and a raft of others.

Any sterility from slick newness is thankfully softened with the accompaniment of original vintage pieces, which successfully illustrates the importance of combining old with new in our homes. Bizarrely, this is unusual practice as most design stores opt for one or the other. I would imagine this confident approach has helped twentytwentyone gain its reputation as one of London's best design shops.

The company acts as a UK agent for various manufacturers and also produces its own collection of furniture and accessories, so what you see here is just a taste of what you can get. Ask for assistance and the attractive staff will present a number of options to help you pinpoint the sort of design for which you are searching.

Viaduct has been trading in contemporary furniture and lighting for 20 years and – with founder James Mair firmly at the helm – has found a comfortable niche within the London design establishment. Located in a 1930s converted printhouse on a Clerkenwell side street, this double-height showroom is home to a fine selection of modern and cutting-edge designs, suitable for the domestic and contract markets. Helping to distinguish Viaduct from the competition is the remarkably dedicated and informative team, who will tap into the company's extensive product database to help guide you through your options.

Viaduct operates as the UK agent for Driade, E15, Maarten Van Severen, Montis, Pastoe and xO, but also supplies dozens of other leading brands, such as Cappellini, moooi, Vitra, Established & Sons and Flos. You'll find the best of the new collections arranged in tidy room displays that invite you to touch, sit and feel as you meander through the long space. A row of chairs runs along the length of one window, representing a cross-section of some of the finest contemporary choices by reputed designers; they're joined by further examples on the mezzanine level that overlooks the main floor.

 VITRA

30 CLERKENWELL ROAD EC1M 5PQ
020 7608 6200
VITRA.COM
MON-THU 9-5.30, FRI 9-5
FARRINGDON

Pioneering German manufacturer Vitra has
been at the cutting edge of commercial furniture
development since its inception in 1950 and
is responsible for introducing many of the
pieces we now consider to be classics – from
Jean Prouvé's *Standard* chair (1934) and Charles
& Ray Eames' *Lounge Chair & Ottoman* (1956)
to George Nelson's *Coconut Chair* (1955) and
Verner Panton's *Panton Chair Classic* (1959). Such
innovations continue with the Home Collection,
including contributions from talents of today,
such as Ron Arad, Jasper Morrison and Hella
Jongerius. A noteworthy recent addition is the
nature-mimicking *Vegetal* chair, itself a production
challenge that was four years in development by
its designers, Erwan and Ronan Bouroullec.

A global network of showrooms help
showcase the Vitra Home Collection and
office systems. The smart David Chipperfield-
designed space in Clerkenwell operates as a
trade showroom, although members of the
public are welcome. Don't be intimidated by the
receptionist – visits from Vitra enthusiasts are
commonplace. After all, where better to view the
full range than at the heart of the UK division?
The only slight nuisance is that, should you
wish to buy anything from this branch of Vitra,
someone will direct you to one of their retail
dealers to place the order.

Eat & Drink

12 6 ST CHADS PLACE 6 ST CHADS PLACE WC1X 9HH
020 7278 3355 | 6STCHADSPLACE.COM
Laid-back urban cool meets the Victorian
warehouse. Retro tables and 50s leather sofas.
Light and airy, great during the day.

13 CICADA 132-136 ST JOHN STREET EC1V 4JT
020 7608 1550 | RICKERRESTAURANTS.COM
A trendy bar-restaurant. The first of the Ricker
restaurants. Strong design. Fun, with inexpensive
Pan-Asian cuisine.

14 THE CLERKENWELL KITCHEN
27-31 CLERKENWELL CLOSE EC1R OAT
020 7101 9959 | THECLERKENWELLKITCHEN.CO.UK
Canteen-style daytime café. Ethical, sustainable
eatery. Fresh ingredients from local producers.

15 COMPTOIR GASCON 63 CHARTERHOUSE STREET
EC1M 6HJ | 020 7608 0851
COMPTOIRGASCON.COM
Gourmet bistro/delicatessen from South West
France. Rustic food. Relaxed with wooden floors
and chic purple chairs. Great for business
lunches or an informal dinner.

16 THE EAGLE 159 FARRINGDON ROAD EC1R 3AL
020 7837 1353
Gastro food in a funky pub environment. Great
energy, open kitchen with North African
influences. Good prices and busy.

17 THE EASTON 22 EASTON STREET WC1X ODS
020 7278 7608 | THEEASTONPUB.CO.UK
A friendly local boozer crammed with
drinking regulars. Intricately etched windows,
smoke-stained wallpaper. Young trendy crowd.
Good food and small but delicious cellar.
Moderately priced.

18 FOX & ANCHOR 115 CHARTERHOUSE ST EC1M 6AA
020 7250 1300 | FOXANDANCHOR.COM
A traditional British pub renovated to its
late-Victorian glory. Simple food done well.
Local, seasonal ingredients. Open from 7AM
for breakfast.

19 THE GUNMAKERS 13 EYRE STREET HILL EC1R 5ET
020 7278 1022 | THEGUNMAKERS.CO.UK
Petite, old unassuming pub on a Clerkenwell
back street. Popular with a local crowd. Can get
very busy and spill onto the pavement. Best for a
drink but food is also quite good if you can find
space to sit.

20 THE HARLEQUIN 27 ARLINGTON WAY EC1R 1UY
07975 652 669 | HARLEQUINPUB.CO.UK
A friendly family pub just behind the Sadlers
Wells theatre. Popular for drink before or after
a performance. Intimate – especially cosy in
winter. Traditional look. Musicians and actors
sometimes pop in.

21 HIX OYSTER & CHOP HOUSE
36-37 GREENHILL RENTS, COWCROSS ST EC1M 6BN
020 7017 1930 | HIXOYSTERANDCHOPHOUSE.CO.UK
Traditional dishes within an old London
sausage factory. The very best of the season's
oysters and a variety of tender meat cuts any
time of day.

22 J&A CAFÉ 4 SUTTON LANE, LONDON EC1M 5PU
020 7490 2992
Modern British cafeteria hidden in the midst
of the East London yards. Friendly, local and
unpretentious. Old-fashioned, rustic feel. Brick
walls, slated ceiling.

23 JERUSALEM TAVERN 55 BRITTON STREET EC1M 5UQ
020 7490 4281 | STPETERSBREWERY.CO.UK
Historic, traditional. London's representative of
East Anglia's St Peter's Brewery. Very small but
full of character. Be prepared to stand outside.

24 KONSTAM AT THE PRINCE ALBERT 2 ACTON STREET
WC1X 9NA | 020 7833 5040 | KONSTAM.CO.UK
Welcoming mix of former Victorian pub and
modern decor. Light, airy open-plan space.
Seasonal food sourced from within the M25
but pricey menu.

25 MEDCALF 40 EXMOUTH MARKET EC1R 4QE
020 7833 3533 | MEDCALFBAR.CO.UK
Situated in a converted turn-of-the-century
butcher shop. Simple and inspired cooking with a
distinctly British theme. Fashionable, scruffy-chic
crowd without an attitude.

26 THE MODERN PANTRY 47-48 ST JOHN'S SQ EC1V 4JJ
020 7553 9210 | THEMODERNPANTRY.CO.UK
Venture from chef/proprietor Anna Hansen.
French bistro cooking with a touch of the
Antipodean and exotica. Designed by London-
based Jump studios. Chairs by Horm. Look out
for lighting by Piet Hein Eek. Enjoyable, relaxed,
informal. The downstairs room great for lunch.

27 MORO 34-36 EXMOUTH MARKET EC1R 4QE
020 7833 8336 | MORO.CO.UK
Great quality Spanish and North African cuisine.
Superb reputation, so always busy. If you can't
get a table, sit at the bar and sample tapas and
sherry. Quite expensive but generous portions.

28 PORTAL 88 ST JOHN STREET EC1M 4EH
020 7253 6950 | PORTALRESTAURANT.COM
Modern Portuguese restaurant. Traditional
yet experimental. Bold interiors with inside-
outside-feel glasshouse design. Bustling open-
plan kitchen. Bar area at the front. Intimate
and stylish meeting point.

29 SMITH'S OF SMITHFIELD
66-77 CHARTERHOUSE STREET EC1M 6HJ
020 7251 7950 | SMITHSOFSMITHFIELD.CO.UK
An always bustling warehouse conversion. Four
floors of modern British food culture. Three

restaurants, a café and a bar. Good food, design and atmosphere – a winning combination.

30 ST JOHN 26 ST JOHN STREET EC1M 4AY
    020 7251 0848 | STJOHNRESTAURANT.COM
Wooden floors, whitewashed walls and high ceilings. Daily-changing menu. Comfortable atmosphere, comforting food. Great for meat from the local market.

31 ST PANCRAS GRAND ST PANCRAS INTERNATIONAL
    NW1 9QP | 020 7870 9900
    SEARCYS.CO.UK/STPANCRASGRAND
Restaurant and oyster bar adjacent to Europe's longest Champagne bar. Sits alongside the Eurostar platform. Upmarket prices and grand decor to match.

32 TART 117 CHARTERHOUSE STREET EC1M 6AA
    020 7253 3003 | TARTBAR.CO.UK
A beautiful old vestry transformed into a stylish restaurant and bar. Good for cocktails or a glass of wine without paying a fortune.

33 VINOTECA 7 ST JOHN STREET EC1M 4AA
    020 7253 8786 | VINOTECA.CO.UK
One of London's most reputable wine bars. Wine shop attached. Seasonal British and European menu. Frequently busy, especially at lunchtime. Sophisticated crowd. Fun wine-tasting.

34 THE ZETTER 86-88 CLERKENWELL RD, ST JOHN'S SQ
    EC1M 5RJ | 020 7324 4455 | THEZETTER.COM
Spacious and light-filled, with floor-to-ceiling windows that overlook the cobblestones of St John's Square. Comfortable retro furnishings. Modern take on classic Mediterranean cuisine.

● Indulge

35 FARM COLLECTIVE 91 COWCROSS STREET EC1M 6BH
    020 7253 2142 | FARMCOLLECTIVE.COM
Fresh, tasty grub not only for the area's hungry drones. Sourcing ingredients from small neighbouring farms (thus the name). Simple and honest, with fresh-faced, friendly staff.

36 KONDITOR & COOK 46 GRAYS INN RD WC1X 8LR
    020 7404 6300 | KONDITORANDCOOK.COM
London's purveyors of luxury cakes and savouries. Has teamed up with five British design talents to bring out a limited-edition range of their signature mini-cakes.

37 MCQUEENS 70-72 OLD STREET EC1V 9AN
    020 7251 5505 | MCQUEENS.CO.UK
Contemporary florist. Also offers creative flower-arranging courses.

38 PEYTON & BYRNE @ ST PANCRAS
    ST PANCRAS INTERNATIONAL NW1 2QP
    020 7278 6707 | PEYTONANDBYRNE.COM
Unabashedly British bakery with a few well-designed pastel shops. Treasure trove of cupcakes, jammy dodgers and gingerbread men and delectable homemade tarts in the Arcade of St Pancras Station.

39 UNPACKAGED SHOP 42 AMWELL STREET EC1R 1XT
    020 7713 8368 | BEUNPACKAGED.COM
A corner shop with a difference – no packaging of any sort on offer. Encourages customers to bring their own containers and fill them up with whatever they need. Sells eco-friendly, Fairtrade and organic products.

40 VIVAT BACCHUS 47 FARRINGDON STREET EC4A 4LL
    020 7353 2648 | VIVATBACCHUS.CO.UK
Wine bar/deli. Walk-in wine cellar and cheese room. South African food specialist. Ideal for a glass of wine and cheese tasting.

● Sleep

41 FOX & ANCHOR 115 CHARTERHOUSE SQ EC1M 6AA
    0845 347 0100 | FOXANDANCHOR.COM
Great British pub that's part of a small chain hotel. Six luxury rooms. Striking facade with terracotta tiling, Art Nouveau flourishes and jutting gargoyles. Dark, handsome Edwardian interior. Cosy, lavish and traditional. Excellent value for money.

42 MALMAISON 18-21 CHARTERHOUSE SQ EC1M 6AH
    020 7012 3700 | MALMAISON-LONDON.COM
Luxury boutique hotel. Lavish example of modern chic. Elegant, classic. On the expensive side but perfect for a stylish city break or business trip. Fine dining.

43 THE ROOKERY PETER'S LANE, COWCROSS STREET
    EC1M 6DS | 020 7336 0931 | ROOKERYHOTEL.CO.UK
All period mid-18th-century charm. Polished wood panelling, stone-flagged floors, rich fabrics and genuine antique furniture. All 33 rooms named after locals of the time. Warm, homely atmosphere. Creative, fun, indulgent crowd.

44 ROUGH LUXE HOTEL 1 BIRKENHEAD ST WC1H 8BA
    020 7837 5338 | ROUGHLUXE.CO.UK
Antithesis of the typical five-star hotel. Expensive designer touches in a totally shabby but grand interior. Straightforward, eclectic. A little bit of luxury in a rough part of London. Small, with shared bathrooms, but reintroducing guests to the personal experience of a night away. Good value for money.

45 THE ZETTER 86-88 CLERKENWELL RD, ST JOHN'S SQ
    EC1M 5RJ | 020 7324 4444 | THEZETTER.COM
Former Victorian warehouse transformed into an example of cutting-edge design. Clever, ironic contrasts of modern styles. Original and affordable. Modest, well-thought-out gateway for the design-orientated traveller.

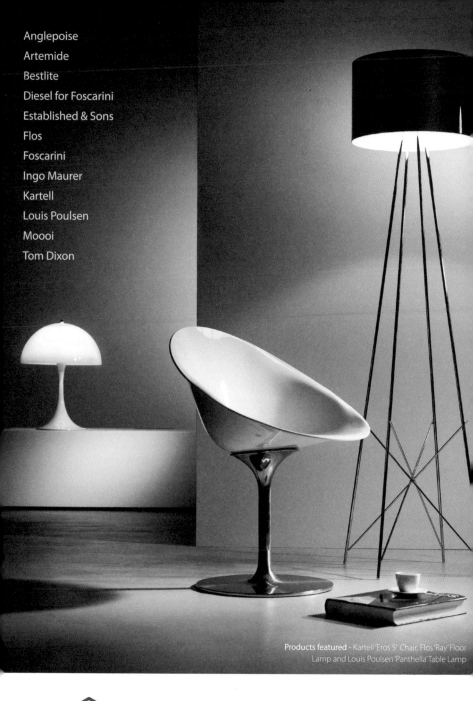

Anglepoise
Artemide
Bestlite
Diesel for Foscarini
Established & Sons
Flos
Foscarini
Ingo Maurer
Kartell
Louis Poulsen
Moooi
Tom Dixon

Products featured - Kartell 'Eros S' Chair, Flos 'Ray' Floor
Lamp and Louis Poulsen 'Panthella' Table Lamp

ICÔNE
DESIGN FOR LIVING

Telephone. +44 (0)1332 866 430
Email. sales@icone.co.uk

www.icone.co.uk

Islington

GIBSON SQUARE

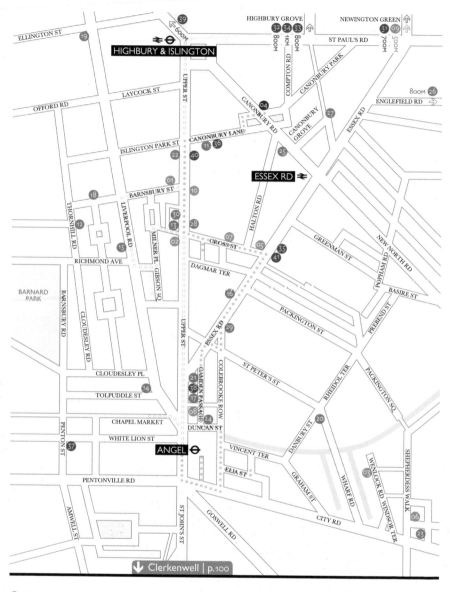

↓ Clerkenwell | p.100

● Design galleries & institutions
● Design shops & C20th vintage

● Eat & Drink
● Indulge
● Sleep
(pp.120-121)

••• Take a walk route

01 ARIA
02 ATELIER ABIGAIL AHERN
03 ESTABLISHED & SONS
04 **ESTORICK COLLECTION**
05 FANDANGO
06 KVADRAT
07 LIVING SPACE
08 ORIGIN MODERNISM
09 THE PEANUT VENDOR
10 TWENTYTWENTYONE

Islington

TAKE A WALK

*Lynda
Relph-Knight* *

As you leave Angel tube station, turn left towards Clerkenwell, then left into City Road and Torrens Street for the Candid Arts Trust and a Gothic experience, an ace hidden café or an art show. Heading on down City Road, turn left into Colebrooke Row then right into Elia Street for the Charles Lamb pub on the corner of Quick Street – good wine list, homemade food and board games. Walk back up Elia Street to Duncan Street and Camden Passage to your right – a walkway flanked by vintage treasures and new fashions. Cross St Peters Street into Colebrooke Row for the Pentagram-designed Cass Art Warehouse.

Turn right into Essex Road, with cafés, bars and Handmade & Found, a frock shop just past Cross Street that was given a makeover by Mary Portas on *Mary Queen of Shops*. Head up Cross Street, with Tallulah lingerie shop, Loop knitting shop and other delights. Detour into Dagmar Passage past the Little Angel Theatre. Continue up Cross Street and turn right into Upper Street for furniture at Coexistence and food at Ottolenghi; at twentytwentyone you'll find more contemporary furniture and accessories. Drop into The Sampler wine shop, just past the town hall, for a tasting, then on to Canonbury Lane and the joys of Canonbury Square, including the Estorick Collection, which features Italian Futurist art and tea and cakes in a delightful garden.

Go back to Upper Street and continue on to Highbury & Islington station, or cross over and turn left past Gill Wing's jewellery, kitchen and giftware boutiques. Turn right into Barnsbury Road for Aria on the right and a sewing class at Make Lounge on the left. Go left into Liverpool Road for Gibson Square, with its Quinlan Terry-designed ventilator shaft. Turn down Milner Passage into Milner Square and an alley set into the terrace to the right that leads to the Almeida Theatre and Terence Conran's Almeida restaurant. Turn right along Upper Street towards the Screen on the Green Cinema, via the wonderful After Noah emporium of toys and trinkets and the historic King's Head Theatre & Pub. Pass the Business Design Centre and cross Upper Street to the Angel tube station, with Chapel Market, a classic London street market, off to your right.

Editor of Design Week
designweek.co.uk

01 ARIA

- BARNSBURY HALL, BARNSBURY STREET N1 1PN
- 020 7704 6222
- ARIASHOP.CO.UK
- MON–SAT 10–6.30, SUN 1–6
- HIGHBURY & ISLINGTON

02 ATELIER ABIGAIL AHERN

- 137 UPPER STREET N1 1QP
- 020 7354 8181
- ATELIERABIGAILAHERN.COM
- MON–SAT 10.30–6, SUN 12.30–4.30
- ANGEL/HIGHBURY & ISLINGTON

Over the years Aria has earned a reputation in Islington for its comprehensive range of contemporary homewares. Located just off busy Upper Street, the two-storey shop benefits from sheer volume in the height of its roof structure; the stripped-back period features of the original 1850s hall provides a textured backdrop that contrasts beautifully with the wide range of products by the likes of Philippe Starck, Ron Arad and Verner Panton. There are displays representing every aspect of home life: living-room furnishings, lighting, bathroom accessories, toiletries and jewellery. There's even an Alessi shop-in-shop, one of the brand's larger concessions in London. Standing out is the colourful plastic furniture from Italian giants Kartell, Driade and Magis, of which Aria's buyers have always been great fans. Furniture by British manufacturer naughtone also receives pride of place.

Aria has created an accessible lifestyle environment with an excellent range of home products and accessories, many of which are suitable for gifts. Not pretending to be a shop for the design elite, Aria has tapped into the market for affordable, well-designed items for those in search of something more unusual than the typical high-street pickings.

Atelier Abigail Ahern is a lifestyle boutique on the busy Upper Street, opened by the interior designer and stylist of the same name. Ahern sources a diverse and unique mix of contemporary and vintage furniture, objects, textiles, handcrafted ceramics, lighting and accessories for the home. Utterly style-conscious and a little tongue-in-cheek, the oversized lamps and trompe l'oeil finishes are representative of the owner's tastes as a designer and reflect her aesthetic approach towards interiors. In essence, this is a montage of the things she loves, a rather haphazard combination of old and new.

Alongside already established designers and brands like Marcel Wanders, Maarten Baas, Zanotta, moooi and Anglepoise, you will find carved-wood Senegalese stools, Moroccan side tables, cabinets made from recycled truck tyres, hand-crafted Tunisian vessels and one-off pieces by emerging young designers such as Jed Crystal and Andrew Oliver.

The product introductions seem to be geared towards a certain sort of female clientele, as might be suggested by the title of Ahern's recent book: *A Girl's Guide to Decorating*. Might that go some way to explaining why, as a man, I struggle to get to grips with this place – and feel even further disengaged by words like 'groovy', 'hip', 'cool', 'glam' and 'yummy' that are used on the website? Nevertheless, it is refreshing to encounter an antidote to the slick, Minimalist look that seems to pervade so many design retail spaces these days.

 ESTABLISHED & SONS

📠 5-7 WENLOCK ROAD N1 7SL
📞 020 7608 0990
🔗 ESTABLISHEDANDSONS.COM
🕐 MON–FRI 9.30-6
🚇 OLD STREET/ANGEL

Established & Sons launched with a bang in 2005 as a serious cutting-edge furniture and lighting producer, promising to put the 'British' back into British manufacturing. True to its name, the company has commissioned both established UK designers (such as Zaha Hadid, Amanda Levete, Jasper Morrison, Industrial Facility, Barber Osgerby and Terence Woodgate) and younger talents like Alexander Taylor, Frank, Klauser & Carpenter, Paul Cocksedge and Shay Alkalay. (They have, more recently, added international designers to the mix.) With the reputation of British design talent flying high but UK manufacturing prowess running low, Established's mission has been to marry the two and create a company that can confidently compete with the European big boys.

The public has recently been granted access to view the Established collection in a showroom at its headquarters, just off City Road. Buzz for entry through a discreet door and you'll be invited to visit the manufacturer's sizable home, a bunker-like shell immaculately fitted out by Angus Pond Architects. Rather uncomfortably, one must pass through the studio and office spaces and past the hard-working staff before reaching the imposing double-height, gallery-like showroom. Don't let that deter you as, indeed, you are welcome to view the changing selection of critically acclaimed furniture and lighting designs – in fact this is the perfect opportunity to interact with the range and ask any questions about it. The immense showroom, which benefits

from an imposing exposed-concrete wall that curves to great effect, provides a strikingly stark yet somewhat theatrical backdrop.

You should be aware that this is not your average shop visit. Everything about this location is unassuming: the area, the street, the building. I wouldn't recommend a visit to aimless browsers but would reserve it for those with serious intent.

Established & Sons also produces a number of high-end limited-edition designs, which can be viewed at its Mayfair gallery (p.055).

04 ESTORICK COLLECTION

- 39A CANONBURY SQUARE N1 2AN
- 020 7704 9522
- ESTORICKCOLLECTION.COM
- WED-SAT 11-6, SUN 12-5
- HIGHBURY & ISLINGTON

05 FANDANGO

- 2 CROSS STREET N1 2BA
- 07979 650 805
- FANDANGOINTERIORS.CO.UK
- WED-SAT 11-6
- ANGEL/HIGHBURY & ISLINGTON/ESSEX ROAD RAIL

The Estorick Collection brings together some of the finest and most important works created by Italian artists during the first half of the 20th century and is Britain's only gallery devoted to modern Italian art. Tucked away in the leafy backstreets of Canonbury, in a quiet Georgian building, the gallery opened in 1998 and is now an established member of the North London art scene. This is a very small, very local gallery based around one man's personal taste – that of American sociologist and writer Eric Estorick (1913-1993). The collection is particularly well known for its core of Futurist work produced in Italy between the 1890s and the 1960s, by such luminaries as Giacomo Balla, Umberto Boccioni and Amadeo Modigliani, to name just a few.

The gallery also runs a programme of temporary exhibitions. Recently the shows *Framing Modernism: Architecture and Photography in Italy 1926-1965* and *Workshop Missoni: Daring to be Different* received excellent reviews in the press. They also represent the gallery's shift from celebrating fine art only to celebrating Italian culture in general.

This is obviously not a venue devoted solely to design, but it is a great source of information about Italy's significant contribution to 20th-century European culture. The building also contains a small Italian-run café, and a bookshop and library with a noteworthy collection of readings on the subject.

The go-to shop for aficionados of original 20th-century furniture, lighting and decorative arts. It is run by Henrietta Palmer and Jonathan Ellis, a like-minded duo forever on the hunt around Europe for beautifully crafted treasures – which they often have restored to their former glory by neighbourhood experts. If you are looking to add some yesteryear style to your home, a vintage piece can contrast nicely with the surrounding contemporary design. And, of course, there are obvious benefits to reusing existing items as opposed to buying new.

Palmer and Ellis currently operate Fandango from two Islington premises: their small Cross Street showroom and their nearby warehouse. The former is a rather awkward triangular-shaped space, which is constantly updated as the team shifts stock and acquires new items. Despite a regular circulation of classics from the likes of Jacobsen and Eames passing through the doors, there is no knowing what will be on sale at any given time. Such is the nature of the business. Recently there has been some emphasis on Dutch Modernism and Italian lighting, as well as postwar design from the 1950s and 60s.

It's always worth popping in to see what is on display, or to chat to the owners if you are hunting for a particular something. Contrary to the published opening hours in Cross Street, one can occasionally arrive to find the shop closed. If this happens to you, take a 10-minute walk to the restoration warehouse at 6A ROSEMARY WORKS, BRANCH PLACE, N1 5PH.

 KVADRAT

10 SHEPHERDESS WALK N1 7LB

020 7324 5555

KVADRAT.DK

MON-THU 9-6, FRI 9-5.30

OLD STREET

Last year Danish textile giant Kvadrat moved its UK operations from small premises in quaint Holland Park to this cavernous showroom off the busy City Road. Happily, more is more in this case. Kvadrat hired the acclaimed architect David Adjaye and the legendary graphic designer Peter Saville to collaborate on transforming this former Victorian factory on Shepherdess Walk into the company's exemplary UK headquarters and showroom.

Unsurprisingly, the result is rather dramatic. As an antidote to his signature dark-grey walls and floors, Adjaye managed to direct plenty of natural light from the vast windows into the basement. To access the lower ground, he has added one of his favourite features: an immense wooden staircase sweeping across the whole length of the space. The stairs are lined in light-refracting glass panels in a variety of colours, which add a welcome injection of interest to a concrete space that might otherwise feel rather cold and bleak.

The bare downstairs space triggers momentary confusion until you realise that Kvadrat's catalogue of textiles is cleverly hidden in tall, narrow pull-out units concealed along one wall. A long concrete table provides a focal point for client meetings.

Needless to say, you aren't likely to come here unless you're in the market for textiles, for use in either furniture upholstery or curtains. But if you happen to have the need, you would be well advised to explore Kvadrat's contemporary collections. They are widely considered to be the best option for quality modern interiors.

07 LIVING SPACE
- 36 CROSS STREET N1 2BG
- 020 7359 3950
- LIVINGSPACEUK.COM
- MON–SAT 10-6, SUN 12-5
- ANGEL/HIGHBURY & ISLINGTON

08 ORIGIN MODERNISM
- 25 CAMDEN PASSAGE N1 8EA
- 07769 686 146
- ORIGINMODERNISM.CO.UK
- WED–FRI 11-4, SAT 10-6, SUN 11.30-4
- ANGEL

Living Space was a welcome addition to this charming Georgian street when it opened 10 years ago, at a time when the local appetite for contemporary design was flourishing. Its staying power would suggest that owner Spencer White has successfully tapped this market. (He has recently opened a second showroom at 53-55 FULHAM HIGH STREET, SW6 3JJ, 020 7731 4114). With a focus on Italian manufacturers, White has introduced high-quality, slick and – dare I say – masculine design to this affluent neighbourhood.

The storefront is rather unsuspecting from the street. The narrow entry space, home to minimal wall-mounted drawer and shelving units with a few choice tables and chairs, suffers from harsh white lighting and plenty of linear, hard surfaces. To escape this, you should head to the out-of-sight showroom at the back, where space, natural light and softer materials come into play. It is here that White displays his selection of sofas, from single-seaters to vast corner settees, some at the price of a small car.

One soon realises that each design is available in myriad configurations and finishes – which sound liberating on the one hand but can be puzzling on the other. The helpful staff recognise how difficult it is to make the right choice, which is why they offer a free interior-design advisory service.

They prefer not to shout about designer labels here, instead allowing the stock to speak for itself. If you are after solid, confident, clean-lined modern furniture that doesn't shout from the rooftops, Living Space is the place to find it.

Hidden behind a modest doorway in this fast gentrifying market street is a wee gem – a treasure chest of beautiful, functional, Modernist design. Origin Modernism specialises in 20th-century furniture, objects and art, with a particular passion for Scandinavian, British and American pieces from the 1930s, 40s and 50s.

Walking into this charming boutique is rather like peeking inside a collector's private room – except, thankfully, you're not intruding. The friendly owner Chris Reen will welcome you in and talk you through his extremely well-sourced and well-edited Modernist stock. The ex-financier, with his obvious affinity for vintage furniture, particularly enjoys dealing with customers and recounting the different journeys that his objects have taken.

Expect to find works by respected 20th-century names like Alvar Aalto, Eero Aarnio, Charles & Ray Eames, Poul Kjaerholm, Mies van der Rohe and Marcel Breuer. But you may also happen upon harder-to-come-by furniture by the likes of Hans Coray, Coen de Vries, Osvaldo Borsani, Pierre Jeanneret and Willi van der Meeren. Stock is shaken up by some Russian avant-garde ceramics and Bauhaus graphic art.

This small, tidy shop shares a devotion to clean lines and restraint with many of the Modernist designers whose gems share space here. Origin Modernism doesn't try to masquerade as anything other than what it is. And with the odd crack in the walls and slightly warn-out carpet adding to its charm, it gives its larger rivals a run for their money.

09 THE PEANUT VENDOR

- 133 NEWINGTON GREEN ROAD N1 5UP
- 020 7226 5727
- THEPEANUTVENDOR.CO.UK
- TUE-THU 10-7, FRI-SAT 10-6, SUN 12-6
- CANONBURY RAIL

10 TWENTYTWENTYONE SHOP

- 274 UPPER STREET N1 2UA
- 020 7288 1996
- TWENTYTWENTYONE.COM
- MON-FRI 10-6, SAT 10-5.30, SUN 11-5
- HIGHBURY & ISLINGTON

The economy had already began to falter when Becky Nolan and Barny Read opened this cosy Newington Green boutique. Nevertheless, their offering of affordable vintage furniture and homewares has, in many respects, arrived at the right time, as locals are increasingly steering towards products with provenance and finding reassurance in a dose of nostalgia. Stepping into the shop – named for a popular Cuban song from the 50s – is rather like time-travelling back to your grandparents' front room. But in the best possible way.

Indeed, the Peanut Vendor plays homage to everything that was great about furniture and product design from the 1940s through to the 70s. Every item in the shop is an original vintage piece, from the tables, sofas and chairs that dominate the tiny space to the mirrors, lamps, clocks and crockery that sit elegantly in the window. Highlights for me were the 1950s Philips bakelite radio, the canary-yellow 50s kitchen unit, the blue Parker Knoll-style winged chair and beautiful 60s Danish teak sideboard.

Each week, the owners trawl markets, junk shops, antique warehouses and auctions for suitable stock. While many pieces can be easily linked to a producer such as Ercol or G-Plan, the owners favour style and quality to collectibility – and the flighty prices that can accompany a designer name. In many instances, the prices here give the high street a run for its money.

The twentytwentyone shop is considered by critics and collectors alike to be a leading exponent in the sale of beautiful, high-quality and timeless furniture, lighting, and accessories. It has been a fixture here for more than a decade, managing to stay put where so many of its peers have failed. As a result, the now legendary spot has developed a strong following of customers attracted to its well-designed objects, homewares and smaller accessories. Choice pieces of furniture and lighting are also available, although more can be found at the nearby warehouse and showroom (p.106). And the delightful staff are happy to assist should you be looking for specifics.

Recently, my favourites here have hailed from Japan – including the perfectly considered stainless-steel kitchen utensils by Sori Yanagi; the charming porcelain pieces from old producer Hakusan; and the minimal *plusminuszero* collection of home accessories that has finally made it to British soil, thanks to twentytwentyone.

The compact interior in this glass-fronted space has the effect of focusing attention on each of the well-edited offerings. I feel as though each piece has been selected with integrity, and I imagine a 'twentytwentyone jury' scrutinising genuine design attributes, looking for a balance of beauty, functionality, material honesty, tactility, longevity and ingenuity. Thankfully, it seems that decisions haven't been tainted by the 'trend factor' or other media hyperbole, which might go some way to explaining why this array of items is not easily found elsewhere.

Eat & Drink

11 25 CANONBURY LANE 25 CANONBURY LANE N1 2AS | 020 7226 0955 | 25CANONBURYLANE.COM

Small, friendly bar just off the top end of Upper Street. Cosy and intimate. Brick walls, wooden floors with contrasting opulent, colourful decoration. Great cocktail list. Always busy. Get there early to snag a couch area at the back.

12 THE ALBION 10 THORNHILL ROAD N1 1HW 020 7607 7450 | THE-ALBION.CO.UK

An old pub with a modern gastro vibe. Old English feel. British comfort food cooked well. Friendly and informal. Large leafy garden gets packed on a sunny day. Great for late Sunday lunch.

13 ALMEIDA 30 ALMEIDA STREET N1 1AD 020 7354 4777 | DANDDLONDON.COM

Sophisticated French eatery. Traditional cuisine with modern twist. Regularly changing menu. Clashing decor of neutral green-grey walls and burgundy booth seating. Opposite the Almeida Theatre. Smart crowd.

14 THE ANGELIC 57 LIVERPOOL ROAD N1 0RJ 020 7278 8433 | THEANGELIC.CO.UK

Glammed-up local gastropub. Classy decor. Dungeon like toilets. Honest British food and a good selection of wine and beers. Mixed crowd and can get very busy.

15 THE BARNSBURY 209-211 LIVERPOOL ROAD N1 1LX 020 7607 5519 | THEBARNSBURY.CO.UK

Smart, neighbourhood pub. Original wood panelling, curving wood bar, bare wood floors, open fireplaces. Relaxed atmosphere and tasty food. Pop into their store – The Barnsbury Grocer – just few doors down at 237 Liverpool Road.

16 BARRIO NORTH 45 ESSEX ROAD N1 2SF 020 7688 2882 | BARRIONORTH.COM

A neighbourhood DJ bar. Latin bar culture with a touch of Britishness. Funky interior by London's Anarchitect. Back-to-front tiles and a stripped-down caravan that's been turned into a booth. Avoid the crowds at weekends.

17 THE BREAKFAST CLUB 31 CAMDEN PASSAGE N1 8EA 020 7726 5454 | THEBREAKFASTCLUBSOHO.COM

On the quest for a best brunch in the area. Anything from scrambled eggs to real American-style pancakes with a mean cup of coffee. Bright and fun. Always a queue outside, but it's worth the wait.

18 THE DRAPERS ARMS 44 BARNSBURY STREET N1 1ER 020 7619 0348 | THEDRAPERSARMS.COM

Local boozer recently reopened with upmarket feel. Clean airy look. A touch of modern in the original Georgian interior. Long wooden tables. Dining room upstairs. For the summer there's a little beer garden at the back.

19 DUCHESS OF KENT 441 LIVERPOOL ROAD N7 8PR 020 7609 7104 | GERONIMO-INNS.CO.UK

Formerly an old-school Arsenal pub reinvented as a trendy, welcoming local boozer. Decent gastropub food. Modern interior with plenty of character. Cosy open fireplaces. Natural wood tables. Comfortable low-slung sofas. Old floor-to-ceiling book cases. Outdoor benches. Simple, comfortable, unpretentious.

20 DUKE OF CAMBRIDGE 30 ST PETER'S STREET N1 8JT 020 7359 3066 | DUKEORGANIC.CO.UK

One of UK's first certified organic gastropubs. Ideal Sunday-brunch haunt in a quiet area close to the Regent Canal. Organic food made from seasonal local ingredients. Bright high-ceiling interior. Menu is written on blackboard instead of paper. Very laidback.

21 THE ELK IN THE WOODS 39 CAMDEN PASSAGE N1 8EA | 020 7226 3535 THE-ELK-IN-THE-WOODS.CO.UK

Popular restaurant with warming, textured British/Scandinavian ski lodge interior. Rustic wooden floors, vivid wallpapers, iron fireplace and even an elk's head mounted on the wall. Unpretentious, well-priced and with great atmosphere.

22 EUPHORIUM BAKERY 202 UPPER STREET N1 1RQ 020 7704 6905 | EUPHORIUMBAKERY.COM

Traditional bakery near the top end of Upper Street. Range of freshly made breads, sandwiches, salads and delicious home-made pastries and cakes. Simple, contemporary decor. Perfect for a quick lunch or a casual meeting, if you can see past the yummy mummies.

23 FIFTEEN 15 WESTLAND PLACE N1 7LP 0871 330 1515 | FIFTEEN.NET

The destination for Jamie Oliver's hearty creative cooking. Tasty ingredient combinations in a true Italian style. A more formal dining room downstairs. Always busy, rustic trattoria on the ground floor.

24 FREDERICKS 106 ISLINGTON HIGH STREET N1 8EG 020 7359 2888 | FREDERICKS.CO.UK

Sophisticated Modern European cuisine. Art Deco salon at the front. Conservatory-like restaurant and open garden at the back. Laidback Parisian feel. Great for early-evening glass of wine or smart yet relaxed sit-down dinner.

25 THE HOUSE 63-69 CANONBURY ROAD N1 2DG 020 7704 7410 | INTHEHOUSE.BIZ

Half pub and half dining room. Delicious modern and fresh menu. Outside area gets popular on a warm summer evening.

26   HUONG VIET   12-14 ENGLEFIELD ROAD N1 4LS
020 7249 0877

Once a modest little community-centre dining room. Today a highly praised Vietnamese canteen. Long cult status in and around Dalston. No-nonsense tasty food. Buzzy atmosphere. Quick efficient service. Easy to miss, but a must place to visit.

27   THE MARQUESS TAVERN   32 CANONBURY ST N1 2TB
020 7354 2975 | MARQUESSTAVERN.CO.UK

An authentic pub on a leafy backstreet of Canonbury. Superb food, famous for its Sunday lunches. Fantastic high-ceiling dining room at back with plenty of ambience and good service. This contrasts with the not-so-special wooden bar area at the front.

28   OTTOLENGHI   287 UPPER STREET N1 2TZ
020 7288 1454 | OTTOLENGHI.CO.UK

A seriously popular revolution in food. Inventive, flavoursome food made from top quality ingredients to eat in or take away. Sumptuous food displays. Menu changes daily. White sleek interiors. Quite pricey but just irresistible (especially the meringues in the window). Limited seating space. Expect queues.

29   S&M CAFÉ   4-6 ESSEX ROAD N1 8LN
020 7359 5361 | SANDMCAFE.CO.UK

Traditional affordable all-day British grub. Hearty portions of the Britain's favourite – sausage and mash. 1950s diner decor and plenty of Formica is another good reason to pop in.

30   WAXJAMBU   144 UPPER STREET N1 1QY
020 7226 7660 | WAXJAMBU.CO.UK

Welcoming and surprisingly relaxed Upper Street cool drinker's bar. Rustic low interior. Exposed-brick walls and heavy wooden tables in contrast with black-leather seating. Open front in summer. Stylish, easygoing and unpretentious but busy at weekends.

● Indulge

31   BELLE EPOQUE PATISSERIE   37 NEWINGTON GREEN N16 9PR | 020 7249 2222 | BELLEEPOQUE.CO.UK

A spirit of 1920s Parisian Art Noveau patisserie. Tasty home made quiches. Small deli counter.

32   FRANK GODFREY   7 HIGHBURY PARK N5 1QJ
020 7226 2425 | FGODFREY.CO.UK

Legendary and without a doubt the best local butcher. Family-run business, trading in the area since 1905.

33   LA FROMAGERIE   30 HIGHBURY PARK N5 2AA
020 7359 7440 | LAFROMAGERIE.CO.UK

A smaller sister to its Marylebone original. Great selection of English, French, Italian and Spanish cheeses in temperature-controlled room. Homemade cakes and delicatessen. Small window table for those who cannot resist and want to taste a few samples.

34   HIGHBURY VINTNERS   71 HIGHBURY PARK N5 1UA
020 7226 1347 | HIGHBURYVINTNERS.CO.UK

Friendly independent wine shop. Great selection of wines from mostly smaller producers.

35   JAMES ELLIOTT BUTCHERS   96 ESSEX ROAD N1 8LU
020 7226 3658

Another local butcher with regular queues outside. Carefully hung beef, free-range chickens, pork and lamb from Devon backed up by a few cheeses, eggs and ice cream from Winters Dairy.

36   MONTE'S   23 CANONBURY LANE N1 2AS
020 7354 4335 | MONTESDELI.COM

Small deli for one-stop shop for fresh Italian cheese, wine, olive oils, antipasti and gourmet foods. Fairly pricey.

37   OLGA STORES   30 PENTON STREET N1 9PS
020 7837 5467

Local Italian delicatessen. A wide range of tasty Italian goods, cheeses and treats makes up for the unassuming shop exterior.

38   PAUL A YOUNG CHOCOLATES   33 CAMDEN PASSAGE N1 8EA | 020 7424 5750 | PAULAYOUNG.CO.UK

Fine artisan chocolaterie on the picturesque Camden Passage. Decadent chocolates made by hand onsite each day, including some unexpected ingredients.

39   LE PECHE MIGNON   6 RONALDS ROAD N5 1XH
020 7607 1826 | LEPECHEMIGNON.CO.UK

Cosy, little and well-hidden French delicatessen. Good food, service and atmosphere. Café and small garden at the back.

40   THE SAMPLER   266 UPPER STREET N1 2UQ
020 7226 9500 | THESAMPLER.CO.UK

A fine wine shop re-writing the wine-selling rules with machines that allow you to taste before you buy. Certainly not the usual stuffy wine shop. Fun and a great place to stop by for sampling before heading out for food.

41   STEVE HATT FISHMONGERS   88-90 ESSEX RD N1 8LU
020 7226 3963

He-has-it-all local fishmonger. Located in straightforward premises on Essex Road. Draws customers from far and wide. Plenty of banter from staff. Prices are on the high-end but the quality and freshness is top.

● Sleep

To our surprise, we have not found any hotels in Islington that we would choose to recommend. Perhaps this is an ideal opportunity for an entrepreneur to introduce a new venture to this desirable area of London.

The word 'modern' is getting its groove back. Today's consumers are gradually shifting away from mass-production and coveting objects with genuine quality and provenance. NINA HERTIG explains

WHAT IS MODERN?

Recently there was an article in a leading newspaper titled 'Modernism – it is so last year'. The article referred to a house that was failing to sell despite having won a TV prize. The surprise is not that the house could not find a buyer, but that the style of the interior was labeled Modernist. Frankly, it was about as Modernist as a page in the now-defunct MFI catalogue. The point was that bland and soulless interiors are no longer selling – even if they are prizewinning.

Now that can only be a good thing.

Le Corbusier said that to combine stone, wood and concrete is 'construction'. But to create something that touches the heart is architecture. This is equally true of design and interiors and sums up what makes a house beautiful. It is the element of art that makes a building or a design relevant to us and gives it some soul that 'touches the heart'. It is also the element missing in so much of design today.

This essential need for art in design was one of the ideas behind Walter Gropius's Bauhaus in Germany. The movement started as a small workshop-based school that connected artists, designers and craftsmen but soon morphed into an institution that designed for industry. Like Bauhaus, but in reverse, design is now turning its focus away from mass-production. We now see designers reconnecting with art and exhibiting their work in galleries around the world, in what is often labeled 'design art'. This could be a return to the values of the early years of the Bauhaus, where small experimental workshops combined art and design to create something new. Or it could be a simple reaction to the reigning years of mass-market, disposable design.

Over the past 50 years we have seen the legacy left by Bauhaus and its marriage

'Modern has come to represent a method of producing rather than a style that reflects our world'

to industrial production – it was so successful, it nearly dominated the market. And it had the gradual effect of allowing manufacturers to define 'modern' as mass-produced. Modern has come to represent a method of producing rather than a style that reflects our world. In my opinion, modern should describe a variety of styles that bear relevance to our lives, regardless of their era.

In the 19th-century, the word 'modern' stood for the mechanical world. Modernism in the 1920s included Filippo Marinetti's Futurist food (sardines and pineapple); abstract revolutionary porcelain by Russian Constructivists for the masses in the newly formed Soviet state; Mies van der Rohe's Barcelona Pavilion; and Bruno Taut's revolutionary walls made from glass bricks. In the 1950s, modern was reflected in the proliferation of skyscrapers, signifying excitement for the future. Today we are modern because our belongings and outlook reflect the world around us. Or so it should be.

The Austrian Modernist Carl Auboeck was the designer of beautiful brass objects skillfully made by hand. He was not famous, but many have chosen to hand down his objects to their children. His work possesses the 'art' of both design and craft, making it timelessly modern. Isn't that why people keep his simple corkscrews for generations?

The fact that the expensive and experimental designs sold as art today are finding an audience must suggest that there are waves of new designers questioning the 'conveyor belt' definition of modern. They know that in order to make design relevant now, it must possess genuine quality and integrity that will make us want it, enjoy it and cherish it.

NINA HERTIG IS THE CO-FOUNDER OF SIGMAR (P.019). SIGMARLONDON.COM

TRUMAN BREWERY / LONDON / UK
FURNITURE / CERAMICS / TEXTILES /
INTERACTION / WALLCOVERINGS /
PRODUCT / GLASS / LIGHTING /
DIGITAL MEDIA / ACCESSORIES

23-26
SEPT
2010

THE
MULTI-FACETED
DESIGN EVENT

WWW.TENTLONDON.CO.UK

TENT
LONDON

Shoreditch & Brick Lane

WHITBY STREET E1

DIRTY HOUSE, WHITBY STREET

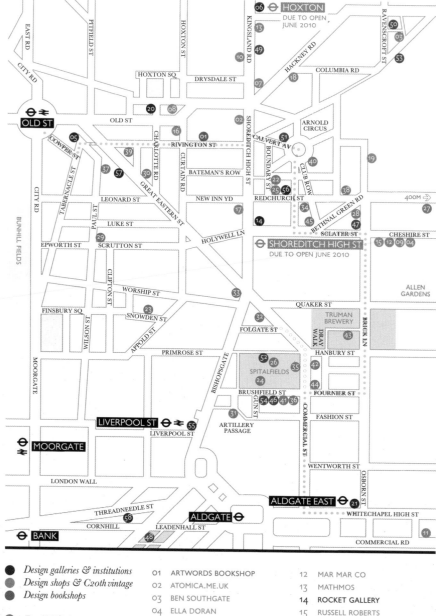

Design galleries & institutions
Design shops & C20th vintage
Design bookshops

Eat & Drink
Indulge
Sleep
(pp.140-141)

••• *Take a walk route*

Shoreditch & Brick Lane

TAKE A WALK
*Duncan Richies** *

Alight at the spaghetti junction-inspired Old Street tube via EXIT 3 and head to No.28 Cowper Street, where you'll find Undercurrents, a treasure of a shop that sells second-hand 20th-century European design. It's bursting at the seams with furniture, accessories, lighting and vintage oddities. Cut back on to Rivington Street and visit Franco's Café – great value, serving the finest in ciabattas, focaccias and freshly made pastas; the jovial staff are ruthlessly efficient and put on something of a performance too. The health-conscious should hop across Shoreditch High Street onto Calvert Avenue, where Lennies Larder offers big salads and big smiles.

Calvert Avenue ends at Arnold Circus, with the Boundary Estate bandstand at its centre. The estate is noteworthy, being the world's first council-housing project, built by London City Council in 1900 to replace the Friars Mount slum. You can take a moment to reflect here while sitting on a Michael Marriott-designed bench next to the bandstand. In truth, the place is somewhat dog-eared and improvements are scheduled for 2010 – though some graffiti on the notice asks: 'What's to improve?' Another architectural gem is just south on Chance Street. *Dirty House* (2002) is one of David Adjaye's early architectural projects. The former timber factory is now a live/work space for artists Tim Noble and Sue Webster. It's a strange, inaccessible slab of a building covered in black anti-graffiti paint with blacked-out windows. The beautiful whitewashed cantilevered roof is actually best viewed from the rarefied air of Shoreditch House, but the building is impressive enough from street level in a showy, you're-not-coming-in kind of way.

Walk south from here on to the ever-evolving Brick Lane. My choice would be to visit Ambala foods for the perfect Asian snack, then head down Fournier Street to the Hawksmoor-designed Christ Church Spitalfields for a piece of local architectural history. From here, a wander south on Commercial Street takes you to Whitechapel Gallery, still the best art gallery in the East End. Alternatively, walk north up Commercial Street and cut across to Bishopsgate via Folgate Street. Then get a well-deserved pint at The Water Poet, a cracking pub on the fringe of the city.

*Writer and brand consultant andassociate.co.uk

01 ARTWORDS BOOKSHOP
- 65A RIVINGTON STREET EC2A 3QQ
- 020 7729 2000
- ARTWORDS.CO.UK
- DAILY 10.30-7
- OLD STREET/SHOREDITCH HIGH STREET

02 ATOMICA.ME.UK
- 125 SHOREDITCH HIGH STREET E1 6JE
- 020 7739 5923
- ATOMICA.ME.UK
- TUE-SUN 11.30-5.30
- OLD STREET/SHOREDITCH HIGH STREET

This small, unassuming shop is a Shoreditch gem and one of the best independent specialists in London. It stocks books, magazines and DVDs on contemporary visual arts and design and keeps up to date with newly published titles from the Continent, North America and Australia. Due to limited space, you may not find older titles here, but the helpful staff can source specific items on request.

I'm a sucker for a good bookshop, such is the business I'm in. For me, it is always a bit dangerous going in here, as I inevitably end up buying something – even if only a small notebook or postcard. Artwords cannot compete with the mega-bookshops, and nor should they. The intimacy of the space coupled with the expertly edited selection is precisely what appeals to the creative community that has become so prevalent here. If you're not hunting for specifics, browse their sizable stock of glossy magazines and niche publications, and pick up a copy of something outside your usual remit.

My advice is to avoid visiting at busy times, as the tiny floor space can feel claustrophobic with more than a few people browsing. Oh, and a small tip: check out the *Resources* section on the Artwords website for a helpful list of galleries in the area.

Atomica occupies small retail premises and has a discrete presence on this busy stretch of Shoreditch High Street. Opened by William Simms in 2001, this is a space that reflects the owner's distinct taste and admiration for 1920s to 1980s vintage furniture, lighting and *objets*.

On an average day you can find original items from the likes of Hans Wegner, Alvar Aalto, Joe Colombo or Eero Saarinen. On my recent visit, there was an emphasis on rosewood furniture, including some stunning 1950s Danish sideboards and tables, an Arne Jacobsen drop-leaf table and Pierre Paulin's 1966 *Oyster Chair*, illuminated by a pair of Louis Wiesdorf copper pendant lights.

Many of the pieces acquired by Simms need some restorative work – a job he can occasionally be found undertaking in the shop. New upholstery is expertly handled at his partner's workshop down the road at 7 Redchurch Street.

A problem inherent to trading in originals: stock levels can fluctuate, meaning the space can sometimes feel cluttered or, just as often, rather thin on the ground. In reality, it is seldom the latter. This delights most visitors, who relish the exciting opportunity to explore this treasure trove. But it may leave others overwhelmed.

Be warned: the opening hours here seem rather sporadic, so I advise calling in advance before making a special journey.

 BEN SOUTHGATE

4 THE COURTYARD, EZRA STREET E2 7RH

07905 960 792

BSOUTHGATE.CO.UK

SUN 9-2.30

OLD STREET/HOXTON

ELLA DORAN

46 CHESHIRE STREET E2 6EH

020 7613 0782

ELLADORAN.CO.UK

WED-FRI 10-6, SAT 12-5, SUN 11-5

LIVERPOOL STREET/SHOREDITCH HIGH STREET

This is the sort of the place you would normally stumble upon or hear about from a friend. Tucked away in a small courtyard off Ezra Street and only open on Sundays, Ben Southgate's furniture shop is a welcome retreat from the chaos of nearby Columbia Road flower market. Coming from a background of furniture restoration, Southgate opened this small shop to sell antique and vintage furniture and a choice of lights, mixed in with the odd curiosity. All items are sourced personally by Southgate – and restored in his East Sussex workshop if necessary.

Most items hail from the 1900s to the 1950s, although it is hard to predict what treasures you will find on your visit. You may come across a beautifully presented 19th-century French table; a clubby leather armchair; polished-steel medical cabinets; oak plan chests; a Bakelite side table; or filing drawers from Senate House, complete with brass card plates and pulls.

You may also find articulated tabletop or wall lights from Anglepoise, Jielde or Mek-a-lek, and elegant French ridged-glass lampshades. And what will most certainly catch your eye are the polished-aluminium film and theatre lamps and heavy-duty ship lights. The selection is spiced up by an intriguing number of vintage games and toys. A set of German-origin stone building blocks and early 20th-century Popular Puzzles are rare finds.

For more than 10 years Ella Doran has steadily risen to prominence for her unique range of coasters, trays, mugs, cushions, mats, stationery, wallpaper and blinds. She cleverly transforms these everyday objects with the simple application of her photographic imagery, and she has been much imitated in the process. Her work is immediately recognisable, sporting imagery that is typically colour-rich and graphically bold and confident – whether it is a photograph of a row of old artist's tools; a close-up of an orchid; or an idyllic green meadow spotted with wildflowers.

Doran's award-winning work is mostly produced under her own label, but she has also developed products under licence for the likes of tableware manufacturer Portmeirion and retailers such as John Lewis. Further commission work has seen the production of two children's books for the Tate and associated giftware collections. She also created a range of products for London Transport and its *All Zones – Routemaster Rocks* project, which celebrates the iconic London bus.

In 2005, Doran took the next logical step and opened a boutique on Cheshire Street, near Brick Lane. The shop carries her entire range of products alongside a handful of complementary creations by other designer friends. When viewed en masse, the mix of styles, patterns and colours are a tad too much. But stand them alone and they provide vibrant accents suitable for gifts or a personal treat.

05 GALLERY FUMI
- 87-89 TABERNACLE STREET EC2A 4BA
- 020 7490 2366
- GALLERYFUMI.COM
- TUE-SAT 11-7, SUN 12-5
- OLD STREET

06 GEFFRYE MUSEUM
- 136 KINGSLAND ROAD E2 8EA
- 020 7739 9893
- GEFFRYE-MUSEUM.ORG.UK
- TUE-SAT 10-5, SUN 12-5
- LIVERPOOL STREET/OLD STREET/HOXTON

Gallery Fumi opened in early 2008 in the heart of Shoreditch and has steadily been building its reputation within the burgeoning market for collectible design. Introducing their own take on the design-meets-art gallery scene are owners Valerio Capo and Sam Pratt, who, as long time Shoreditch locals, had spotted an opening for a design gallery amid the area's already thriving creative community. The duo doesn't tend to gravitate towards established names, instead choosing to commission emerging design talents to produce one-off and limited-edition furniture, lighting and accessories.

The gallery is populated by unusual pieces chosen on the criteria that, if the gallerists would live with it in their own home, they would sell it here too. Keep an eye out for the primitive honesty of Max Lamb's chairs; the sculptural geometry of Francisco Sarria's tables; the glass globules of Pieke Bergman's 'infected' lighting; and mesmerising electroluminescent mirrors by Marcus Tremonto. Recent additions include the characterful but fragile-looking gum paper and cast-bronze *Les French* furniture series by Studio Glithero. These play nicely against the high-quality, minimal aluminium furniture by Paul Kelley.

The two-storey space is all bare-brick walls, wood floors and muted paint colours. Thankfully, this relative newcomer on the scene lacks the pretension – and astronomical prices – of some of its rivals. Fumi will no doubt attract you back for more.

The Geffrye is a glimmering gem on this otherwise downtrodden stretch of Kingsland Road. Fronted by enormous gardens, the elegant 18th-century almshouses are dedicated to domesticity and house a permanent collection of quintessentially London room layouts exhibiting the ever-changing style of home interiors in middle-class England from 1600 to the present day.

The first room-scene at the start of a narrow corridor running the length of the building is a 17th-century heavily oak-panelled living room. Continue and you come across the refined splendour of the Georgian period, followed by the high style of the Victorians. A contemporary extension, designed by Nigel Coates, houses room-sets charting the evolution of interior decoration across each decade of the 20th century.

The extension is also the site of a café and shop, plus temporary exhibition and event spaces. On my visit, I saw Mark Cowper's photography exhibition, which offered a voyeuristic glimpse into every apartment in the Battersea tower block in which he lives. Shows like this illustrate the museum's ongoing dedication to documenting our contemporary domestic interiors.

The Geffrye offers a snapshot of how life in Britain has progressed. With painstaking attention to detail, the displays encompass every aspect of home life, from furniture, lighting, artwork and textiles to bricks and mortar and heating. The challenge for the museum will be to continue to source 'typical' rather than exceptional objects from each passing era.

 JASPER MORRISON SHOP
🖝 24B KINGSLAND ROAD E2 8DA
📞 N/A
🖊 JASPERMORRISON.COM/SHOP
🕐 MON–FRI 11–5
🚇 OLD STREET/HOXTON

Some may claim that Jasper Morrison is the top living industrial furniture and product designer in the world. And I would be one of them. This British success story consistently comes up with simple, elegant, functional and timeless products that are devoid of any egotistical fanfare or excess. Morrison products are the sort of products that sit quietly and confidently – almost anonymously – before the untrained eye.

Particularly anonymous is Morrison's very own shop, installed in an unused corner of his London studio. On a rather shabby stretch of Kingsland Road, surrounded by take-away joints, rowdy bars and sultry nightclubs, stands the black-painted doorway of 24B. Press the buzzer for entry to the immaculately presented shop, which carries examples of Morrison's homewares and other functional objects he has picked up on his travels.

The shop theme is an extension of the *Super Normal* exhibition Morrison co-curated with Japanese contemporary Naoto Fukasawa. The exhibition encouraged visitors to appreciate quietly efficient design. 'I wanted a continuation of the contact that [*Super Normal*] provided me with everyday, useful things,' said Morrison of his motivations for opening the shop.

Here you can pick up some of Morrison's signature designs, such as his perfectly plain Rosenthal crockery, straightforward cutlery and stainless-steel tableware and cooking pots for Alessi, plus his cork stools for Vitra. Some of the merchandise is by fellow designers like Sori Yanagi and Konstantin Grcic. But it is the most

anonymous objects that delight, including the iconic Bialetti coffeemaker; the orange-handled Fiskars scissors from Finland; the colourful Ellepi staplers from Italy; and the beautifully shaped Italian *Pastorino* hammer and plastic oil can from Japan.

The Jasper Morrison Shop does not advertise; the designer relies on positive word-of-mouth to gain footfall. The telephone number remains unpublished as calls would interrupt the day-to-day work flow of the studio. But send an email to shop@jaspermorrison.com if you have an enquiry.

For better or for worse, you're not likely to keep this place quiet once you discover it. Just be a bit cool about who you tell. And be warned: the policy is cash only.

08 KK OUTLET
- 42 HOXTON SQUARE N1 6PB
- 020 7033 7680
- KKOUTLET.COM
- MON–FRI 9-6, SAT 12-5
- OLD STREET/SHOREDITCH HIGH STREET

09 LABOUR AND WAIT
- 18 CHESHIRE STREET E2 6EH
- 020 7729 6253
- LABOURANDWAIT.CO.UK
- WED, FRI 11-5, SAT 1-5, SUN 10-5
- LIVERPOOL STREET/SHOREDITCH HIGH STREET

A relative newcomer to design hub Hoxton Square, KK Outlet is a shop and gallery named after KesselsKramer, the Amsterdam-based communications agency that produces witty advertising solutions for clients like Diesel, J&B and MTV. This dynamic agency believes that great communication ideas come from a variety of disciplines, which it aims to nurture in this small studio that doubles as the London office.

The hybrid environment was designed as an 'outlet' for different aspects of the KK portfolio, from advertising to product development, from design to publishing. On display against white-tiled shelving at the entrance are some of KesselsKramer's eye-catching titles – like the *Useful Photography* series, which documents collections of found photography in beautifully bound tomes. The gallery regularly showcases projects from its own talented staff, as well as by neighbourhood artists, designers and photographers like Jennifer Skupin, whose playful marshmallow *Soft Porn* creations are here.

True to its form, this is no ordinary space either. Designed by architectural practice FAT (who have also recreated the publisher's Amsterdam office), the space has been divided in half by a plywood wall. On one side is a plain white space which is split by a plywood wall concealing a number of unexpected, brightly coloured and richly-decorated spaces.

Everything about this multifunctional workspace seems simultaneously random and cool. Whatever you make of KK, its output will offer a glimpse into the minds and imaginations of the KesselsKramer family.

Classic English meets old-fashioned reliability at the original Labour and Wait store off Brick Lane. The local institution propagates a simple, honest approach to design, where quality and utility are intrinsic in every product. The quaint shop sells carefully chosen artisanal household items, from brooms and vintage watering cans to kitchen and tableware. All products have a timeless quality: hard-wearing, made-to-original designs sourced from specialist makers from around the world – many of whom continue to use traditional production methods.

Visiting Labour and Wait is like stepping back in time, embracing a bygone era that seems rather apropos for the nostalgic mood of today. Everything holds a sense of old-world charm: the enamel mugs and measuring jugs, stainless-steel kettles, vintage teapots, linen dishcloths, horn combs, vintage needle and thread packets... Each item is a classic in its own right, mixing the modern with the traditional. This calm shop celebrates functionality at its most simple, which seems a world away from much of the over-designed gadgetry of today. New doesn't always mean better here.

The ordered aesthetic of the space is likely to awaken your childhood memories of shopping for doorstops, watering cans, and dishcloths with mother. Such common household tools take on new meaning at Labour and Wait.

In addition to this flagship, there is a shop-in-shop at Dover Street Market (p.054).

10 LIFESTYLEBAZAAR
- 11A KINGSLAND ROAD E2 8AA
- 020 7739 9427
- LIFESTYLEBAZAAR.COM
- MON-SAT 11.30-7.30, SUN 12-6
- OLD STREET/HOXTON

11 LIGNE ROSET CITY
- 37-39 COMMERCIAL ROAD E1 1LF
- 020 7426 9670
- LIGNE-ROSET-CITY.CO.UK
- MON-SAT 10-6, THU 10-7, SUN 12-5
- ALDGATE EAST

Following the success of their debut Soho location (p.069), London-based design team Laurent Nurisso and Christopher Curtis were moved to launch a second outlet in the East End design Mecca of Shoreditch.

Located in the heart of the neighbourhood, taking over a converted Victorian boot factory, Lifestylebazaar Shoreditch is the edgier of the two locations. You'll spot the interior from blocks away, wrapped as it is in colourful fluorescent lighting, which updates the old brick building squatting under a crumbling railway. Chipboard floors, exposed brick work and original fireplaces provide a contrast that is very much in keeping with the surrounding urban look of the area.

Nurisso and Curtis have shopped the world for their unusual mix of furniture, lighting, decorative objects, accessories and gifts. Large cage-like lights by La Corbeille dominate the space, along with a *Sodom & Gomora* steel screen by Pulpo and the owner's favourites: multi-hued acrylic chairs – the *Frilly*, *Thalya* and *Papyrus* – produced by Kartell. Next to these you'll discover all manner of curiosities, from iBride's surreal legged *Bambi* tables and the eccentric *Blaue Blume Tea Set* by Tina Tsang to Dominic Wilcox's *War Bowl*. Products range in price from an affordable £10 to a hefty £4,000, making this a place for a quirky birthday gift or a permanent home fixture.

Lifestylebazaar is a welcome retail addition to Shoreditch – a feat, considering the area's high standards. Happily, it lacks the pomp or snobbery that some of its neighbours succumb to. Thus it makes the contemporary design scene more accessible to a wider audience.

Showroom spaces are seldom large enough for vast collections of furniture, lighting, and accessories, as catalogued by interiors brand Ligne Roset. When it opened its largest UK showroom in 2003, spanning 750-square-metres, such a limitation was resolved even if this enormous space occupies a rather odd location on this main London artery road.

For several years, I've been of the impression that Ligne Roset's art direction has been improving, with an assortment of individual designs reinforcing my judgement. Wandering around this space, whilst still of the same opinion, I was slightly perturbed to find a fair share of rather bourgeois, suburban furniture. Usually, these sorts of pieces tend to consist of a palette of polished chrome, either mocha brown or clammy leather upholstery, and plenty of dark-wood veneers mixed with frosted glass. For me, this type of design lowers the tone of the stronger pieces.

That said, it is clear that a swathe of accomplished French designers have introduced new designs to the range which have helped to raise the bar in the minds of design snobs like me. After freely perusing this spacious showroom, I came to the conclusion that the sofas, tables, chairs, storage, lighting, rugs, beds, and accessories offer, in general, a good quality starting point for anyone wanting to introduce modern design to their home, free from the showy elitism that is characteristic of some other furniture brands.

12 MAR MAR CO
16 CHESHIRE STREET E2 6EH
020 7729 1494
MARMARCO.COM
FRI-SAT 12-6, SUN 11-5
LIVERPOOL STREET/SHOREDITCH HIGH STREET

13 MATHMOS
96 KINGSLAND ROAD E2 8DP
020 7549 2700
MATHMOS.COM
MON-FRI 9.30-5.30, SAT 10.30-6
OLD STREET/HOXTON

That Mar Mar Co is a collaboration between two graphic designers is hardly surprising. The small Cheshire Street shop is filled with pretty pattern and interesting combinations of colour, a natural sum of the interests of the two owners, Mark Bedford and Marianne Lumholdt (get the origin of the name?).

The boutique is organised in vignettes, each item carefully selected and in many cases exclusive to the store. The emphasis is on timeless, well-considered products made by independent designers from around the world, but the duo also celebrates larger, more established producers.

Mar Mar Co is an inviting place with accessible pricing, where you can buy smaller well-priced items such as the slick spherical *Birdfeeder* by DWR; a hot-pink *Pigeon Lamp* by Ed Carpenter; or Rob Ryan's colourful vinyl wall stickers. I've got my eye on the minimal *Maku* kitchen collection designed by wunderkind Sami Ruotsalainen, a couple of glossy-black pendant lamps by Cecilie Manz and pair of primitive-looking trestles made entirely of thin chestnut logs.

From its cosy spot on this market street lined with independent shops, Mar Mar Co attracts a following of loyal customers, as well as a curious crowd of weekend passers-by who come for a quick fix of Cheshire Street's unique aesthetic. This is a destination shop that doesn't try to pack in too much, instead adopting a more confident approach to its curated gallery of products.

Mathmos is the producer of the original and now iconic lava lamp, the colourful, mesmerising rocket-shaped accessory of choice in the 60s, 70s and beyond. The company's challenge has always been to evolve past this initial success and grow into a diverse design force. Well, once again it has succeeded. Over the last decade Mathmos has gone from strength to strength – the lava lamp recently enjoyed a futuristic makeover by British designer Ross Lovegrove.

Of course, there is only so far you can take the 'glow in the dark theme'. So Mathmos has tapped into the brilliance of some London-based innovators – including Azumi and Two Create – who, in my opinion, hit the mark with new designs that incorporate the company's Airswitch technology. The products harness motion sensors, so you can switch on the glass lights and adjust the light intensity simply by moving your hand through the air above them. One recent collaborator, El Ultimo Grito, tackled the eyesore that is the bare hanging lightbulb. The result was an elegant spun-aluminium lampshade with a slit in the side that allows for the shade to be slipped over existing light fittings quickly and easily. It is now ubiquitous in London.

Also in the Mathmos range are LED lights, space projectors, outdoor lights and candle lights, some of which are a bit gimmicky for my tastes, and some of which have been spoilt by the prominent placement of a logo.

But whatever your preference, the entire range of colourful, playful lighting can be viewed and purchased in the new flagship on Kingsland Road – also the site of the company's head office.

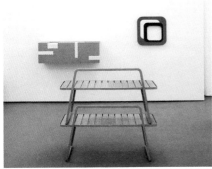

 **ROCKET GALLERY**
🚇 TEA BUILDING, 56 SHOREDITCH HIGH STREET E1 6JJ
☎ 020 7729 7594
➤ ROCKETGALLERY.COM
🕐 TUE-FRI 10-6, SAT 12-6
⊖ LIVERPOOL ST/SHOREDITCH HIGH ST

(15) **RUSSELL ROBERTS**
🚇 8 CHESHIRE STREET E2 6EH
☎ 020 7613 3355
➤ 8CHESHIRESTREET.COM
🕐 THU-SAT 12-6, SUN 11-4
⊖ LIVERPOOL STREET/SHOREDITCH HIGH STREET

Rocket Gallery is a stalwart in this fast-morphing neighbourhood. It was established in the mid-90s by Jonathan Stephenson, who developed a reputation for his sensitive overlap of contemporary art, photography and design, and now resides in a crisp white gallery in the newly converted Tea Building.

In this sparkling-clean post-industrial room, Rocket offers a calendar of rotating exhibits of Minimalist painting and photography, abstract art from the 60s and 70s and mid-century and contemporary furniture. Some recent exhibition highlights in the realm of design include a comprehensive presentation of 1950s *Krenit* bowls by Danish designer Herbert Krenchel; a mini-retrospective of mid-century furniture by my favourite Danish designer Poul Kjaerholm; and *Merger: New Minimal Painting in Dialogue with Contemporary Furniture Design*, featuring the work of younger artists and designers Lars Wolter, Richard Roth, Corinna Warm, Oliver King and Tom Lovegrove.

The gallery recently dedicated a private viewing room to its stock of furniture and objects that can be perused on request. Here you will find those colourful *Krenit* bowls, Jens Risom's curvaceous sofas, Hans Wegner's masterpiece armchairs, even Arne Jacobsen's *Munkegaard* chair and desk.

In addition to the offerings in the main-gallery, be sure to check out the bookshop, which stocks signed and deluxe editions of art, photography and design tomes.

Celebrating beautiful mid-century modern originals in his intimate shop on Cheshire Street is the ever-passionate Russell Roberts. The son of furniture dealer Tommy Roberts and brother of Keith Roberts, co-owners of vintage shop Two Columbia Road (p.137), Russell enjoys an illustrious background that prepared him well for opening his own shop.

The unassuming storefront is deceptive; inside is an impressive collection of highly regarded 20th-century furniture, lighting, art and collectibles. The range changes constantly but always manages to combine some iconic creations with a few lesser-known surprises. Those after collectible names may well unearth chairs by Hans Wegner, Finn Juhl, Arne Jacobsen and Charles & Ray Eames. On my visit, I was delighted to find a 1960s Ercol *Daybed* in good condition, complete with its original wool upholstery. From the same decade, a stunning rosewood sideboard by Danish talent Arne Vodder also caught my eye. A bright-orange multifunctional children's chair from the 1970s by Luigi Colani living in the window added an element of lightheartedness to the store – as did the selection of cup-holding 1980s robots.

Having grown up surrounded by vintage designs, the friendly and chatty Roberts possesses a clear idea of what constitutes a brilliant find. And he points out the importance of evaluating a piece's condition, provenance, authenticity and price before making a purchase. Needless to say, he can claim to have done his due diligence, and more, in selecting his own stock.

16 SCP EAST

📠 135-139 CURTAIN ROAD EC2A 3BX

📞 020 7739 1869

↖ SCP.CO.UK

🕐 MON-SAT 9.30-6, SUN 11-5

🚇 OLD STREET/SHOREDITCH HIGH STREET

SCP has been on the design radar since 1985, when Sheridan Coakley started selling re-editions of 1930s tubular-steel furnishings produced in a small East London workshop. Since then the initials SCP (Sheridan Coakley Products) have become synonymous with the production and retail of finely crafted contemporary British furniture. After all, Coakley was one of the first to commission some young British talents who have gone on to become established names in the industry (think bright lights like Matthew Hilton, Jasper Morrison, Tom Dixon, Terence Woodgate and Konstantin Grcic). More recent talents on his roster include Russell Pinch, Alex Hellum, Donna Wilson and Peter Marigold. Functional, timeless, classically characterful: these are some of the recurring traits you'll notice across his range.

The growth of Coakley's production business saw the natural evolution into retail. This original SCP store on Curtain Road is one of the early success stories of the East End creative boom. In the mid 90s it was one of the few spots in London where you could buy a Saarinen table or a Panton chair. Today, it remains the company's creative hub and very much a part of the establishment in this area.

Across the voluminous two-floored shop, the SCP home collection is displayed alongside designs from a raft of other well-known suppliers, including Magis, Hay, Cappellini and Kartell. While most of the first-floor space is given over to furniture, the ground floor is the place for smaller, more affordable items including glassware, bathroom accessories, rugs, toys, books, kitchenware and stationery. There's a corner dedicated to lighting from the usual suspects: Artemide, Anglepoise, Louis Poulsen, Bestlite and Flos. But you'll also find choice pieces by Tom Dixon, Harri Koskinen and Ingo Maurer.

For the trade, SCP also runs a successful contract division from the offices upstairs. Those nearer West London should check out the Notting Hill store (p.031).

SQUINT

- 178 SHOREDITCH HIGH STREET E1 6HU
- 020 7739 9275
- SQUINTLIMITED.COM
- MON–FRI 10–6, SUN 1–5
- LIVERPOOL STREET/SHOREDITCH HIGH STREET

18 TWO COLUMBIA ROAD

- 2 COLUMBIA ROAD E2 7NN
- 020 7729 9933
- TWOCOLUMBIAROAD.CO.UK
- TUE–FRI 12–7, SAT 12–6, SUN 10–3
- OLD STREET/HOXTON

Former sculptor and painter Lisa Whatmough embarked on a new career path when she opened Squint in 2005. But her longtime initial passion for collecting antique textiles took over and triggered the idea of combining her stash of luxe fabrics with period furniture. The result is a range of over-the-top plush furnishings in exuberantly coloured patchwork upholsteries. Whatmough will cover such classics as a plump Victorian chaise longue, a Chippendale stool and the iconic *Egg* chair by Arne Jacobsen – as well as all manner of market finds, from mirrors and bed heads to lighting. By virtue of the unique mix of contemporary and vintage fabrics, each piece is reliably one-off.

Every design is meticulously handmade in Squint's showroom-slash-gallery-slash-workshop. Whatmough uses traditional upholstery techniques, including tied springs and hand-stitched seams. Currently everything is made to commission, and the team works closely with clients to reach the final desired design – an eclectic collage of patterns, bold and striking colours, textures and random composed shapes.

Nobody expects the Squint style to appeal to everyone's tastes. My impression is that you either love it or hate it. And, by the way, that is by no means a criticism. Indeed, some of the most enchanting design – like some of the most successful designers – is confident, outspoken and commanding, with its own concept, aesthetic and point of view. So, for those reasons, Squint is worth a visit.

Heading down Hackney Road, it is hard to miss the tantalising shop window at this prominent corner spot at the junction with Columbia Road. Inside, it is bliss for anyone who gets excited by 20th-century originals: a feast of mint-condition tables, desks, seating, storage, lighting and artwork.

Two Columbia Road is a family business, operated by Keith Roberts and his father Tommy (owner of 60s cult interiors shop Kleptomania and later Tom Tom). In the past few years the space seems to have become tidier – which is not easy to achieve when you're dealing with ever-changing stock and a mix of styles from half a dozen different eras.

As with all shops supplying original design, it is impossible to guarantee the availability of a particular piece. When I was there, sitting proudly in the window was an original Eero Saarinen *Womb* chair in bright-red upholstery. Next to it, my favourite Modernist design, the timeless *PK22* chair by Poul Kjaerholm, was perched elegantly atop an immaculate rosewood table. There was a teak and oak table by Hans Wegner, complete with six matching chairs, alongside a linear Arne Vodder sideboard from the 1950s, adorned with tactile *Krenit* bowls by Herbert Krenchel. It would also seem that the shop is starting to source some pieces from the 1980s: Marc Newson's *Felt* chair (1989) and Ron Arad's *Rocking* chair (1988) are examples.

The reliable website keeps treasure-hunters abreast of new stock. And should you be searching for something specific, staff can help source it for you.

19 UNTO THIS LAST
- 230 BRICK LANE E2 7EB
- 020 7613 0882
- UNTOTHISLAST.CO.UK
- DAILY 10-6
- LIVERPOOL STREET/SHOREDITCH HIGH STREET

20 WHITE CUBE
- 48 HOXTON SQUARE N1 6PB
- 020 7930 5373
- WHITECUBE.COM
- TUE-SAT 10-6
- OLD STREET/SHOREDITCH HIGH STREET

In 1860 John Ruskin wrote *Unto this Last*, railing against the industrial revolution, advocating a return to the local craftsman's workshop. A century and a half later, visionary entrepreneur Olivier Geoffrey shares the same ideology. In his Brick Lane workshop he employs the latest technologies to design, produce and sell inexpensive furniture, lighting and accessories.

His distinctive shelving, chairs, tables, lighting and beds are made from sheet materials, mostly birch plywood. Using 3D modeling software, he transfers the designs from computer directly to an onsite digital CNC cutting machine, where the components are cut from the plywood. Finally, the design is assembled and refined for customers, who trek from the more popular end of Brick Lane just to shop here. The whole process is closely supervised to ensure utmost efficiency of time, materials and space – which keeps prices remarkably competitive. On an environmental level, waste is kept to a minimum and shipping miles are virtually non-existent.

Unto This Last carries no overstock here, producing on demand and selling direct to the public from the showroom at the front of this converted pub. Customers can choose among various finishes and discuss bespoke dimensions, after which the pieces are produced and ready for pick-up within a week or two.

This is a fascinating concept, and it is satisfying to know that the merchandise is being constructed onsite, rather than in some cheap foreign factory. Geoffrey's method has been carried over to his second showroom space in Battersea (p.156).

For years now Hoxton has been a hub for the capital's creative movers and shakers. So it was only a matter of time before the White Cube moved into this vaulting space in Hoxton Square. Many would admit that its arrival helped transform the area from a creative backwater to a fully-fledged cool-kid capital.

Esteemed art dealer Jay Jopling founded White Cube in 1993 at the heart of London's art world, Duke Street. At the time it was one of Europe's smallest exhibition spaces, occupying a single 'white cube' room. But it has grown into, arguably, one of most influential commercial galleries today, with a purpose-built outpost at Mason's Yard in Mayfair and this slightly older sibling.

Jopling's artists include the likes of Chuck Close, Mona Hatoum, Ellsworth Kelly and Hiroshi Sugimoto, all exhibited here in turn. White Cube offers a window onto the cream of international contemporary art, and has been instrumental in promoting the Young British Artists of the 1990s, including Damien Hirst, Tracey Emin and Gary Hume.

Why is an art gallery in a design guide? The White Cube was a catalyst for change in Hoxton Square, and regardless of what you think about the area's subsequent influx of wannabe trendies, it is important to recognise that the gallery helped bring a whole new audience to Shoreditch. For me, that alone warrants its inclusion.

21 WHITECHAPEL GALLERY

77-82 WHITECHAPEL HIGH STREET E1 7QX

020 7522 7888

WHITECHAPEL.ORG

TUE-SUN 11-6, THU 11-9

ALDGATE EAST

Whitechapel has been a force in controversial art in London's East End for more than a century – long before the current surge of contemporary artists arrived in the area. The influential space reopened to acclaim in 2009 following a two-year multimillion-pound expansion. Under the watchful eye of Belgian architects Robbrecht en Daem, the gallery has doubled its size and the original exhibition spaces have been carefully renovated to provide unprecedented free access to important art collections.

This is where 20th-century greats like Frida Kahlo, Jackson Pollock, Mark Rothko, and Jasper Johns made their London debuts. And where most of Britain's most significant contemporary artists – from Gilbert and George to Lucian Freud and David Hockney to Mark Wallinger – have premiered new work.

Among the dozens of contemporary-art galleries that have emerged in the East End in the past several decades, the established Whitechapel enjoys A-list status. But, let's not neglect the building itself. The Grade II-listed facade, designed by Charles Harrison Townsend, is an imposing beacon on an otherwise grim stretch of the high street. Once you're inside and sheltered from the noise of the city, the individual galleries feel surprisingly calm, and the refreshed white walls form a clean backdrop for the important artworks on show.

In addition to the changing programme of exhibitions and educational events, visitors also benefit from a sleek new bookshop. And if the gallery itself doesn't offer rejuvenation enough, rest your legs and grab a drink and a snack in the café, or make an occasion of it with a proper meal in the restaurant.

It is worth pointing out that, strictly speaking, the Whitechapel Gallery infringes on the entry criteria for this guide, as it handles fine art as opposed to design. In this instance I have decided to turn a blind eye. The positive impact that the revitalised gallery has had on the up-and-coming neighbourhood, coupled with my personal fondness of the institution, makes it hard to ignore.

● *Eat & Drink*

22 ALBION 2-4 BOUNDARY STREET E2 7DD
020 7729 1051 | ALBIONCAFF.CO.UK
A bakery, grocers and café all in one. Casual but stylish. Exposed brick complemented by white walls, wooden tables. Great for relaxed brunch. Open front.

23 L'ANIMA 1 SNOWDEN STREET EC2A 2DQ
020 7422 7000 | LANIMA.CO.UK
Contemporary Italian cuisine. Sleek and sophisticated design. A great place to relax in style and comfort.

24 BEDALES 12 MARKET STREET E1 6DT
020 7375 1926 | BEDALESTREET.CO.UK
A wine shop and wine bar with wine-tasting – plus tasty tapas. Decor is rather rustic. Wine cellar downstairs.

25 THE BOUNDARY 2-4 BOUNDARY STREET E2 7JE
020 7729 1051 | THEBOUNDARY.CO.UK
Part of Conran's much talked-about Boundary Project. Classic French menu. Elegant design. Vaulted ceilings, exposed-brick walls, intimate booth seating. Rooftop restaurant is a big draw in summer.

26 CANTEEN 2 CRISPIN PLACE E1 6DW
0845 686 1122 | CANTEEN.CO.UK
Simple, locally sourced food served in hearty portions. Glass-fronted, open space in the heart of the new Spitalfields Market. Bubbling atmosphere and excellent service.

27 E PELLICCI 332 BETHNAL GREEN ROAD E2 0AG
020 7739 4873
Tiny family-run Art Deco café appealing to locals. Consistently rated by city magazines. Tasty, cheap, authentic-Italian meals. Must try their *Full British Breakfast*.

28 FIKA 161A BRICK LANE E1 6SB
020 7613 2013 | FIKALONDON.COM
Decently priced Swedish fare. Eye-catching interior. Painted trees and woodland animals on the walls. Small but very friendly with a chilled atmosphere.

29 FOX DINING ROOM 28 PAUL STREET EC2 4LB
020 7729 5708 | THEFOXPUBLICHOUSE.CO.UK
Honest gastropub menu and careful selection of beers and wines. An excellent homemade pie. Simple and relaxed atmosphere – loud and cheerful downstairs, more sedate in the upstairs dining lounge.

30 GREAT EASTERN DINING ROOM
54-56 GREAT EASTERN STREET EC2A 3QR
020 7613 4545 | RICKERRESTAURANTS.COM
Accomplished and impossibly chic pan-Asian eaterie. Generous frontage, high windows, prime corner location.

31 GRAPESHOTS 2-3 ARTILLERY PASSAGE E1 7LJ
020 7247 8215 | DAVY.CO.UK
Traditional British wine bar. Intimate subterranean dining room. Tucked away in cosy Artillery Passage.

32 HAWKSMOOR 157 COMMERCIAL STREET E1 6BJ
020 7247 7392 | THEHAWKSMOOR.CO.UK
The best elements of American and British cuisine meet here. Supersized portions and quality cocktails, all served with a smile. A discovery to boast about.

33 LOUNGE BOHEMIA 1E GREAT EASTERN ST EC2A 3EJ
07720 707 000 | LOUNGEBOHEMIA.COM
Avant-garde cocktails, great Eastern European beers and Czech-inspired canapés. Homely Bohemian-style interior. One of Shoreditch's best-kept secrets.

34 LOUNGELOVER 1 WHITBY STREET E1 6JU
020 7012 1234 | LOUNGELOVER.CO.UK
Decadent decor with eccentric elements. Taxidermy is ever-present. Expert lighting. Book well in advance.

35 LUXE OLD SPITALFIELDS MARKET, 109 COMMERCIAL STREET E1 6BG | THELUXE.CO.UK
Shoreditch's newest hip evening venue. Bar and restaurant, plus a programme of music and arts, all under one roof. Located on the fringes of the Old Spitalfields Market. Lively and cool but still rather sophisticated.

36 MARKET COFFEE HOUSE 50-52 BRUSHFIELD STREET E1 6AG | 020 7247 4110 | MARKETCOFFEEHOUSE.COM
A taste of old-fashioned English café culture a stone's throw from the City. Traditional English staples like crumpets and ginger beer. Warm, woody interior.

37 THE PRINCESS OF SHOREDITCH
76 PAUL STREET EC2A 4NE | 020 7729 9270
THEPRINCESSOFSHOREDITCH.COM
Bustling gastropub with upstairs dining room. Hearty British favourites. Iron spiral staircase.

38 THE REDCHURCH 107 REDCHURCH STREET E2 7DL
020 7729 8333 | THEREDCHURCH.CO.UK
A tucked-away late-night bar. Decorated with Victorian flourishes (think velvet banquettes). Intimate and personal, not loud and showy.

39 RIVINGTON GRILL 28-30 RIVINGTON ST EC2A 3DZ
020 7729 7053 | RIVINGTONGRILL.CO.UK
Back-to-basics British cooking. Comfortable loft-style dining environment. Whitewashed walls, stripped-wood floors. Local and relaxed.

40 ROCHELLE SCHOOL CANTEEN
ARNOLD CIRCUS E2 7ES | 020 7729 5677
ARNOLDANDHENDERSON.COM
Shoreditch's best-kept secret. Hidden behind the walls of a converted schoolhouse. Great home-cooked food. Buzz the door open.

41   S&M CAFÉ   48 BRUSHFIELD STREET E1 6AG
    020 7247 2252 | SANDMCAFE.CO.UK

Perfect sausages and mash, as the name suggests. A great British tradition, modernised. Generous portions. American diner feel.

42   ST JOHN BREAD AND WINE
    94-96 COMMERCIAL ST E1 6LZ | 020 7251 0848
    STJOHNBREADANDWINE.COM

Unpretentious, interesting food in a welcoming environment opposite Spitalfields market. Simple, refreshing decor. Ivory walls, wood tables. Packed at peak hours.

43   STORY DELI   3 DRAY WALK E1 6QL | 020 7247 3137

No-nonsense organic pizzeria and café in the shadow of the Old Truman Brewery. Long-time student favourite. Small warehouse space, unvarnished wooden tables, boxes as seats. Rough-edged but uber-cool.

44   TEN BELLS   84 COMMERCIAL STREET E1 6LY
    020 7366 1721

Traditional British haunt with the atmosphere of a modern bar. Overshadowed by the Gothic Christ Church Spitalfields.

45   LES TROIS GARCONS   1 CLUB ROW E1 6JX
    020 7613 1924 | LESTROISGARCONS.COM

Linked to Loungelover, located on the street to the rear. Fine French fare. Known for its over-the-top opulent decor. Stuffed animals on the walls; huge, sparkling chandeliers hanging from the ceilings. Quirky and kitsch but always worth the visit.

● Indulge

46   A GOLD   42 BRUSHFIELD STREET, LONDON E1 6AG
    020 7247 2487

British deli with antique fittings. Everything from traditional sausages to jelly babies. Charming without being twee.

47   BEIGEL BAKE   159 BRICK LANE, LONDON E1 6SB
    020 7729 0616

The oldest and probably the best bagel shop in London. Open 24 hours. Social hotspot. Great for a late-night bite.

48   CHEESE AT LEADENHALL
    4-5 LEADENHALL MARKET EC3V 1LR
    020 7929 1697 | CHEESEATLEADENHALL.CO.UK

Dedicated fromagerie with more than 100 different British and continental cheeses. Soak up the scent. Wine bar next door. Friendly atmosphere.

49   THE GROCERY   54-56 KINGSLAND ROAD E2 8DP
    020 7729 6855 | THEGROCERYSHOP.CO.UK

Local, organic and fairtrade food. Impressive vaulted ceilings and brick walls. Sit down for a quick lunch.

50   JONES DAIRY   23 EZRA STREET E2 7RH
    020 7739 5372 | JONESDAIRY.CO.UK

A bustling café attached to an excellent cheese shop. On the premises of a former Welsh dairy.

51   LEILA'S SHOP   17 CALVERT AVENUE E2 7JP
    020 7729 9789

Small deli and café with affable owners. Supports small, local producers. Seasonal produce, organic, biodynamic and artisan products. No packaging.

52   TEASMITH   6 LAMB STREET, LONDON E1 6EA
    020 7247 1333 | TEASMITH.CO.UK

Specialist teashop with a tea bar. A wide variety of leaves from Assams to Earl Greys.

53   TREACLE   110-112 COLUMBIA ROAD E2 7RG
    020 7729 0538 | TREACLEWORLD.COM

Teatime treats ranging from traditional British favourites to the famous cupcakes – hand-crafted and beautifully decorated.

54   VERDE & CO   40 BRUSHFIELD STREET E1 6AG
    020 7247 1924 | VERDE-AND-COMPANY-LTD.CO.UK

Iconic gourmet-food emporium. Fine, high-quality produce in an authentic Georgian atmosphere and rustic setting.

● Sleep

55   ANDAZ   40 LIVERPOOL STREET EC2M 7QN
    020 7961 1234 | ANDAZ.COM

A 21st-century hotel experience behind a striking red-brick Victorian facade. Ultra-modern interiors with few original details. Monumental fireplaces, plaster moldings. The ultimate city-hotel experience.

56   THE BOUNDARY   2-4 BOUNDARY STREET E2 7JE
    020 7729 1051 | THEBOUNDARY.CO.UK

Converted Shoreditch warehouse. Seventeen guest rooms adjacent to the well-reviewed Conran restaurant. Each room has a different decor inspired by legendary designers or style movements. Reasonable prices.

57   HOXTON HOTEL   81 GREAT EASTERN STREET
    EC2A 3HU | 020 7550 1000 | HOXTONHOTELS.COM

Urban living meets country-lodge lounging. Large glass front. Double-height foyer often displays art installations. Get yourself a deal – a few £1 rooms are released every three months.

58   THREADNEEDLES HOTEL
    5 THREADNEEDLE STREET EC2R 8AY
    020 7657 8080 | THEETONCOLLECTION.COM

A grand former banking hall built in the City in 1856. Rooms decorated in chic contemporary style but with many original features still in place. Intricate stained-glass central dome and lounge. Luxurious sanctuary in the heart of the financial district.

The Internet has opened up a much broader platform for the democratic dissemination and exchange of design ideas. GILLIAN RUSSELL explores the web's potential and points out where it currently falls short.

DIGITAL DIALOGUE

'One half of the world does not know how the other half lives,' Jacob A Riis reminded us, referring to the rampant issues of economic divide in America in the 1880s. Years later this very same statement can be applied to the context of design. Up until the advent of the Internet it would seem that design discourse and debate were predominantly reserved for members of the design world, leaving the general public unaware of the greater meanings of the objects they confronted regularly in their day-to-day lives.

Although design itself has long been intended for the masses, the discourse surrounding its contexts, intentions and values was not. Before the introduction of the Internet, aesthetics, price and functionality were our only considerations when trying to understand design. Even if one hoped to learn more, the resources were not available. Design discourse was seen as belonging to the classroom and the studio, and not open to the public's perception.

The past decade has brought about many changes in the way the subject is disseminated. Today the rules that govern our understanding of design have shifted. Characterised by a series of exemplary manifestations – blogs, wikes, 'zines and social networking sites – Web 2.0 has cultivated a culture of participation and engagement, where the creative process of knowing is extended to the 'other half' – or at least those with access to the Internet.

Thanks to this information revolution, design now sits in a new paradigm driven by accessibility, communication and collaboration. Today's design supports open interaction and knowledge exchange. It invites individuals to participate in the creation and enhancement of their experiences and understand it in ways never before imagined.

In this technological arena, typified by the international free exchange of trade and ideas, the vocabulary of the design language is changing. While promoting the construction of new narrative forms, the Internet has offered the design world the potential to engage in a dialogue, exchange and collaboration with people beyond the capitals of design.

'As technology advances and web platforms improve, we will see this shift in the evolution of design consciousness grow'

This burgeoning online world has brought with it a new means of representing manufactured goods. Our knowledge is no longer constrained simply to functionality and aesthetics. Rather, it has broadened to include cultural values, contextual specificities and social accountability. This is not to say that aesthetics and functionality are without significance in this day and age. Yet, in order for these qualities to remain relevant in our society as a whole, it is crucial to develop a discourse that encompasses a more comprehensive understanding of design's various meanings, values, intentions and implications.

As technology advances and web platforms improve, we will see this shift in the evolution of design consciousness grow. However, as the Internet continues to play a larger role in the dissemination of design, the need for a critical examination of the nature of communication will grow as well.

Undoubtedly there is a need for new perceptions and dialogues with design. Nevertheless, our current relationship to online technology – while encouraging participation and collaboration – is still lacking a thorough and ordered approach to critical discourse. As the public embraces its newfound voice, we must begin to encourage a dialogue founded on deeper understandings.

To a large extent, while improving accessibility to design and design discourse, these virtual spaces have continued to promote a descriptive commentary – based mainly on mundane observations and superficial drivel – rather than creating a strategy for critical exchange.

If we truly wish to develop a collective design consciousness, we need to focus on creating a discursive space for design, while building up our critical discourse around the discipline – a discourse with the ability to foster far deeper and more meaningful dialogues than ever before.

GILLIAN RUSSELL IS EDITOR OF **DETNK.COM**

100%**design**
london

Create your environment
23–26 September 2010
Earls Court London

100%**design**
100%**futures**
100%**materials**
100%**detail**

Elsewhere

Design galleries & institutions
Design shops & C20th vintage

01 CHAPLINS
02 CIRCUS ANTIQUES
03 **DAVID GILL GALLERIES**
04 **DESIGN MUSEUM**
05 DESIGNS OF MODERNITY
06 GALLOP
07 **HELEN YARDLEY GALLERY**
08 IKEA
09 LASSCO
10 LOOPHOUSE

11 OXO TOWER WHARF
12 PLACESANDSPACES
13 PLANET BAZAAR
14 PRIMROSE HILL INTERIORS
15 RETROUVIUS
16 **TATE MODERN**
17 UNTO THIS LAST
18 VITSŒ
19 **THE WAPPING PROJECT**

Elsewhere

INTRODUCTION
*Max Fraser**

This chapter is dedicated to all of the design shops, galleries, and institutions that are located away from the key areas of geographical concentration highlighted in previous chapters. Whilst there is a lot to be said for the power of association brought about through proximity to like-minded businesses, there are also virtues for creating a destination, which is what this chapter celebrates.

Some people forget just how vast a city London has become. Its offerings are constantly in flux. Its neighbourhoods and communities morph and shift at variable rates, attracting transient followings and changing demographics. Keeping on top of these changes has been a non-stop challenge when researching for this guide, not least for this chapter. After all, the city is spread over 600 square miles and is essentially made up of numerous interlocking villages that have merged organically over time, making it extremely difficult to feel like you've covered every base.

Furthermore, London is a frustrating city in which to travel. Despite some positive changes implemented since the introduction of a mayor in 2000, the transport network remains plagued by its old infrastructure. Crossing the city can take up considerable chunks of time, which is why so many Londoners become localised and somewhat insular – the age-old rivalry between north and south London a stereotypical reminder.

Researching this chapter has taken me on the odd wild-goose-chase and into many sub-standard places. That said, the more I have travelled, the more it has left me wondering how many destinations I have simply missed out. This is the first year of this guide and I fully expect subsequent editions to support more entries in this wide-reaching chapter, rather incongruously titled Elsewhere. Of course, I rely on external sources for such information and would encourage you to feed any suggestions to info@londondesignguide.com

*Editor of London Design Guide
londondesignguide.com

 CHAPLINS

🚊 477-507 UXBRIDGE RD, HATCH END, MIDDX HA5 4JS
📞 020 8421 1779
🏹 CHAPLINS.CO.UK
🕐 MON-SAT 10-6
🚇 HATCH END RAIL

 CIRCUS ANTIQUES

🚊 60 CHAMBERLAYNE ROAD NW10 3JH
📞 020 8968 8244
🏹 CIRCUSANTIQUES.CO.UK
🕐 MON-SAT 10-6, SUN 11-4
🚇 KENSAL RISE

I hadn't visited the Chaplins furniture and lighting showroom for several years, so when the time came to return for this review I was rather reluctant to endure the full afternoon in the car from central London to the premises in Hatch End (ZONE 6, to you and me). It was deemed best that I go alone – my colleagues understandably put off by the traffic, my road rage and the relentless views of suburban sprawl. More than an hour of expletive-filled travel later and I was ready to hate this place, but I knew it couldn't be ignored.

After all, Chaplins is probably the largest 'modern contemporary' design showroom in the UK, spread across three floors and two buildings amounting to over 2,500-square-metres. For more than 15 years it has successfully showcased leading European furniture and lighting and has grown to include some 190 brands. The high-street site caters to all aspects of modern interiors, and is complemented by the UK's largest B&B Italia and Maxalto shop-in-shop (check out the comprehensive website for a full list of suppliers). Presumably these premises were chosen for size, coupled with their proximity to the wealth-belt of suburbia.

Meandering through the more high-end offerings I came across a room called the Chaplins Design Museum, only to find a Vitra shop-in-shop with a smattering of other 20th-century additions. With the R'N'B music challenging my patience, I acknowledged the strength of the range, then made a swift exit.

The retro carnival-inspired branding caught my eye at this busy Kensal Rise junction and prompted me to park the car and get out for a closer inspection. The prominent corner location clearly benefits Circus Antiques; there seems to be a high level of footfall here, with locals popping in regularly to survey the ever-changing stock of antique and vintage seating, storage, lighting, mirrors, artwork and *objets*.

Owner Mark Slade operates with a mission to marry unusual treasures from both the 19th and 20th centuries. Circus doesn't kowtow to the popular lineup of Modernist masters, preferring a more varied selection without hefty pricetags that come with designer names.

On my visit an ornate 19th-century French settee was accompanied by an elegant chaise longue from the same era. Next to that, a pair of slender 1950s wood-framed Italian chairs were guarded by a vintage mannequin, and a honey-oak haberdashers shop counter stood alongside an imposing Victorian butcher's meat safe. At the rear of the shop was the recent addition of vintage clothing and accessories – an unnecessary distraction, in my opinion.

A nostalgic mood is effectively captured here, particularly by the True Grace candle collection, whose scents waft through the room. If you have a taste for eccentric Old World charm sometimes overlooked at other shops, Circus is worth a trip. As, incidentally, is Niche (at 70 Chamberlayne Road) and Howie & Belle (at No.52).

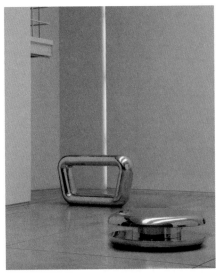

 DAVID GILL GALLERIES

3 LOUGHBOROUGH STREET SE11 5RB

020 7793 1100

DAVIDGILLGALLERIES.COM

MON-FRI 10-6, SAT BY APPOINTMENT

VAUXHALL

David Gill has been a leading advocate of the cutting edge in contemporary decorative arts since the 80s, when he opened his first gallery on Chelsea's Fulham Road. Inspired by 20th-century furniture while working in modern and old master prints for Christie's, Gill struck out on his own with a collection of largely French pieces by top names such as Charlotte Perriand, Jean Prouvé and Eileen Gray. He soon added works by Donald Judd, Yves Klein and then-newcomers like Tom Dixon and Ron Arad. The year 1989 marked a turning point for Gill when he started a series of collaborations with French artists Elisabeth Garouste and Mattia Bonetti. This helped to establish his reputation as a producer, not just a dealer.

The original Chelsea space remains open by appointment only, the larger gallery on Loughborough Street in South East London has been Gill's home base for more than a decade. The immense, sleek-white warehouse-like space has put on some spectacular shows in the past years, with exhibitions of limited-edition furniture by Marc Newson; Jaime Hayón; Grayson Perry; and Ettore Sottsass. Zaha Hadid exhibited her enormous *Dune Formations* here. And there have been well regarded solo shows from Fredrikson Stallard, Oriel Harwood and Barnaby Barford.

Gill has managed to remain a pioneer with a vision to commission extraordinary designs; and he was doing so long before the recent explosion of the art-meets-design trend. Giving designers creative carte blanche enables them to explore unusual and challenging materials and processes, while still pushing the boundaries of their own self-expression – free from the constraints of serial production. The results speak for themselves in this stunning gallery, which attracts return visits from a parade of loyal collectors.

Aware of his position in this market, Gill rolls his eyes at the wave of newcomers who have jumped on the 'design art' movement as if it were a new phenomenon. For now he can rest comfortably and observe the jostling of egos in this burgeoning market, content in the knowledge that he has been provoking this debate for the past 21 years.

 **DESIGN MUSEUM**
- 28 SHAD THAMES SE1 2YD
- 020 7403 6933
- DESIGNMUSEUM.ORG
- DAILY 10-5.45
- TOWER HILL/LONDON BRIDGE

05 DESIGNS OF MODERNITY
- CRYSTAL PALACE ANTIQUES, JASPER ROAD SE19 1SJ
- 07966 285 694
- DESIGNSOFMODERNITY.COM
- MON-SAT 10-6, SUN 10-5
- GIPSY HILL/CRYSTAL PALACE RAIL

Design's leading entrepreneur, Terence Conran, launched the Design Museum in the basement of the V&A (p.021) in 1982 before relocating it to Shad Thames at the end of that decade. Now housed in a Bauhaus-inspired building benefitting from magnificent views along the Thames, the museum has become a beacon in London's creative landscape.

Operating under the directorship of Deyan Sudjic, the institution continues to promote and debate the ingenuity of furniture, graphics, architecture, fashion and industrial design through the 20th century and into the 21st. Each year there is a schedule of retrospectives featuring legends living and past, as well as an annual showcase of trailblazing projects titled Designs of the Year.

At the end of your visit, pop into the museum shop for a focused – and affordable – selection of books and designer housewares that are a welcome departure from the usual dross carried in museum shops. If you need to recharge, stop at the ground-floor café or indulge in a meal at the Blueprint café upstairs.

It seems hard to imagine now, but the Design Museum was one of the first institutions to exhibit mass-produced items for daily use, a subject once ranked low on the cultural hierarchy. With luck, the government will increase subsidies to the museum as it wakes up to the fact that design is a major contributor to the British economy and helps to distinguish us on the world stage.

I'm not going to lie. I wasn't much looking forward to travelling to Crystal Palace – not least because it involved the dreadful overground rail network. It took some time to find myself in front of a worn-out white-brick façade, thinking: 'This had better be good.'

Phew. Designs of Modernity is a treasure hidden in the 100-square-metre basement of Crystal Palace Antiques & Modern, a Victorian warehouse home to a dozen dealers with different specialities. I was struck by the sheer quantity of items on offer here – everything from 17th-century lighting to 20th-century sideboards.

I met the knowledgeable owner, Ben Adams, who regularly scouts the UK and northern Europe for 20th century furniture, decorative items, posters and lighting. On my visit he had an endless number of mid-century beauties to show me. A particular favourite was a round-topped Hans Wegner table surrounded by four shell chairs by Eames for Herman Miller, all illuminated by the tiered enamel pendant lamp from Fog & Morup. In the corner, a 1960s teak and rosewood sideboard by Ib Kofod-Larsen for G-Plan caught my eye. It was topped with a brass clock and a German polished-brass desk lamp.

So, I might have moaned about the journey but, thankfully, it was well worth the effort.

06 GALLOP

- 198 DEPTFORD HIGH STREET SE8 3PR
- 020 8694 8601
- GALLOP.CO.UK
- MON-SAT 8-7
- DEPTFORD RAIL

07 HELEN YARDLEY GALLERY

- A-Z STUDIOS, 3-5 HARDWIDGE STREET SE1 3SY
- 020 7403 7114
- HELENYARDLEY.COM
- TUE-FRI 11-4
- LONDON BRIDGE

A few years ago Clare Page and Harry Richardson, partners in the design studio Committee, took on this derelict space nestled between a takeaway joint and a solicitors' office. Over time they personalised it and developed it into this shop-gallery-venue, which now hosts a curious mix of design-centric activities.

The duo have tiled the walls in a collage of various whites, inspired by the famous Manze's Pie & Mash shop a few doors down. Drawers and display cabinets are cleverly embedded in the walls, creating a witty relief. The Committee workspace has moved here, but Gallop also offers refreshments at the bar (with a selection of coffees, teas, ice cream, pastries, cheese, ham, breakfasts and aperitifs), a one-man film booth, a small display area for 'matters of interest' and a magazine rack selling obscure titles.

Page and Richardson met during fine art studies and since then have followed their instincts rather than any defined career path – which is why they've come to design products as varied as lighting, rugs, ornaments, furniture, textiles and wallpaper. Their work pushes the boundaries between art, craft and design, and their pragmatic creative approach is best experienced in this gem of a space in an unsuspecting corner of South East London.

This 200-square-metre Bermondsey showroom specialises in its own-design range of rugs, carpets and wall-hangings. It occupies a Victorian warehouse flooded with natural light and whitewashed to form a calming backdrop for Yardley's abstract-impressionist creations.

The atelier is more than 25 years old and has amassed a distinguished following of private and corporate clients. The allure of Yardley's handiwork comes from the painterly effect of her designs – sweeping brushstrokes and swathes of colour echoed in hand-tufted wool, hand-knotted needlepoint or stitched and printed felt.

The rugs are essentially drawings for the floor – collages of colour and shape, some lifelike, some geometric. I struggle with the notion of walking on these artworks, which may go some way to explaining why so many clients choose to hang them on the wall.

Many bespoke pieces are commissioned here; otherwise you'll find a good-sized collection of standard designs available 'off the peg'. Undoubtedly the joy of visiting this showroom in person is that you can also observe first-hand the manufacturing process and take a peek into the creative nerve centre: the studio.

 IKEA

🚆 CROYDON, EDMONTON, WEMBLEY

☎ 0845 358 3364

↖ IKEA.COM/GB

🕐 (SEE WEBSITE)

🚇 (SEE WEBSITE)

LASSCO

🚆 BRUNSWICK HOUSE, 30 WANDSWORTH RD SW8 2LG

☎ 020 7394 2100

↖ LASSCO.CO.UK

🕐 MON-SAT 10-5, SUN 11-5

🚇 VAUXHALL

Nowadays the 'rack it and stack it' flat-pack revolution needs little introduction. IKEA has furnished millions of homes and, in the process, changed the interior vernacular of the buying public. This monstrous global brand has spawned nearly 300 megastores in 36 countries with group sales of more than 21 billion euros. So many of us loath the out-of-town shopping experience but can, nonetheless, still be found dodging trolleys here on a Saturday afternoon.

With literally thousands of choices here, covering every area of the home, it is necessary to weed out the unnecessary filler to find the top treasures. The brand's blond-wood stereotype remains a dominant feature, but is by no means exclusive these days – think trendy white and black, even 'teak'. Every few years, IKEA releases the Post Scriptum (PS) collection – a more imaginative 'designer' addition, including recent contributions from Swedish quartet Front and Dutch design star Hella Jongerius.

While I acknowledge that IKEA's affordability has made contemporary Scandinavian design more democratic, I can't ignore the huge burden that cheap furniture place on our planet. According to IKEA's 2008 figures, nearly 1.3 million tonnes of CO_2 are emitted, directly and indirectly, across their total operations. In the same year, the company printed 198 million catalogues using just 5.2 per cent recycled fibres. We, the consumers, are fuelling this demand. If we shifted away from our culture of cheap and disposable to one of durability and quality... Ah. Wishful thinking perhaps, but thinking I would urge you to practice.

Lassco has become one of London's largest resources for 'architectural antiques, salvage and curiosities' since its founding by Adrian Amos in 1979. Scouring demolition and refurbishment projects, they aim to recover architectural gems that possess characteristics unique to a certain era or with a noteworthy story linked to its provenance.

I travelled to Lassco's premises in Vauxhall to discover an elegant Georgian mansion full of treasures from marble fireplaces, cinema seating, and museum cabinets to cast iron radiators, church fittings, hinges, and even the kitchen sink, not to mention a whole array of outdoor miscellanea. Beside the array of furniture and curiosities, they also supply a range of renovation materials, including stone tiles, wooden floorboards, and iron ornaments for an entrance gate. I'm no expert on the pricing of such items but I was struck by some seemingly high price tags on a few occasions.

The mansion is a miracle of existence amid the hideous urban planning and traffic of Vauxhall roundabout. Perhaps most surreal is that the listed building is totally overshadowed by one of London's ugliest riverside developments – St George Wharf – yet it stands defiant. The presence of a business like Lassco, which supports the preservation and continued use of old materials and products, makes for a bizarre contradiction to the newness of its surroundings, and a visit here all the more intriguing.

Further to Brunswick House, Lassco has two more branches: a flooring warehouse in Bermondsey and a showroom in Oxfordshire.

10 LOOPHOUSE
- 88 SOUTHWARK BRIDGE ROAD SE1 0EX
- (020 7207 7619
- LOOPHOUSE.COM
- MON-FRI 9-5
- BOROUGH

11 OXO TOWER WHARF
- BARGEHOUSE STREET SE1 9PH
- (020 7021 1600
- COINSTREET.ORG
- TUE-SUN 11-6
- BLACKFRIARS/WATERLOO/SOUTHWARK

Making a decision on which flooring to install in your home is a troubling and often expensive dilemma. Over the past couple of decades, more of us have stripped out fitted carpets in favour of the modern feeling of wood, but in doing so we have also experienced large swathes of unforgiving surfaces need some softening. Cue the contemporary rug collection at Loophouse, which offers warm, tactile and deliciously coloured solutions for your floor.

Of course rugs are like functional artworks, so choosing an off-the-shelf design can prove dissatisfying and the hunt frustrating. Thus it is easy to understand why the bespoke commission service at Loophouse has attracted a growing list of private and corporate clients tapping into the wisdom of the energetic and enterprising founder, Lorraine Statham.

At this studio and showroom in Southwark, Statham's collections illustrate the diversity of styles, textures, and techniques that can be incorporated into a design. On the whole, colour is the main driver of Statham's output, with bold floral and geometric patterns standing out as the prominent feature. More intriguing are the designs incorporating various pile heights and changes in weave textures.

Should you wish to discuss any bespoke options with Statham, it is wise to make an appointment in advance. Otherwise, pop round to Southwark Bridge Road and check out Loophouse's additional offerings: vibrant cushions, beanbags and throws, bold wall art and spectacular wallpapers.

Walking along the South Bank, you can't miss the distinctive 1930s OXO Tower Wharf, with its illuminated OXO lettering on the tower. This riverside landmark was once home to the infamous gravy producer of the same name. It was converted in 1984 and now houses a community of design studios, as well as cafés, restaurants and an exhibition space.

The first and second floors house more than 30 ateliers, which also function as retail showrooms for their wares. Here, the public has the opportunity to observe designers at work and commission or purchase a wide variety of products spanning fashion, furniture, lighting, textiles, jewellery, ceramics and glass. On the first floor, ceramics maestro Bodo Sperlein showcases his range of sculptural tableware and lighting, and salt displays its ethereal handwoven fabrics. Up a level, you'll discover contemporary giftware from w2 Products, including those popular Pantone mugs. Next door, Anne Kyyro Quinn sews her graphic, sculptural cushions, throws, and blinds. Do the tour and you'll spot Joseph Joseph, J-Me, Black + Blum and Innermost, each specialising in unique and affordable giftware and home products.

There are no official opening hours; each studio operates on its own schedule. So don't be discouraged if some shops are closed when you visit. Get your fix at gallery@oxo on the ground floor, or head to the eighth floor for a drink in the Oxo Tower restaurant and bar, which commands some of the best views of London.

12 PLACESANDSPACES

🠖 30 OLD TOWN SW4 0LB

📞 020 7498 0998

🔖 PLACESANDSPACES.COM

🕐 TUE-SAT 10.30-6, SUN 12-4

⊖ CLAPHAM COMMON

13 PLANET BAZAAR

🠖 ARCH 68, STABLES MARKET, CHALK FARM RD NW1 8AH

📞 020 7485 6000

🔖 PLANETBAZAAR.CO.UK

🕐 MON-WED 12-6, THU-FRI 11-6, SAT-SUN 10-6

⊖ CHALK FARM

This place and space is the highlight of a small stretch of shops at one corner of Clapham Common. Originally a simple neighbourhood boutique with a decent selection of retro furniture and lighting, it got a contemporary injection by new owner Laura Slack, who elevated its standing as a prized retail destination in this part of the city.

The premises are small, but this doesn't inhibit Slack from showing off a cross-section of her favourite interior products, from lighting and furniture to wallpaper and gifts. She excels at combining timelessly modern, Scandinavian-style furniture with sculptural lighting and touches of more vibrant, almost tongue-in-cheek, accessories. On my visit I was presented with a selection by the 20th-century masters (Castiglioni, Breuer, Panton, Eames, Aalto) and a few of today's talents (Barber Osgerby, Dixon, Morrison, Wanders). If these names mean nothing to you, you'll certainly have no problem enjoying everything at face value.

And if you like what you see but are after something more specific, be sure to talk to the informed staff, who operate a sourcing service to pinpoint that perfect-sized sofa, coffee table or storage cabinet. Or you can check out their website for a categorised breakdown of the placesandspaces range; it also features the shop's own-label collection.

The old brick arches of Planet Bazaar provide a fitting vintage backdrop for this colourful collection of original 20th-century furniture, lighting, glass, ceramics and 'urban art'. 'Curated' by former artist Maureen Silverman, a passionate fan of the Sixties look, the iconic collection has rightfully earned this space its reputation as London's 'top pop shop'. Indeed, there is a definite bias here towards the vibrant pop aesthetic of the 1960s and 70s.

The treasure-trove is full of covetable originals, from classic mid-century collectibles to affordable tabletop items, yet it is accessible to a variety of budgets. There is a laidback attitude here, free from the pretense that can infect vintage dealers. Irreverent designs from the likes of Verner Panton, Gaetano Pesce, Eero Aarnio and Pierre Paulin are joined by earthier wood pieces by Alvar Aalto, Arne Jacobsen and British manufacturers Ercol and Gordon Russell.

Silverman carries some more generic offerings, like Murano glassware, children's mechanical toys from the 1960s and poster prints from Andy Warhol and Jamie Reid. It's dark and cave-like here, but you'll be guided by the famous selection of sculptural, stylised and highly functional lighting.

Planet Bazaar recently moved from its Islington store to these larger premises in the newly developed Horse Hospital complex. A word of warning: don't be put off by the more tacky features of the Stables Market development – it is aimed at tourists.

 PRIMROSE HILL INTERIORS

115 REGENT'S PARK ROAD NW1 8UR

020 7722 6622

ESSENTIALVINTAGE.COM

TUE-SAT 11-6, SUN 12-5

CHALK FARM

RETROUVIUS

2A RAVENSWORTH ROAD, KENSAL GREEN NW10 5NR

020 8960 6060

RETROUVIUS.COM

MON-SAT 10-6

KENSAL GREEN

Phil Cowan's upmarket collection of vintage 20th-century furniture, lighting, accessories and art is expertly and elegantly styled. It began life in Camden's Stables Market before maturing and graduating to larger premises in smarter and wealthier Primrose Hill.

Hunting down originals is an ongoing challenge that Cowan seems passionate about, his enthusiasm for the pieces is infectious. He seems to have a penchant for Scandinavian pieces, and boasts a comprehensive collection of rosewood sideboards, dining tables, chairs and desks from the region's collectible 1950s period.

Any emphasis on wood is offset by sleek and sculptural European lighting from the 1950s through the 1980s, and accents of colour are picked out by one-off glass and ceramic accessories. On the walls, decorative pier mirrors from the 19th century are mixed with op-art prints by Victor Vasarely and 20th-century oils.

If you're into 70s walnut and chrome furnishings, you're likely to find some top examples by British design house Merrow Associates, or more rare abstract Modernist pieces from Willy Rizzo. Personally, I veer towards the softer and more tactile contours of the 50s by Hans Wegner and Ico Parisi, Danish and Italian respectively.

Cowan also offers an interior-design service, which might explain why the presentation in this two-storey shop is so tidy and artfully composed. It has certainly come a long way from the clutter of Camden.

Retrouvius is an architectural salvage and design business, set up by partners Adam Hills and Maria Speake in 1993 with the motto 'bridging the gap between destruction and construction.' The duo have carved out a niche selling reclaimed treasures and integrating it with an architecture and interiors studio. Operating initially from a characterful warehouse on the residential Ravensworth Road, the duo seized the opportunity to expand into the neighbouring shop unit when it became available around the corner on Harrow Road.

Now nestled between a house clearance shop and a catering equipment supplier and with no sign over the door, their premises are most unsuspecting. This turns out to be part of the charm as you enter into a long and expansive room, home to the likes of Victorian library chairs, cast iron lion heads, oak library steps and even a Central Line tube sign as well as wall panelling, fireplaces, columns and reusable materials – marble, flooring, and wood. Needless to say, the stock fluctuates depending on the vagaries of demolition.

As you might expect, the textured space itself was built from reclaimed materials – pine joists from Wales, oak floors from Middlesex Courts off Parliament Square, lighting from Rover factory in Longbridge, and doors from a demolition in Marylebone. The office rooms upstairs accommodate the design side where Speake and team work on client projects, putting the salvage items and other new pieces to good use.

16 TATE MODERN

- BANKSIDE SE1 9TG
- 020 7887 8888
- TATE.ORG.UK/MODERN
- SUN-THU 10-6, FRI-SAT 10-10
- SOUTHWARK

17 UNTO THIS LAST

- QUEENS CIRCUS SW8 4NE
- 020 7720 6558
- UNTOTHISLAST.CO.UK
- DAILY 10-6
- BATTERSEA PARK RAIL

During London's millennium celebrations, the once disused Bankside Power Station was reopened as the home of Tate Modern, the younger sibling of one of Britain's leading art institutions: Tate Britain. Nowadays the only thing generated in this modernised megastructure is enthusiasm, from the record numbers of museum-goers who come from around the world to explore the vast galleries dedicated to international modern art from 1900.

The Tate collection covers all the major art movements of the 20th century. Three levels of galleries, organised around four key periods, exhibit historically significant masterpieces from Picasso and Matisse to Dali, Rothko, Pollock and Judd. Special exhibitions that explore the works of individual artists or more niche themes complement the permanent displays.

The somewhat overwhelming cavernous space within the brick-clad structure – transformed by Swiss architects Herzog & de Meuron – is awe-inspiring from the sloping main entrance through the Turbine Hall and beyond. Annual commissions that use the immense Turbine Hall as a canvas have included ambitious site-specific sculptures from Louise Bourgeois, Anish Kapoor, Olafur Eliasson, Rachel Whiteread and Carsten Höller.

For respite, head to the ground-floor café or enjoy the views from the top-floor restaurant. But before you leave, it is the bookshop you must visit. It stocks more than 10,000 titles and carries one of the largest selections of art, design and architecture books in the country – a significant resource for London's art and design devotees.

It is the vision of Olivier Geoffrey, owner of Unto This Last, to demystify the manufacturing process by moving it into the city and making it directly accessible to the consumer. He has successfully exploited this business model for years at the original Brick Lane premises (p.138), and he has steadily developed more efficient micro-production facilities for a growing range of furniture, lighting and accessories. He recently expanded the model to South London.

Upon entering this unit under the railway tracks in Battersea, the first thing you encounter is the automated CNC machine precision-cutting shapes and components from sheet wood. It is mesmerising to watch. Then, mere metres away, the components are hand-assembled into the finished product, be it a table, chair, pendant light or cabinet.

Interestingly, you have to pass through this production area before you reach the concealed showroom at the back of the cavernous arched unit. Here, having had a taste of the production process, you are left alone to browse the uncomplicated designs.

Apart from a few smaller accessories, this outlet does not carry any overstock. Most pieces are made to order, which allows customers to choose between specific finishes and dimensions. At the moment, the production is limited by the use of sheet materials. But I predict that, very soon, Unto This Last will embrace the neverending possibilities of 3D printing.

18 VITSŒ

- CENTRIC CLOSE NW1 7EP
- 020 7428 1606
- VITSOE.COM
- MON–FRI 8-6, SAT 10-6
- CAMDEN TOWN

19 THE WAPPING PROJECT

- HYDRAULIC POWER STATION, WAPPING WALL E1W 3SG
- 020 7680 2080
- THEWAPPINGPROJECT.COM
- MON–FRI 12-10.30, SAT 10-10.30, SUN 10-6
- SHADWELL DLR / WAPPING

In our age of built-in obsolescence, disposability and short attention spans, it is a miracle to find a company that has sustained a successful business from a single design for more than 50 years. That product is the *606 Universal Shelving System* by the legendary German designer Dieter Rams.

The story goes that Danish furniture entrepreneur Niels Vitsœ and German furniture-maker Otto Zapf teamed up with Rams when he was only 28. The result was this fully modular system of aluminum tracks that supports shelves, cabinets and a table. The components lock together and can be easily moved, repaired, altered or updated as needed – like a kit of parts.

The secret of its success comes down to the fact that the design is unobtrusively stylish, unquestionably functional and limitless in its configuration. But it's just shelving, I hear you mutter. Indeed it is, but when you really start to investigate, you quickly realise that most systems pose limitations. And if they don't, they are often very ugly. If you don't believe me, visit this Vitsœ showroom, bizarrely located in a warehouse-like building, and you'll soon be converted.

The company slogan – 'live better with less that lasts longer' – seems incredibly prescient as society is now waking up to the fact that we should invest in quality with longevity. If you buy into this way of thinking, check out Vitsœ's *620 chair*, also by Rams.

The formerly industrial area of Wapping, near London's docklands, wouldn't necessarily be on your design radar. At least not until distinguished theatre director Jules Wright transformed the derelict Wapping Hydraulic Power Station into a cultural-hybrid of contemporary-art gallery, performance venue and fine-food restaurant. Wright and her crew, who undertook to convert the cavernous space, were motivated by a resistance to change – specifically the whitewashing of this historic district. The spacial drama here has been enhanced by the introduction of a few contemporary details, which help to focus your attention on the original features and your imagination on the prior life of this Grade II-listed building.

In the Engine and Turbine Houses, corpses of the decommissioned machinery are now the centrepiece of the restaurant, laying idle among diners who perch on slick Vitra furniture. Enjoying a daily menu in the echoing space, one also benefits from the visual splendor of a bygone era: rusty chains, Victorian pipes, giant hooks and mysterious valves.

Descend into the dark, bare-brick Boiler and Filter Houses to the imposing art space, used to showcase performances, live events and commissioned works by visual artists, choreographers, composers, writers, poets, designers and filmmakers. One of many recent highlights was an exhibit from French *Vogue*'s famous photographer Guy Bourdin.

If you're turned on by niche art titles, make sure you check out the tiny bookshop, located in a greenhouse in the garden.

In today's materialist culture we have become addicted to the constant allure of the 'new'. MAX FRASER argues that now is the time to change our game

THE STATE OF STUFF

Over the past decade or so we have lived well beyond our means, propped up by easy access to credit and an attitude that we can have what we want, when we want it. Today we wallow in a culture of uncontested consumerism. As Richard Girling wrote in his book Greed: 'We acquire, accumulate, and consume so far in excess of "need" that the word itself has fudged its meaning.' [1]

Girling has a point. We belong to a generation that has never had to go without, and along the way we have created an invisible monster that feeds off our over-indulgence and wastefulness. It looms on the horizon of Western consciousness, yet we live with the belief that we are somehow immune to the problems it conceals.

The current recession (bemoaned by many of the businesses compiled in this guide) has brought some designers to the consensus that now is the time to address our culture of aimless consumption in the hope of restoring a marketplace with a healthier and more sustainable outlook than before.

As it stands the design industry seems to blindly produce more 'stuff', clambering at every opportunity to capture our attention amid a sea of homogeneous and derivative products. It is by no means the only industry that simultaneously creates desire and fuels disposability; in general, the vast majority of 'stuff' is only adequately designed and manufactured and capitalises on its own planned obsolescence. We recognise this – the burden on the planet is discussed endlessly – yet until it smacks us in the face, calls for change are likely to go unheard. In the main, we are hypocrites; we know we need to reduce but we feel doubtful that as individuals we can make any difference.

Could we ever move away from consumption altogether? I hear you ask: Why would he, the editor and publisher of an annual guide that ultimately encourages consumption, suggest such a thing?

True, this thinking is naive and short sighted. Trade is engrained in our culture. Our finely tuned production cycle should be credited for providing us with an ever-important source of income – which, in turn, helps keep society's wheels in motion. Production

'More than ever before, society needs to embrace moderation and readdress the reality of our needs'

should not be considered a 21st-century scourge; innovation and technology offer infinite possibilities to a forward-thinking society.

It is also important to recognise that human nature is at its finest when creating. It gives us a sense of purpose. Throughout history our country has spawned pioneers we can thank for everything we value as great. These innovators deserve kudos, not the imitators who follow in their wake. However, as Richard Girling rightfully warns: 'We salute excellence, but excellence is seldom born of modesty, and still less of moderation.' [2]

More than ever before, society needs to embrace moderation and readdress the reality of our 'needs'. But only when we seriously question why we have mountains of stuff cluttering our shelves (as well as our minds and, ultimately, the rubbish tips) will we be able to start changing our consumption patterns. It is time to move away from the concept of disposability and promote quality and longevity, repair and reuse. Consumption is fine, as long as we buy better quality products less often and place value on emotional resonance – the sorts of things featured in this guide. The future should be seen as rich with opportunity, but conditional on a move away from today's self-destructive trajectory. Along the way we need to excite and empower one another and sidestep those who hesitate.

As things stand today, I get the feeling we are just treading water, waiting for others to make the first move. An army of creative entrepreneurs is eager to advance, but seems held back by risk-averse corporations and government. As our history tells it, however, it is during the hard times that human beings have best responded to new challenges. There is every reason why now is the time for change.

1 Richard Girling, *Greed. Why We Can't Help Ourselves* (2009), p.64

2 Richard Girling, *Greed. Why We Can't Help Ourselves* (2009), p.83

MAX FRASER IS EDITOR OF LONDON DESIGN GUIDE. **LONDONDESIGNGUIDE.COM**

RETAIL
FACILITY
WWW.RETAILFACILITY.CO.UK

products designed by **INDUSTRIAL FACILITY**. available online.

Design Tribes

The question is often asked: 'What are the characteristics of British design?' More often than not, the response comes with a scratch of the head and a slight pause: 'Well, er, its quite eclectic, isn't it.' On one hand this is a cop-out, but on the other hand it is an apt account of the sheer diversity of talented, visionary and individually minded designers working in London.

That said I wanted to identify some key trends that might help define individual designers today and group them by their various approaches and philosophies. The research involved in doing so was massive and the outcome ran the risk of being hugely subjective, so I called upon a group of expert journalists to filter down the data into definable groupings with representative designations. The project was given the title Design Tribes. Stacks of images, reams of paper, several bottles of wine and a great deal of debate later, we reduced about 30 possible tribes down to five.

One impression we all came away with after our conversations was that designers are distinctly individual, making it difficult and unjust to rigidly divide them. Likewise, designers hate to be categorised. Thus we have tried to steer away from pigeonholing individuals into specific tribes, preferring instead to highlight projects that represent a specific tribal genre. Most certainly, it is a subjective area with lots of overlapping. Our categories should be regarded as open-ended, food for thought.

You will notice that plenty of big-name designers have been omitted from the following pages. They are not included because their work defies placement – they are ever-present, ever-pioneering and ever-innovative. We toyed with adding them to a tribe called the Signature Innovators, but quickly realised that this would take up the whole book. One thing that became very clear is that London prevails as a treasure trove of leading creative talent. And, thankfully, there seems to be little risk of that changing.

We would like to thank Anna Bates, Laura Houseley, Dominic Lutyens, Lynda Relph-Knight, Nicole Swengley, and Henrietta Thompson for their valuable contribution.

WORDS BY MAX FRASER AND ANNA BATES

mod*us*

SHOWROOM
28-29 GREAT SUTTON STREET
LONDON EC1V 0DS

HEADOFFICE
5 WESTCOMBE TRADING ESTATE
ILMINSTER TA19 9DW

+44 (0)1460 258590
info@modusfurniture.co.uk
www.modusfurniture.co.uk

THE NEW MODERNISTS

01

Year after year, designers vie for the attentions of manufacturers in the hope that their new design proposal will come up trumps against the rest. Mass production still represents the holy grail of success. Yet amid a sea of competition and marketing noise, it becomes rather easy to miss the designs that are most likely to sustain the industry on a commercial level. Provocative, entertaining and sensationalist design – a tiny but loud segment of the market – has tended to overshadow the more pragmatic work of hardworking designers.

That said, there is still a pulse in the area of commercial production that concerns itself with subtle – as opposed to seismic – improvements and advancements in our everyday material landscape. Refined, pure and formalist. Classic and timeless in visual language. Pragmatic in functionality, sometimes with a smattering of irony. This is the work of the New Modernists.

01 (P.163) BASEL CHAIR, JASPER MORRISON FOR VITRA

02 SPOT TABLES, TOM DIXON

03 W084T, STUDIOILSE FOR WÄSTBERG

04 THE CRATE, JASPER MORRISON FOR ESTABLISHED & SONS

As the name suggests, the New Modernists reference the focused language of their Modernist predecessors, who were concerned with the implementation of 'form follows function' rules. This may be considered an age-old principle in today's designscape, where influences are far-reaching and varied. But the quest for production efficiency still remains a commercial imperative. Designers working at the mass-market end of the spectrum are presented with production constraints that don't allow for frivolous and excessive gestures. With this in mind, functionality is a core concern in the design phase, after which the character of the final product takes shape.

Jasper Morrison has always been a careful contributor to our material world, preferring not to design for design's sake. He is not on a quest to radically alter the face of design. Rather, he favours quiet refinements, which some might indeed deem Minimalist. He references familiar archetypal forms and updates their material qualities. This can be seen in the *Basel Chair*, where he has rejuvenated a classic wooden chair, lifting a familiar, 'anonymous' design and making it his own. More controversially, Morrison took the image of the classic wooden wine case and issued it in superior Douglas fir. With *The Crate*, the designer felt no need to improve on the existing design, claiming the dimensions were already perfect for a myriad of domestic uses.

Much of the output of the New Modernists captures the essence of form with graphic clarity, eschewing superfluous ornament or pattern. A good example of this is Barber Osgerby's *Tab*

05

06

07

Lamp, whose confident, proportional composition masks the complexity of its construction. The shape of the lamp itself is reminiscent of a bird taking flight. Such zoomorphic references also feature in a great deal of Matthew Hilton's work – his *Light Table*, for instance, whose top perches on two webbed feet.

The new millennium has seen a shift from slick, artificial finishes to a more honest use of texture and material; warmth and tactility reign. Take the *w084t* table lamp by Studioilse, or Benjamin Hubert's concrete *Heavy Light*, antidotes to harsh, austere lighting of the mid 20th century. Indeed, any suggestion of austerity is dismissed. Cost cutting is not the objective.

Tom Dixon's *Utility* collection hits a particularly timely note with a visual language that places function and material honesty at the forefront. His *Spot Tables* – visually slender side tables – are constructed from cast iron with enamelled tops. The simple geometric shapes are made of materials from bygone eras, yet applied with a fresh approach. The tables are heavy, strong and solid, imbued with the notion of stability that seems particularly reassuring in turbulent economic times.

The tactile elements of a product and the attention to finite detailing are ways of communicating quality for this tribe. Unfortunately, these days the uninitiated public doesn't always pick up on such nuances. Nor do they always understand the high prices that such pieces can command. The challenge for the New Modernists will forever be justifying the elite categorisation of designs that are often dubbed, simply, 'anonymous'.

lead crystal chandeliers dipped in rubber
perfume made from $960,567 a gallon crude oil
one off machine made books
bulletproof brooches
bronze cast, gold plated pen caps
crucifix shaped scrubbing brushes
mcdonalds lawsuits
museum collections
rogue retail interventions
repurposed forest thinnings made into tables
concrete doorstops cast from designer vases
terrorist weapons
culturally curated retail
handmade corporate logo quilts
sex toys

Make sense?
www.citizen-citizen.com

CITIZEN : Citizen

| Design Tribes |

THE ESCAPISTS

01

Disenchanted with the monotony of household objects in an oversaturated market, a new generation of designers who strive for more creative self-expression has recently emerged. These players have individualist attitudes and go about expressing their own distinctive concepts and narratives with the freedom and independence of artists.

The Escapists rebel against tradition, boundaries and narrow definitions, rejecting the notion that 'a gap in the market' should be the primary motivation for designing something new. They are storytellers who don't necessarily want to respond to someone else's brief, rather preferring to set their own agenda. They work with the materials, processes and techniques of their choice and push the envelope; they have no limits. High labour costs are not a hindrance to the Escapists – to these mavericks, value is measured by the strength of ideas. Mass production is a distant concern; many designs are rolled out as one-offs or limited editions. Above all, the work of the Escapists is free of constraints; it injects poetic flair into the mundane; it is all about theatricality, a touch of magic and surreal sensationalism.

01 (P.167) CRYSTAL CANDY SET, JAIME HAYÓN FOR BACCARAT

02 RUG 'THE LOVERS', FREDRIKSON STALLARD

03 MY BEAUTIFUL BACKSIDE, DOSHI LEVIEN FOR MOROSO

04 CITYCATTV CAMERA, MATTHIAS MEGYERI FOR SWEET DREAMS SECURITY™

05 DE LANK GRANITE CHAIR, MAX LAMB

One member who regularly escapes into his own fantasy world is Jaime Hayón. The Spanish artist-designer freely applies the stories in his head to a 'plasticine baroque' material aesthetic. A flurry of ideas emerges from his reverie and these physically manifest themselves as high-quality, refined objects with playful naivety and characterful gestures (see his *Crystal Candy Set* for Baccarat). Hayón is at ease combining the skill sets of specialist craftsmen with high-tech industrial processes.

Similarly, Nipa Doshi and Jonathan Levien of Doshi Levien will happily merge craft and industrial processes that echo the convergence of their cultural differences (Doshi's origins are in India and Levien was trained as an industrial designer in England). A smorgasbord of stories and contemporary reinterpretations infiltrate their work. Take, for example, the *My Beautiful Backside* sofa for Moroso, filled with subtle references to time and place that could hardly have come from any other duo.

Some designers concentrate on the playful interpretation of otherwise mundane objects. The *Little Crawly Thing* benches by Carl Clerkin look as if they're about to scurry away. Gitta Gschwendtner's *Uncanny Lamps* distort the form of traditional pleated lampshades, allowing them to escape up walls and wrap around table legs. Matthias Megyeri added a humorous and kitschy element to security devices such as railings, razor wire, and CCTV cameras in his *Sweet Dreams Security* collection; his is a social commentary on the brutish presence of security and surveillance in a post-9/11 society. In Megyeri's world, cartoonish rabbits, donkeys and penguins made of cast-iron adorn the tops of railings – though they do have threateningly sharp beaks and ears.

Design duo Dunne & Raby aren't afraid to

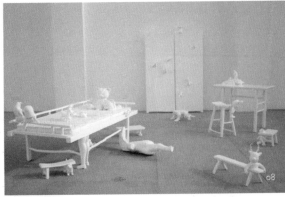

06 HUGGABLE ATOMIC MUSHROOM, DUNNE & RABY
   AND MICHAEL ANASTASSIADES
07 UP THE WALL LAMP, GITTA GSCHWENDTNER

08 MADE IN CHINA, WOKMEDIA
09 COW BENCH, JULIA LOHMANN

deal with taboo subjects. The polyester-filled *Huggable Atomic Mushroom* cushion designed in collaboration with Michael Anastassiades provides literal comfort from the threat of nuclear detonation in the form of a throw pillow shaped like a mushroom cloud. WOKmedia's *Made In China* furniture collection distorts happy childhood memories with surreal scenes of chaos and confusion; seemingly innocent toy characters invade tables, benches and stools in a landscape of derailed trains and drowning babies.

Julia Lohmann confronts mortality and challenges our relationship to animals with her *Cow benches*; they serve as a memento mori for the cows that gave their lives for the leather used in their fabrication. Duo Fredrikson Stallard created the '*The Lovers*' rug, comprising conjoined pools of red urethane that represent the quantity of blood in two average human

beings. By instilling mundane materials with new meaning, these designers shift the established conventions of how objects should communicate and function.

One designer who places materials and processes at the centre of his vocabulary is Max Lamb. He manages to escape the conventions of furniture production altogether, primitively chiselling armchairs from polystyrene (*Soft Poly Chair*), crudely carving them from boulders (*De Lank Granite Chair*) or building them from extruded biodegradable material (*Starch Chair*). The effect is rugged, raw and intense.

By virtue of their individualist tendencies, this tribe is extremely difficult to group. Their personal manifestos are constantly shifting, so running a thread between their collective works is virtually impossible. It is their ability to continually 'escape' convention that, of course, gives the Escapists their definition.

| Design Tribes |

THE REACTIVISTS

01

Today's designers have to find a place within a paradox: while their aim is to produce, they don't want to add to the spill-out from manufacturing plants, most of which is destined for landfill. There is already some 109 square miles of rubbish beneath our feet, the result of 27,000,000 tonnes of waste we tuck under the ground each year in the UK.

Some designers address this problem by making sure the materials they use are biodegradable or can be melted down safely, then carrying on as usual. But a more curious group of designers have made themselves at home among scrap yards, junk shops and rubbish bins. Some are fascinated with the consumer tat that lurks there and some are puzzled by our set of values: what makes some materials fit for rubbish and others valuable? There are those who are simply looking for free supplies for their craft, because being a designer in London is very expensive. Yet others enjoy using readymades for the richness and history the pieces hold. The latter group are the Reactivists.

01 (P.171) MELTDOWN CHAIR 'CABLE TIE', TOM PRICE
02 KEBAB LAMP 'OVER THE HILLS AND FAR AWAY', COMMITTEE

03 OPTICAL, STUART HAYGARTH
04 TIDE, STUART HAYGARTH
05 IF ONLY GIO KNEW, MARTINO GAMPER

These designers don't necessarily have an environmental agenda; they simply enjoy manipulating objects that already exist. And with a little design alchemy they can transform objects we thought we knew into something completely different.

The design duo Committee belongs in this category. Committee's Harry Richardson and Claire Page hunt down kitsch and junk, piecing together their findings to make totems to our material culture. In *Kebab Lamp* they juxtaposed pieces in a way that celebrates their colour and form and encourages us to look at them in a new light. In the end, the whole is far greater than the sum of its parts – a *Kebab Lamp* recently sold at Christie's for nearly £6,000.

The work of Karen Ryan is a direct reaction against the burden of society's waste;

she struggles with the notion of adding more 'superfluous' objects to our world. The designer has always scavenged through rubbish and pulled out random pieces of broken furniture that she then transforms into intriguing hybrid compositions. The Technicolor hybrids from her *Custom Made Furniture* collection feature second-hand parts masked behind vibrant and glossy paint finishes that 'customise' them.

Stuart Haygarth's work is similar in principle. The designer has been known to comb beaches looking for anything the sea might have washed up. He took this approach with *Tide*, a chandelier made entirely from clear and translucent plastic objects found at the coast. His *Optical* chandelier was a bit less exotic – he visited local opticians and asked if they had any old glasses hanging around. With meticulous

06 100 CHAIRS IN 100 DAYS, MARTINO GAMPER

07 CUSTOM MADE CHAIR 2006, KAREN RYAN

precision, Haygarth hung the individual lenses around a bulb. When switched on, the lenses reflect and refract the light in a way that makes the air appear to melt. In doing so they transcend their initial function and become something aesthetically stunning.

Other Reactivists like to keep their hands a little cleaner. Martino Gamper uses cast-offs to create three-dimensional collages, which he likens to a song remix, or a cover by a different musician. He dismantles furniture – anything from a £3 plastic garden chair to a *Thonet* bentwood chair – and reappropriates it, challenging our concept of taste in the process. For his project *If Only Gio Knew*, Gamper assumes the role of a rebellious teenager by sawing up a the work of Gio Ponti and turning it into something new.

For some designers it is not so much about the object as it is about the material. Tom Price uses various forms of plastic for his ongoing *Meltdown* series. He wants us to remember that polypropylene rope, a nylon cable tie, fleece clothing and a plumbing tube are all made out of the same material – one that we consider cheap, nasty and environmentally damaging. Price heaps the material into a ball, then dents it with a heated seat-shaped former, which, in a simple sweep, upgrades the material from landfill to auction house.

The Reactivists take a holistic approach to designing, by valuing what is already made. Once these alchemists have finished with their raw material, we look at the individual components with new appreciation and realign our tastes.

VOID WATCHES

www.voidwatches.com

V01ELCO

V01ELBR

V01ELBL

V01ELGO

Size: 36x42x9 (WxHxD) I Material: 316 Stainless Steel I Strap: Leather
Waterproof: 3ATM/30M I Warranty: 1 Year I Functions: Time/Date/Light

Visit www.voidwatches.com for retailer locations and more information.

| Design Tribes |

THE DIGITALISTS

01

Until the past decade, only those with specialist knowhow were really capable of meddling with electronic technology. And so, only those with vast amounts of money – namely, large corporations – had access to it. But thanks to open-source software and the Internet, that elite knowledge isn't a must in the workplace. Technology, once accessible only to diehard engineering geeks, is now in the realm of the designer.

A group of enterprising creatives has run with this relatively new opportunity and made technology central to their craft. It is the mission of these designers to imbue technology with personality, emotion and, most importantly, interactivity. Software, sensors and circuit boards are fundamental to the Digitalists.

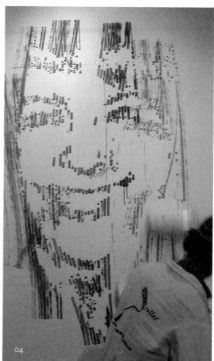

01 (P.175) 'VOLUME' AT THE V&A, LONDON, UNITED VISUAL ARTISTS

02 BY ROYAL APPOINTMENT, MORITZ WALDEMEYER

03 POWER UP, JASON BRUGES STUDIO

04 PIXEL ROLLER, RANDOM INTERNATIONAL

The Digitalists are such a young tribe that defining them is difficult. Some of them exploit the mystery factor of technology like magicians. Others harness its interactivity or its decorative potential. For still others, technology is a vehicle for social commentary.

Moritz Waldemeyer was one of the first to bring advanced technology into the design world. The trained engineer applied his wizardry to Zaha Hadid's touch-sensitive *Z.Island Corian* kitchen, and he gave Ron Arad's *Lolita* chandelier the ability to receive and display text messages. He wired up Hussein Chalayan's sculptural skirts, which accordion'd out at the press of a button. Waldemeyer's first independent design, *By Royal Appointment*, is a chair that glows to match the clothing of the person seated.

The installation titled *Volume*, created by design collective UnitedVisualArtists, integrates a complex sensory system that responds to human movement; a veritable forest of LED columns, it 'greets' passers-by with an exquisite orchestration of sound and light. Jason Bruges Studio is also known for designs that interact with their environment. Bruges's *Power Up* employs variations in light to reflect the demand for power in the local area – a poetic way of sharing data.

Artificial intelligence is an emerging feature in design. The organic *AI Light* by Assa Ashuach has five sensors that pick up light, sound and movement and cause the light to morph accordingly. Simon Heijdens's *Lightweeds* is a computer-generated garden that 'reads' the weather and actually responds to sunshine, rainfall and wind; projected onto a wall, the plants sway in the breeze, lose their seeds and 'fertilise' other walls throughout the space.

Other digital designs dream up new uses for basic technology, making us reexamine some tools we've come to take for granted. Take rAndom International's *Pixel Roller*. A handheld printer in the shape of a simple paint roller, it

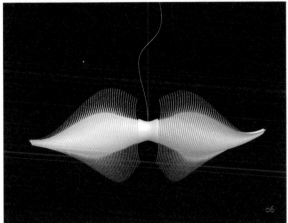

05 LIGHTWEEDS, SIMON HEIJDENS
06 AI LIGHT, ASSA ASHUACH

07 CLOUD, TROIKA
08 S.O.C.D, DUNNE & RABY WITH MICHAEL ANASTASSIADES

allows you to print digital imagery directly onto the wall with a simple motion.

Design trio Troika takes a similar approach. Frustrated by the relentless updating of technology, the studio prefers to hearken back to older technologies and question why they have been made redundant. Troika's kinetic *Cloud* sculpture for Heathrow Terminal 5 uses flip-dot technology commonly associated with old 2D information boards. More beautiful than the sequence of patterns that moves across it is the fluttering sound it makes. Here Troika plays on the emotional, nostalgic resonance of yesterday's technology to make us ask ourselves: are plasma screens really necessary?

Because technology interacts so effectively with spectators, it makes a powerful vehicle for social commentary – or 'critical design', as Anthony Dunne and Fiona Raby of Dunne & Raby prefer to put it. Dunne & Raby are leaders of the pack in this field. They use technology to engage with the 'real world' – particularly the

more inconsistent and hypocritical aspects of it. One of the team's more recent installations, s.o.c.d, designed in collaboration with Michael Anastassiades, contains a device intended for people who enjoy pornography but feel guilty about watching it. A DVD player is connected to a rubber mechanism with an in-built sensor; when the viewer is aroused, the picture and sound blur, so in order to continue watching, he must dampen his enthusiasm.

Anthony Dunne is the head of Design Interactions at the Royal College of Art and has passed along his design philosophy to his disciples throughout the years. Many of the Digitalists, including Troika and rAndom International, are former students of his. In fact, RCA graduates are among the top designers today using technology to ask questions about the medium itself. As Dunne explains it, the movement is about 'designing relationships'. How funny that relationships were the one thing alienating technology once served to hinder.

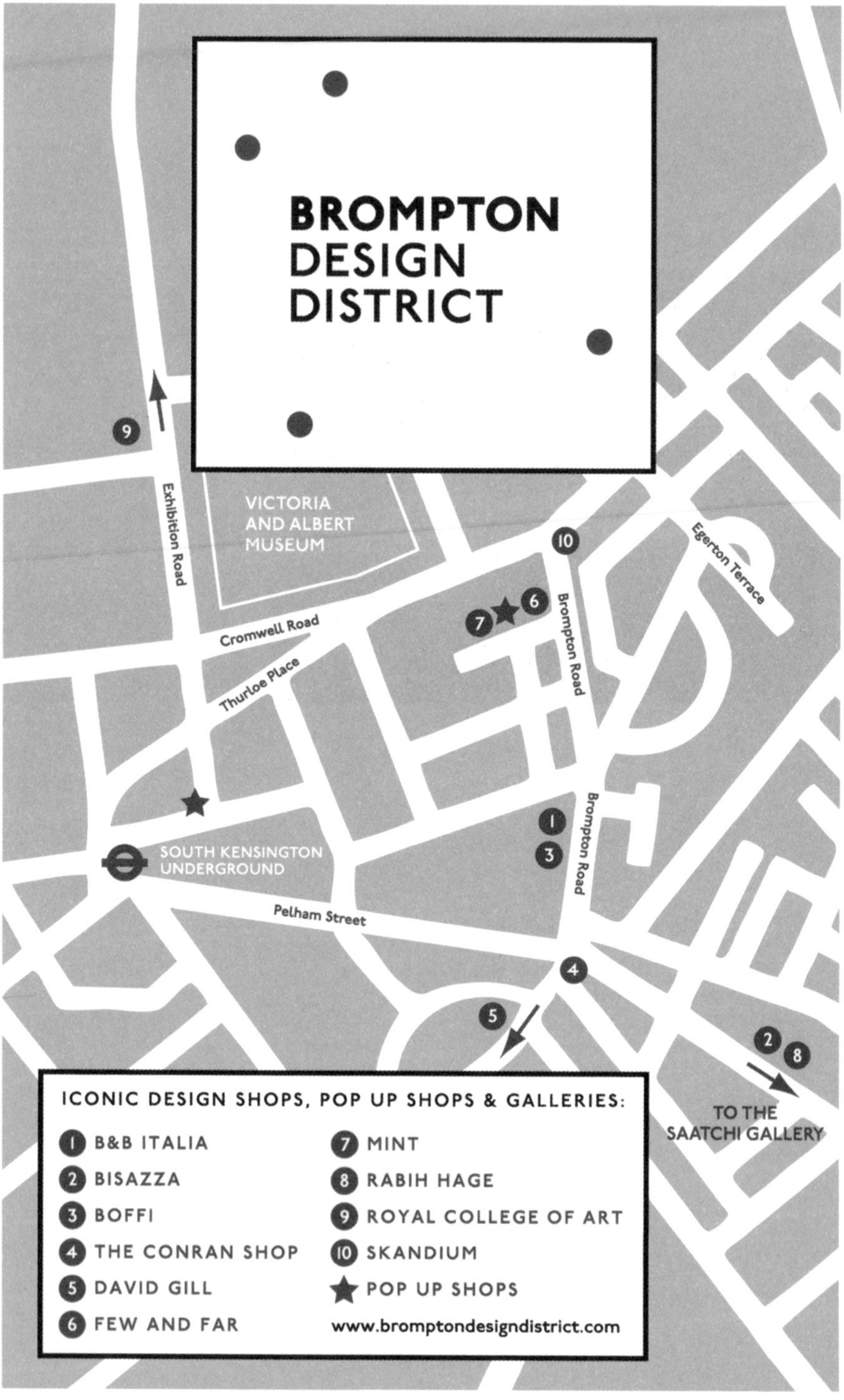

BROMPTON
DESIGN
DISTRICT

Exhibition Road

VICTORIA AND ALBERT MUSEUM

⑨

⑩

Egerton Terrace

Cromwell Road

⑦ ★ ⑥

Thurloe Place

Brompton Road

★

Ⓣ SOUTH KENSINGTON UNDERGROUND

①
③

Brompton Road

Pelham Street

④

⑤

② ⑧

TO THE SAATCHI GALLERY

ICONIC DESIGN SHOPS, POP UP SHOPS & GALLERIES:

① B&B ITALIA

② BISAZZA

③ BOFFI

④ THE CONRAN SHOP

⑤ DAVID GILL

⑥ FEW AND FAR

⑦ MINT

⑧ RABIH HAGE

⑨ ROYAL COLLEGE OF ART

⑩ SKANDIUM

★ POP UP SHOPS

www.bromptondesigndistrict.com

| Design Tribes |

THE REVIVALISTS

A designer's professional existence relies on introducing new things. But many creatives struggle with the notion of constant newness or the sterility of mass-production. Still others mourn the loss of traditional craftsmanship. The homogenous 'catalogue' look – devoid of personality or individuality – is the last thing on the minds of many designers seeking to connect more emotionally to the consumer, often with nostalgic references to yesteryear.

Indeed, a new wave is reassessing the traditional role of the designer. They strive to reappropriate the forgotten or overlooked; reinvigorate a genre from an earlier era; refresh a style, material, technique or approach that is no longer in vogue; or reference heritage and provenance. With honesty and authenticity as their core principles, these designers are the Revivalists.

01 (P.179) GEORGE 3: CHEST OF DRAWERS, GARETH NEAL
02 BASED UPON MAM, BASED UPON
03 PLANT CUP, GITTA GSCHWENDTNER FOR THORSTEN VAN ELTEN

04 BROUHAHA, DAVID CLARKE
05 VINTAGE PENDANT LIGHTS, KATHLEEN HILLS
06 VICTORIAN DAMASK WING CHAIR, HELEN AMY MURRAY

A Revivalist design comes in various guises. Sometimes the outcome is quite referential, invigorating an old-fashioned, even kitsch, object by lending it contemporary relevance. *George*, by the English designer Gareth Neal, is a good example; it takes on the silhouette of an archetypal chest of drawers, but realises it in an otherwise modern, ghostly veneer. Another popular Revivalist approach is the mutation of traditional objects to form a new definition – like David Clarke's *Brouhaha* vase, which distorts the form of a late 19th-century teapot and repurposes it as a vase. Other designs reference archetypal forms simply by stripping them of their original detailing or exaggerating their scale. This is an effective and often humorous way of redefining context and function, and is best illustrated by Gitta Gschwendtner's *Plant Cup*.

Some designers choose to recreate vintage designs with contemporary interventions.

Kathleen Hills's *Vintage Pendant Lights*, for instance, reimagine old glass pendant lamps with specially designed contemporary bone-china fixtures. Helen Amy Murray customises antique furniture with her distinctive textiles, which are 'carved' into sculptural relief; a damask-patterned leather adorns the back and sides of her *Victorian Damask wing chair*. Similarly, design studio Based Upon will take an existing object and apply its unique metalising process to the surface in order to capture and seal its personal history; *Based Upon Mam* gives new significance to a small cabinet, reviving our appreciation of the familiar form, and toys with our perceptions of value.

Of course the Revivalists also make new designs that merge traditional English craftsmanship and period features with a modern aesthetic, to create a style that is familiar and comforting while also being distinctly fresh and original. This approach can be seen

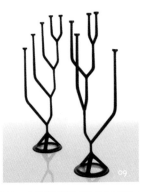

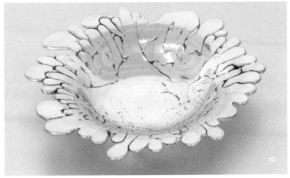

07 BLACKWELL, RUSSELL PINCH FOR SCP
08 HEREFORD, MICHAEL MARRIOTT

09 SPIN CANDELABRA, TOM DIXON
10 SPLASH BOWL, TIM PARSONS FOR AR WENTWORTH
(SHEFFIELD) LTD

in the furniture collections of Russell Pinch, Alex Hellum and Kay + Stemmer – as well as in Michael Marriott's recent *Hereford* chair, a contemporary reworking of a classic Windsor chair. These results, distinguished by subtle yesteryear references and fabric choices, come very close to the work of the New Modernists.

A preference for involving hands-on human skill in craft is a recurring trend among the Revivalists. They embrace variations in production and respect the idea that a personal touch is an important antidote to the uniformity of machine assembly. Take Tim Parson's *Pewter Drip-Casting* collection: he gives the old-fashioned pewter look a fresh lease of life by hand-casting individual bowls and platters with specialist artisans. He also introduced a pioneering way of drip-casting molten pewter; by virtue of this new process, no two pieces are ever the same. The final product celebrates the material's once liquid state and provides a decorative snapshot

of the production process, of which the outcome is never exactly the same.

Another material enjoying new limelight after a century out of vogue is cast iron, most commonly associated with the productivity of the Industrial Revolution. Tom Dixon rejuvenated the material in a number of his recent creations, including his *Spin Candelabra*. The Spin not only reinvents the fading tabletop heirloom for a present-day setting but also boldly replaces the traditional ornate brass variation. The desirable contemporary cast-iron alternative makes this rather rough and brutish material covetable once again.

On many levels the Revivalists help to sustain existing standards of production that have become threatened by the modern notion of progress. Their work provides a refreshing reminder that traces of our cultural evolution needn't be wiped out by society's overwriting quest for the new.

Not just for outdoors.

LONDON
DESIGN GUIDE
.com

Register your details to receive monthly news
updates, promotions and special reader benefits
throughout the year.

Design books from **Thames & Hudson**
Inspiration, innovation, ingenuity

Sixty Innovators
Shaping Our Creative Future

Showcases 60 innovators at the forefront
of: Interiors & Exteriors • Street World
Built World • Green World • Graphic Design
Advertising • Fashion • Photography
New Media • Visual Arts • Applied Arts
& Materials

ISBN 978 0 500 514924   £35.00 hb

The Independent Design Guide
Innovative Products from the New Generation

Laura Houseley

A one-stop sourcebook that showcases over
400 of the most exciting objects created by
young, emerging designers around the world.

ISBN 978 0 500 514573   £24.95 hb

Thames & Hudson
Sixty years of making a splash

www.thamesandhudson.com

DESIGN RESOURCES

ABITARE ABITARE.IT
Italian magazine focused on architecture, interior design and innovative construction techniques. Features profiles of projects around the world, interviews with top designers and architects, information on new products and commentary.

ARCHINECT ARCHINECT.COM
Website connecting designers and architects from around the globe to introduce new ideas from all disciplines. Features, news, views, image gallery and event calendar.

ARCHITONIC ARCHITONIC.COM
A growing resource for architects, designers and private individuals hunting for the latest materials, products and fixtures, with a choice of 55,000 searchable items.

BLUEPRINT BLUEPRINTMAGAZINE.CO.UK
A 25-year track record as one of the leading magazines for architecture and design. Takes a parallel approach to the different design disciplines, believing that fashion, product, furniture and architecture can share ideas. Published monthly.

THE COOL HUNTER THECOOLHUNTER.CO.UK
Website that champions style and culture from around the world. Shares today's most dynamic movements, styles and trends, and covers genres including fashion, music, urban living and designer trends.

COOLHUNTING COOLHUNTING.COM
Daily online update on ideas and products from the cultural intersection of art, design and technology. Regular video content gives an inside look at the work of various designers and artists.

CORE 77 CORE77.COM
Established online magazine dedicated to the practice and produce of industrial design. Practical resource for information as well as a venue for essays and reports on the topic of design in general.

DAILY ICON DAILYICON.NET
Online magazine featuring profiles of designers, architects and products as well as regular weekly posts on the latest happenings in architecture, interiors, art and travel. Special focus on furniture and accessories for home.

DESIGN ADDICT DESIGNADDICT.COM
Extensive design portal and comprehensive source of information on 20th-century product design. Index of designers and manufacturers. Great design blog.

DESIGN AND DESIGN DESIGNANDDESIGN.COM
Independent, non-profit venture helping designers promote their work. Features graphic and product design of the day.

DESIGNBOOM DESIGNBOOM.COM
A leading online independent publication for key contemporary issues and critique of all aspects of art and design. Snapshot reports from international design shows, interviews and portraits of today's leading design protagonists. Plus design history and even a design shop.

DESIGN OBSERVER DESIGNOBSERVER.COM
Blog site featuring critical writings on design, communications, arts and popular culture. Editorial by design connoisseurs Michael Bierut, William Drenttel and Jessica Helfand.

DESIGNSPOTTER DESIGNSPOTTER.COM
Online magazine dedicated to everything related to young, modern contemporary design, including product and interior design, fashion, residential architecture, exhibitions and publications. Offers a platform for publication and publicity for designer makers.

DESIGN WEEK DESIGNWEEK.CO.UK
Essential weekly magazine for designers and design professionals. The very latest news, features and exclusive commentary from the design industry. A regular must-read.

DETNK DETNK.COM
Online think tank dedicated to contemporary design and interiors, with a marketplace for the trade and acquisition of collectible design. Daily news is accompanied by regular video interviews with leading designers from around the world.

DEXINGER DEXINGER.COM
Online portal delivering design-related news, events and competitions as well as a design directory and database. Also available as a free iPhone and iPod touch application.

DEZAIN DEZAIN.NET
Weblog by Tokyo-based design journalist Eizo Okada, with links to architecture, furniture, textiles and other design-led content.

DEZEEN DEZEEN.COM
Online design and architecture magazine providing a daily overview of the latest news from designers and architects around the world. Also includes a job section for those hunting for work in these areas.

DOMUS DOMUSWEB.IT
Historically acclaimed Italian design and architecture magazine, first published in 1928. Bilingual, with articles printed in both Italian and English. Full of contemporary design and ideas, reviews of architecture, new products on the market and topical articles covering current events.

DWELL DWELL.COM
A popular us homes and interiors magazine. Delivers fresh, intelligent coverage of modern residential architecture and design, presenting examples of well-designed spaces that integrate the residents and their ideas and values. Published 10 times a year.

ELLE DECORATION
Monthly style magazine for luxury modern interiors. Showcases the leading designer trends and inspirational ideas in home furnishings, architecture and the decorative arts.

FRAME FRAMEMAG.COM
A bimonthly review of interior architecture and design. Focuses on cutting-edge corporate and public interiors, particularly retail, exhibition, hospitality and workplace design.

FX FXMAGAZINE.CO.UK
Extensive products database featuring the latest furniture, lighting, materials, fixtures and finishes for the contract interiors and interior-design market. Published monthly.

ID ID-MAG.COM
International critical design magazine, published in New York since 1954. Covers the art, business and culture of design. Published seven times a year.

ICON ICONEYE.COM
uk design and architecture magazine that tackles controversial topics with a strong critical edge. Website offers news and a selection of features from the magazine.

INTERNI INTERNIMAGAZINE.IT
Italian design magazine famous for selecting and documenting those works that are influential to Italian and international design culture.

INTRAMUROS INTRAMUROS.FR
Bimonthly and bilingual French/English magazine. Covers mainly French but also international design news and trends in the furniture, objects, interior design, fashion and new technology sectors.

MARK MARK-MAGAZINE.COM
Quarterly report on architecture and interior news. Another slick publication from the makers of *Frame* magazine.

METROPOLIS METROPOLISMAG.COM
us magazine examining contemporary life through design, architecture, interiors, product, graphics, crafts, planning and preservation.

MOCOLOCO MOCOLOCO.COM
A web magazine dedicated to modern contemporary interior design including furniture, accessories, lighting, floor and wall coverings, books, websites, audio and video, with online and retail stores.

MONOCLE MONOCLE.COM
A monthly publication from ex-*Wallpaper** editor Tyler Brûlé, covering international affairs, business, culture and design. Mainly targeted at wealthy cosmopolitan readers.

OBJEKT OBJEKT.NL
A premium quarterly publication for interior design and architecture with editorial features from around the world.

SURFACE SURFACEMAG.COM
An American design, fashion and lifestyle magazine. Known for its creative inspiration, coverage of the burgeoning design world and cutting-edge design trends, and profiles of the emerging designers.

TED TED.COM
Technology, Entertainment, Design. Non-profit event where the world's leading thinkers and doers gather to discuss design, entertainment, technology, business, science and other global issues. All talks uploaded onto the site and available to watch for free.

TREEHUGGER TREEHUGGER.COM
A prominent sustainability website offering the latest news, solutions and product information on green design.

TREND HUNTER TRENDHUNTER.COM
The world's largest trend-spotting site. Fuelled by a global network of thousands of trend-spotters and cool-hunters.

WALLPAPER* WALLPAPER.COM
International design lifestyle magazine. Features the biggest developments in the worlds of interiors, design, architecture, travel and fashion. Published monthly. Also publishes travel guides.

YATZER YATZER.COM
Online design magazine featuring the very latest and most unique items from all the creative fields, including architecture, art, interiors, industrial design, graphics and fashion.

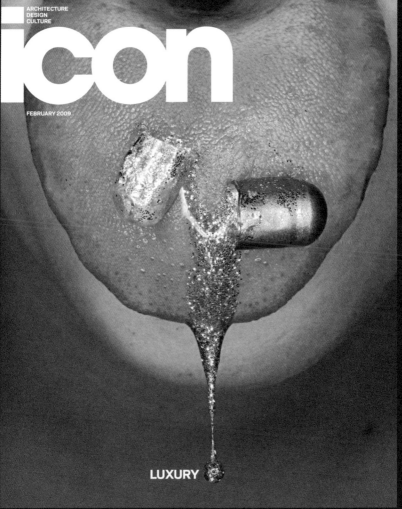

Hidden Art.

Transforming Passion into Products

Hidden Art helps designer-makers and designers transform their passion into products.

We do this through promoting and supporting members to place their products both nationally and internationally, through the Hidden Art E-Shop, international trade fairs, global press coverage, Hidden Art Awards, our Annual Pre-Christmas Open Studios Event and networking and one-to-one training sessions.

www.hiddenartshop.com • www.hiddenart.com/membership

Index

"Modern life demands,
and is waiting for,
a new kind of plan,
both for the house
and the city"

Le Corbusier

sigmar 265 kings road

SPOTLIGHT PRESS

Published in 2009 by Spotlight Press Ltd
londondesignguide.com

Editor's acknowledgements:

*This book is dedicated to my mother, Anne.
I wish you were still here to enjoy it.*

The editor would like to thank all of the shop owners
and their staff, designers, manufacturers, photographers,
PRS, advisors and contributors who gave their time to this
book. Thanks to Tim Bill at Tabs Creative for finding
us the right print deal in the UK, and Emily Palmer and
Sarah Haviland at Cultureshock Media for their work
on advertising sales. Likewise, thanks to the advertisers
for supporting this guide in year one. Thanks also to
any companies who sat on the fence and the many
bureaucrats who wasted our time – you have taught me
exactly what to avoid in business.

More specifically, a huge thank you to Ida Viznerova
for her tireless dedication to this project and her
patience, loyalty and faith; Richard Ardagh for his
calm professionalism and vision for the design; my
girlfriend Hannah Martin for her unfaltering belief,
motivation, love and head scratches; my father John and
sister Annabel for their unconditional support; and the
numerous friends and family for their encouragement.

Printed in the UK by Butler Tanner & Dennis, Frome

Butler Tanner & Dennis uses paper products that are
environmentally friendly, from well managed forests and
mills that are FSC accredited.

Trade orders: Central Books, orders@centralbooks.com
centralbooks.com For further distribution details and
advertising enquiries, visit: londondesignguide.com

ISBN 978-0-9563098-0-8

Publisher's acknowledgements:
Spotlight Press would like to thank all contributing shops,
galleries, institutions, designers, manufacturers and
photographers for their kind permissions to reproduce
their images in this book.

⊖ © ® Transport for London
Underground Roundel logo reproduced by kind
permission of Transport for London

Photography credits: (10) left Andrew Lamb; right Federico Cedrone; (11)
Boffi Chelsea showroom; (12) left Ammar Syed; (13) left David Mellor Design;
right De Parma; (14) left Designers Guild; right Alastair Hendy; (15) All
Annabel Elston; (16) left Uli Schade; right Jorge A. Herrera – Courtesy of
Phillips de Pury & Company; (17) left Jeremy Enness; right Potterton Books
London Ltd; (18) left Brian Benson; right Royal College of Art; (19) left The
Serpentine Gallery/John Offenbach; (21) left TASCHEN Store London/
Luke Hayes; right Morley von Sternberg/© V&A Images; (30) left Howie
Houghton; right Rachael Benjamin; (31) left Nick Sharp; right SCP Ltd;
(32) left Peter Wood; right Henry Bourne; (33) left Ester Segarra; top right
Christoph Lehmann; bottom right Olle Johansson; (40) left Alfies Antiques
Market; right Century Design; (41) left The Conran Shop; right Marimekko
Corporation; (42) left Selfridges & Co; (43) all Uli Schade; (52) left Alessi; right
David Koppel; (53) left Armani/Casa; right Courtesy Carpenters Workshop
Gallery, London; (54) all Dover Street Market; (55) left Kalpesh Lathigra; right
Gagosian Gallery; (56) bottom right Marcus Leith; all Courtesy of the ICA;
(57) Paul Smith; (66) right Lucy Pope (67) left Habitat; right iittala (68); top
Ed Reeve; (69) left Yael Fachler; right The Photographers' Gallery, London;
(76) left and top right Shira Klasher; all Aram Designs; (78) all Molteni & C;
(79) left and bottom right The Edmond J. Safra Fountain Court at Somerset
House – Gideon Mendel; top right Skin+Bones at Somerset House – Richard
Bryant; (88) right Agnese Sanvito; (89) left Image courtesy of CAA; right Guy
Drayton; (90) right Ligne Roset; (91) left Minotti London; right MUJI; (92)
left Lee Paton; right Janet Hall/RIBA Library Photographs Collection; (93)
left and bottom right Rama Knight/Wellcome Images; top right Wellcome
Images; (99) Richard Ardagh; (102) left Lyndon Douglas – Courtesy of
Barbican Art Gallery; right Gagosian Gallery; (103) left Mario Carrieri; right
James Finch; (104) left Anthony Parkinson; (105) left Leon Chew; right Toby
Summerskill; (106) left twentytwentyone; right Jonathan Barrie; (107) left Alex
Griffiths; all Vitra; (114) left Julie Williams-Krishnan; right Abigail Ahern; (115)
all Callum Toogie; (116) left Estorick Collection; right Asa Taulbut; (117) all Ed
Reeve; (118) left Living Space; (119) left Leo Cackett; right twentytwentyone;
(125) Duncan Riches; (128) right Steve Nyman; (129) left Ben Southgate;
right Ella Doran; (130) left Melissa Duarte; right The Geffrye Museum,
London/David Clarke & Marcus Leith; (131) all Morrison Studio; (132) left
KK Outlet; right Andrew Moran; (133) left Natalie Pecht; right Ligne Roset
City; (134) left Mar Mar Co; right Mathmos Ltd; (135) left Paul Tucker; right
Russell Roberts; (136) all SCP Ltd; (137) left Squint; right Keith Roberts/Two
Columbia Road; (138) left Polly Braden; right Stephen White/Courtesy White
Cube; (139) left Gavin Brown; top and bottom right Richard Bryant;(148) left
Chaplins; right Cody Burridge; (149) all Thomas Brown/Courtesy of David
Gill Galleries; (150) left Design Museum, London/Luke Hayes; right Ben
Adams; (151) left Matthew Hollow; (152) left Inter IKEA Systems B.V.; right
George Amos; (153) left loophouse; right Peter Durant/arcblue.com; (154)
left Ian Rippington; right Kristina Haslund; (155) right Tom Fallon; (156) left
©Tate, London 2009/Andrew Dunkley; right Sharon Green; (157) left Vitsoe;
right Thomas Zanon-Larcher; (163) Vitra/Marc Eggimann; (164) left Henry
Bourne; top right Wastberg/Philip Karlberg; bottom right Established &
Sons/Peter Guenzel; (165) top benjamin hubert studio; bottom left Matthew
Hilton/De La Espada; bottom right Piero Fasanotto; (166) Baccarat; (168) top
left Courtesy of David Gill Galleries; bottom left Moroso; top right Matthias
Megyeri; bottom right Max Lamb; (169) left Michael Anastassiades; top
right WOKmedia; bottom right Julia Lohmann; (171) Christoph Bolten; (172)
top middle and right Stuart Haygarth; bottom right Angus Mill; (173) left
Courtesy Nilufar Gallery, Milan; right Karen Ryan; (175) John Adrian; (176)
top left Moritz Waldemeyer; right Kristina Haslund Gallery Libby Sellers; bottom left Julian Abrams;
right rAndom International; (177) top left Simon Heijdens; bottom left Assa
Ashuach; top right Alex Delfanne/Artwise Curators; bottom right Francis
Ware; (179) James Champion; (180) top left Based Upon/Mark Henderson;
top middle David Clarke; top right Alun Callender ; bottom right Marcos
Bevilacqua; (181) top left SCP Ltd; bottom left Lisa Linder; top right Henry
Bourne; bottom right Leigh Simpson.